Gun Craft

Fine Guns & Gunmakers
in the 21st Century

Gun Craft

Fine Guns & Gunmakers in the 21st Century

Vic Venters

A SHOOTING SPORTSMAN BOOK

www.shootingsportsman.com

ISBN 978-0-89272-907-4

Designed by Lynda H. Mills

Printed in China

5   4   3   2   1

Library of Congress Cataloging-in-Publication Information
available on request

A SHOOTING
SPORTSMAN
BOOK
www.shootingsportsman.com

Distributed to the trade by National Book Network

For My Grandfather,
Who Started It All

Wayne Victor Venters
July 13, 1903 - June 10, 1980

Gun Craft

Fine Guns & Gunmakers
in the 21st Century

GUNS

GUN PROOF & PROOF MASTERS

OLD GUNS & RESTORING THEM

APPENDICES

Foreword

About 25 years ago, gunmaker John Wilkes remarked to me that traditional gunmaking is a 19th Century craft struggling to survive in the Space Age. Looking around his little shop at 79 Beak Street in the Soho section of London, I could not see much evidence of Space Age intrusion. It reminded me more of some image out of Dickens. The tiny front shop was stacked nearly to the ceiling with well-worn gun cases of oak and leather, with perhaps three or four newly completed guns on display. Through a doorway beyond lay an even tinier business office and a narrow stairway leading to the workshops above.

There again, two rooms, fitted with workbenches that were mostly cluttered with hand tools. The atmosphere was redolent with the smells of gun oil, linseed and fresh walnut shavings. Wads of tow, some fluffy and some blackly soaked with oil and solvent, lay scattered about. All told, it was about as traditional a shop as one could find in London. Even then, the more high-tech makers worked in digs tidy as operating rooms. Times change.

John Wilkes, Gun and Riflemaker, no longer occupies No. 79. Having no sons to whom they could pass the business, the Wilkes brothers, John and Tom, closed it some years ago—ending a tradition that began in 1830 and ultimately made Wilkes the oldest London gunmaker still owned by the founding family. I don't know what the building houses now, probably some trendy boutique. And I don't really want to know, as I prefer to remember it the way it once was.

But as Hamlet says, "The past is prologue." Having what I hope is a reasonably good grasp of what came before, I can't help wondering what the future will be.

My long-time friend Vic Venters has wondered this as well. The book you're about to read is the result of his curiosity, his boundless enthusiasm for finely built guns, and his admiration of the craftsmen who create them. It also derives from his hard-headedly practical approach, free of the breathless gushing that too often taints the writing on this subject. Whether his topic is historical or technical, you'll find no sappy fantasizing here, just lucid thinking expressed in clear, cleanly crafted language.

You will find it neither dry nor pedantic. Vic's love of fine guns comes through at every turn. A writer of long experience and great skill, he achieves the balance between thought and feeling to which all of us who ply the word trade should aspire.

When we get it right, as Vic has done, the readers will be the prime beneficiaries. So, this is your book. I trust you'll enjoy it as much as I have.

—*Michael McIntosh*

Acknowledgements

My grandfather was a bird hunter born and bred—the bird hunted being bobwhite quail. He kept a passel of dogs kenneled out back—setters and pointers and the occasional "drop"—and in a cedar-lined closet off the screened-in back porch was a rack of guns and shelves stacked with ammo and old hunting equipment. The closet was large enough for me to crawl into when I was a kid, and in it I could spend hours messing around with guns and gear and dreaming of the day I'd be old enough to take them afield.

Like many Southerners of his generation, my grandfather had switched from a double to an autoloader in the years following the Second World War. But he kept his side-by-sides—a couple of Field Grade L.C. Smiths, one a 12, the other a 20. My Dad grew up shooting the latter, mostly at squirrels, because he found the tightly choked Elsie less than an ideal bird gun.

To the eyes of a youngster, however, the Elsie had few flaws and, accompanied by my Granddad, I used it to shoot my first wood duck and woodcock in the lowlands of coastal North Carolina. I did miss my first quail with it, so it must have had a quirk or two—but his stewardship and that old gun, worn silver from use, stoked a passion in me that in a real sense has resulted in the book in your hands. To my Granddad, then, I owe the first round of thanks.

Ralph Stuart, *Shooting Sportsman's* Editor in Chief, hired me back in 1996—which meant a move to Maine, a state teeming with grouse and woodcock, to write about guns. It was a dream job come true. It was Ralph who cajoled me into compiling, revising and updating the articles that make up the chapters in *Gun Craft*. Not only has it been a privilege to work with Ralph—and designer Lynda Mills—over the past decade and a half, but I also have appreciated being given the editorial freedom to tackle subjects divorced from commercially dictated interests of advertising. In an era of media increasingly being driven by the latter, I cannot emphasize how important this has been.

In the writing trade, fellow *Shooting Sportsman* editors Ed Carroll, David Trevallion, Silvio Calabi, Bruce Buck, Clair Kofoed, Chris Batha and Steven Dodd Hughes always have been generous in sharing their expertise. Michael McIntosh, the dean of America's fine-gun writers, has many times offered useful counsel, and Douglas Tate has likewise provided much valuable advice and informed perspectives on British gunmaking. John Ian Gregson has played perfect host (and de facto taxi-driver) on my many visits to the UK gun trade. British gun photographer David Grant likewise has been a great host, and he took many of the photos that illustrate this work. Elena Micheli-Lamboy and her husband, Stephen, were invaluable with contacts and translations in the Italian trade. Engineer/writer Don Amos has rescued me from any number of technical flubs. *Blue Book* author S.P. Fjestad generously shared photos proprietary to his publishing company.

I also owe thanks to Larry Earley, Bill Kempffer, Wes Dillon, Abby Mouat, Carol Barnes, James J. Baker, Jim Stubbendieck, Alex Brant, G.O. Baker, Ray Poudrier, Bill Poteat, Charles Rucker, Steve Wilson, T.E. Nickens, Raiford Trask, Chip Robinson, Loran Johnson and Dr. Drew Hause for assistance through the years. My boss at *Wildlife in North Carolina*, Jim Dean, has been a mentor in the best sense of the word and Dr. James Leutze provided inspiration at a time in my life when I needed it.

In the UK, Dr. Derek Allsop, David Baker, Donald Dallas, Richard Rawlingson, Chris Holloway, Nigel Brown, John Payne, Mike Yardley and Diggory Hadoke all responded to my inquiries. Editors Mike Barnes and Will Hetherington have been good enough to see my work into print in *Fieldsports* and *The Shooting Gazette*, respectively.

Without the cooperation of craftsmen and others associated with the gun trade, this book would have been utterly impossible. Over the past two decades I often have intruded upon the valuable bench time of craftsmen in England, Italy, Belgium, Spain and the US. None have complained when I interfered with production, and all have generously shared their hard-earned expertise. Ultimately, this book is a tribute to them and their skills—and also to the craftsmen who came before. In the gun trade I owe special thanks to:

Atkin Grant & Lang, Ltd.—Ken Duglan, Alan Bower, Carl Russell and Ian Sweetman.

Manufacturas Arrieta—Manolo Santos, Asier Arrieta and Juan Carlos Arrieta.

Pedro Arrizabalaga—Alberto Garate.

The Birmingham Gun Barrel Proof House—Roger Hancox, C.W. Harding and Roger Lees.

Boss & Co.—Graham Halsey.

A.A. Brown & Sons—Robin Brown, the late Albert and Sidney Brown, and the late Harold Scandrett.

David McKay Brown (Gunmakers), Ltd.—Alexe & David McKay Brown.

E.J. Churchill—the late Don Masters (and widow Valerie).

Cogswell & Harrison (Gunmakers) Ltd.—Alan Crewe.

Connecticut Shotgun Manufacturing Co.—Tony Galazan.

John Foster Gunmakers—John Foster and Graham Bull.

Auguste Francotte—the late Ivan de Stoop.

Armas Garbi—Jesus Barrenechea.

Gavin Gardiner, Ltd.—Gavin Gardiner.

W.W. Greener Ltd.—David J. Dryhurst, Richard Tandy and Graham Greener.

Griffin & Howe—Guy Bignell, Luc Vander Borght and Bob Beach.

Heritage Guns—Toby Barclay.

Holland & Holland, Ltd.—Daryl Greatrex, Russell Wilkin, Steve Denny, Roland Wild, Paul Faraway, Dean Burman, Mike Birch, George Woodruff, Warwick Dauncey and Steven Cranston.

Holloway & Naughton—Andrew Harvison.

Holt's Auctioneers—Nicholas Holt.

Independent Craftsmen (North America)—David Trevallion, Abe Chaber, the late Alfred Gallifent, Michael Ehinger, Claudio Opacak, Dale Tate, Bill Harvey, Hugh Lomas, Jack Rowe, Doug Turnbull, Leslie Paul and Dewey Vicknair.

Independent Craftsmen (UK & Europe)—Mike Smart, Paul Stevens, Stephane Dupille, Henri Laurent, Bill Blacker, Gary Hibbert, Alex Torok, Alan Wey, Mark Sullivan, Mick Kelly, Richard St. Ledger and Roelof Lucas.

Independent Gun Dealers—William, Dan and David Moore; Bill Bryan; Richard Raymond; Jack Jansma and Bryan Bilinski.

Independent Gun Engravers—Alan & Paul Brown, Phil Coggan, Barry Lee Hands, Peter Spode, Keith Thomas, Ken and Marcus Hunt,

Charles Lee, Gianfranco Pedersoli, Firmo Fracassi, Gian Marco Sabatti and Mario Terzi.

Kennedy Gunmakers—Tony Kennedy.

Lebeau-Courally—Cornelis 'T Mannetje.

Liège Arms Museum—Claude Gaier.

P.V. Nelson (Gunmakers)—Peter V. Nelson.

William Powell & Sons—Peter Powell.

James Purdey & Sons—Richard Purdey, Nigel Beaumont, Peter Blaine, Ian Clarke, Bob Nicholls and Ian Andrews.

Turner Richards Gunmakers—Bob Turner.

Westley Richards & Co.—Simon & Karena Clode, Keith D. Thomas, Chris Soyza, Ken Halbert and Anthony Alborough-Tregear.

D.H. Sinnerton Gun & Rifle Maker—David Sinnerton.

Watson Bros. Gunmakers—Michael Louca.

T.R. White & Co.—Tony White.

William & Son—William Asprey and Paul West.

Finally, without the patience, love and support of my parents and wife, Leigh, and son, Ian, this would all be for naught. Thank you.

—*Vic Venters*

Gun Craft & Gunmakers

I.
The Unknown Gunmaker:
Bob Turner

Birmingham gunmaker Bob Turner in 2009. (David Grant)

Agunmaker lifts the lid of a felt-lined leather case that rests on a table in his living room. Into view comes a sidelock—a beautifully proportioned action filed up by hand with double bars and beads and wed to a stock of highly figured walnut. With barrels attached, the gun almost dances in the hands, so lively is its balance. Ejectors are perfectly timed, the shift of the safety is simultaneously crisp but buttery, and the fit of metal to metal is as flawless as human hands are capable of. On each side of the foliate-engraved action is the maker's name: Turner Richards.

Turner *who*?

Bob Turner may just be the finest English gunmaker you've never heard of. In five decades on the bench he's built only a handful of guns under his own company's name—the gun described perhaps his last. Turner's craftsmanship, however, has appeared in guns and rifles bearing Britain's best names: Boss & Co., Churchill Atkin Grant & Lang, Dickson & MacNaughton, William Evans, Holland & Holland, P.V. Nelson, William Powell and Westley Richards.

Like legions of anonymous British craftsmen before him, the 70-year-old Birmingham native spent his entire career courting neither fame nor fortune, but rather perfecting his craft as "maker to the trade," supplying other firms with components and actions and guns that they would stock, engrave and finish under their own names.

Beauty, it has been said, makes presence shine. Turner's handicraft positively gleams, whether its presence bears his name or not.

Almost retired now, Turner met me for his first-ever interview last November at the Ewe & Lamb, a bustling pub on the outskirts of Bromsgrove, a town of 35,000 southwest of Birmingham that has been his home since 1964. Clad in a spotless white cable-knit sweater and wearing glasses, the smiling, soft-spoken craftsman might easily have passed for a retired minister.

Robert E. Turner was born October 3, 1939, a block from the Westley Richards factory in Birmingham. His passion for guns, however, came first from the country. "I was a war baby," he said. "When the Germans began bombing Birmingham, I was put out to live with my grandparents in the country. By three or four I was going with my grandfather, a gun over his arm, when he went out for a rabbit or pigeon for the pot. I've had a passion for guns and shooting since."

Turner never formally apprenticed with another maker, something that differentiates him from almost every other working craftsman of his era. Over fish and chips and mushy peas washed down with a pint of ale, he outlined the circuitous road he took into gunmaking. "As a lad, I began hanging around the 'old hands' at Westley Richards," he said. "Harry Payne was really my mentor."

Payne was a "stock, screw & finisher" and one of Westley's most experienced craftsmen, the son of Harry (Henry) Payne Sr. and the firm's works manager before the Second World War. "I was 15 and was very keen to learn about gunmaking," Turner said, "and I pes-

Harry Payne Jr., a seasoned craftsman at Westley Richards,
was Turner's mentor in the 1950s. (Courtesy of John Payne)

tered the life out of Harry to teach me how."

The '50s were hard times for British gunmakers. Inexpensive guns
made overseas were killing domestic demand for the sort of mid-
priced product Birmingham excelled at. Youngsters coming into the
trade were scarce, and older craftsmen who had kept their jobs normally were loath to share their skills with interlopers. Payne, however,
took the enthusiastic teenager under his wing.

"He came to realize I could do a job after he'd given me instruc-
tion," Turner said. "I'd go home and practice the projects he'd given
me in my little shed, then bring the work back and he'd correct me."

When Turner was about 18, Payne showed him a Leslie B. Taylor-
patent Westley selective single trigger—one of Britain's best triggers

but an intricate mechanism in which, in the words of Major Sir Gerald Burrard, "every part must be fit with absolute accuracy." It has been likened to the Swiss watch of single triggers.

"When you get better," Payne told him, "you can move on to clever work like this."

"I blurted out, 'Oh, I can make that,'" Turner said. "Of course, I didn't know if I could or couldn't . . . ."

"Then take it away and build me one like it," Payne replied.

Turner went home, stripped the 31-part mechanism, made some sketches of its dimensions, got to work making components, and in time returned with a gleaming new trigger.

"After Harry examined it, he gave me a little smile and said, 'Hold on,' then, clutching it, disappeared downstairs." He returned soon after with Harry Rogers, Westley's managing director. "Rogers handed the trigger back and said, 'Can you make us half a dozen?'"

A pupil so ardent and mechanically adept seemed destined for glory in the gun trade, but Turner's father virtually forbade him to enter. "'No future in it,' I was told."

So he did the next best thing: "I went into the machine-tool trade." Turner apprenticed with H.W. Ward & Co., then a prominent Birmingham manufacturer of capstan and turret lathes, spending five years on the floor learning to make machine tools and components, then another 14 years as a draftsman creating the engineering drawings used by machinists to transform concepts on paper into components of steel.

In 1964 he married Barbara Westwood, moved to Bromsgrove and built a small workshop alongside his house. The want of young craftsmen coming into the gun trade had become manifest during the 1960s, and in the shortfall Turner found opportunity. In his spare time he made single triggers and began "fitting in" (or jointing) new barrels to existing guns for a number of makers. "This gave me a foothold into the trade," he said.

Jointing is a time-consuming process that matches the bearing surfaces of the barrel assembly to the action and, if skillfully performed, assures the longevity of the gun through time and over tens of thousands of rounds. "By 1973 I had more work than I could sensibly cope with," Turner said. In October of that year he gave his notice at Ward's and launched a full-time career in gunmaking.

A new 12-bore Turner Richards sidelock—one of a handful of guns made that bear Turner's name. (David Grant)

Birmingham's William Powell & Sons was at the time overhauling its gunmaking operations, with many of its craftsmen either retiring or approaching the age at which they could. "Where to find a best actioner who could complete all aspects of a new sidelock now that our best furniture and ejectorwork men had died, retired or been put out to grass?" reflected Peter Powell, who in 1973 was a new director succeeding his recently retired father, Bernard.

Turner, it turned out, was that actioner. "I was introduced to Bob, and I was impressed by his skills and liked his intelligence, honesty, integrity and thirst for knowledge," Powell said. He presented Turner with an order for a dozen sidelocks, his first large commission for complete guns (sans stocks) rather than piecework. Since then, Turner has actioned almost all of Powell's best-quality English-made No. 1 model sidelocks (including the pair engraved by Alan Brown and pictured on the cover of Nigel Brown's *British Gunmakers, Volume Two*).

As Turner's reputation spread, orders followed from some of Britain's most famous makers—some for guns and actions, others for smaller projects like making "furniture" (components) for Boss single triggers and such. Turner never felt compelled, however, to make guns under his own name, except for a handful under the banner of Turner Richards (the name resulting from a short-lived business partnership, with Turner keeping the name for trading purposes once the partnership dissolved).

If retail buyers barely know his name, Turner has earned respect from his peers. "While Bob didn't enjoy a traditional gunmaking apprenticeship, his love of guns and rifles coupled with his talent and engineering background enabled him to work his way up to true 'gunmaker' status," said Robin Brown, of Birmingham's ultra-traditional A.A. Brown & Sons.

Said Powell: "There have been few who have mastered almost all of the aspects of building a truly 'best' gun—jointing, making and fitting leverwork and ejectors and safeties, filing up action fences—ball and bead—and single- or double-bar shoulders, and fitting lockwork. Bob is one of them. I believe he could finish the stock were he given enough time to meet his standards of perfection."

Exquisite guns often spring from surprisingly tight confines: Turner's workshop of 46 years measures 9' x 14'. A small lathe, a horizontal and vertical miller and a drill press comprise Turner's conventional machinery. Neatly organized boxes of components fill drawers and shelves above and below his bench. On the wall hang stock templates, rifle barrels, big-bore single-shot actions, reloading equipment (Turner is an obsolete-caliber rifle buff), even a barreled action of a Westley Richards-type hand-detachable he's been working on for 40 years. "One day I'll finish it for myself."

To the right of his bench is a full drilling setup salvaged from a dentist's office. A dentist's drill? "I use it for some of the artistic work," Turner said. "With a cutting head, I can use it for fine sculpting, also for getting into corners and slots hard to reach with a chisel or file."

To the left, on shelves up high, are files and notebooks filled with engineering drawings he has drafted over his career. These drawings would go to specialist firms, such as Phillipson & Nephew, to have action bodies and forend irons machined out to his specifications.

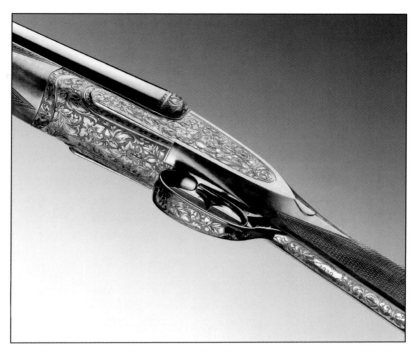

Built on an assisted-opening Holland-type action, Turner's sidelock was engraved with bold foliate scroll by John Barratt. (David Grant)

More than anything, perhaps, Turner's engineering background distinguishes him from other artisanal gunmakers. "Craftsmen traditionally had nothing on paper to build guns from," Turner said. "Each craftsman worked from his own set of templates, jigs and gauges copied from those of the man who taught him.

"As far as I am aware, I am the only practical gunmaker who has actually done his own drafting. The principle behind engineering and drafting—to be extremely accurate—has seen me all the way through gunmaking."

This expertise led to one of Turner's last big jobs for the trade. In 1997 he was hired by Scotland's James MacNaughton to help the firm revive production of its Edinburgh model gun. Turner reengineered it for modern production—notably improving the MacNaughton by incorporating Southgate-type ejectors in place of the original fragile design. He also made the first new 20-gauge MacNaughton. When MacNaughton purchased John Dickson in 1999 to form Dickson

& MacNaughton, Turner also worked on reengineering the former's Round Action.

In 2001 Turner returned to college to learn CAD (computer-aided design) programming. "I was obviously the oldest in my class . . . ."

As one of 15 elected Guardians of the Birmingham Proof House, Turner remains engaged in the gun trade, but his career is winding down. The last gun he built—the Turner Richards sidelock—was made for a cousin, not the trade. There is the Westley-style droplock he'd like to finish and a couple of rifles—but if completed, they will be his and not sold.

Turner's career, in retrospect, presages the high-tech revolution that has transformed fine gunmaking in the past couple of decades. The British trade (aside from that of the Basques) remained arguably the most traditional the longest, with craftsmen regarded as distinct from engineers. By contrast, Turner has been fully in both camps his entire working life, his success predicated in part on ambidexterity in mastering metal with each set of skills.

That such an integrated approach dominates contemporary gun-making was shot home a couple of days after my visit with Turner, when my tour of Purdey's London factory revealed engineers in the firm's sophisticated machine shop having appropriated many of the tasks once reserved for bench-trained artisans. For example, the goal of old-fashioned actioning—in essence, ensuring the mechanical integrity and function of the gun—nowadays can be written into CAD/CAM programs and substantially achieved through CNC machining, with the craft of actioning increasingly an adjunct of assembly work and fine finishing.

Dual skills for tomorrow's artisan gunmaker will not be an exception, as was the case with Turner, but a necessity. "Any youngster coming into the trade today not only will need gunmaking skills but also will have to be computer literate and definitely have knowledge of CNC machining," Turner said.

That an unknown gunmaker helped blaze the way should be better known.

II.
Jointing & The Circle

Man has for a long time recognized that the number "three" possesses special properties. Pythagoras considered it the perfect number, the embodiment of harmony and masculine strength. Classical mythology held that three gods ruled the world: Jupiter (heaven), Neptune (sea) and Pluto (Hades). Christianity's God has a triune nature—Father, Son and Holy Ghost—and the Old Testament, New Testament and Apocrypha comprise the Bible. All stories have a beginning, middle and end, and any carpenter worth the steel in his saw knows that a three-legged stool is more stable than a comparable one made with four.

Gunmaking has its own rules of three, starting with what are traditionally a gun's elemental components: its lock, stock and barrel. Another application concerns "jointing,"

In traditional craft gunmaking little has changed in the past century in jointing a gun: a W.W. Greener actioner at work in the early 20th Century, and Richard Tandy performing same today. (Courtesy Richard Tandy/ W.W. Greener)

the process of fitting the barrel assembly into the action so that the bearing surfaces of each mate in ways that make the gun durable, safe and easy to operate. To accomplish these three goals in a shotgun, an actioner brings surfaces to bear at three critical locations: at the hinge pin, on the action face and at the bolt.

Allied with sound design and high-quality steel, a triadic joint is the front-line defense against a gun shooting loose—that is, coming "off the face" at the barrel breeches and action face. A gun severely off the face will show daylight between the breech surfaces, and there invariably will be play at the hinge.

Every time a gun is fired, a slew of violent physical forces generated by the combustion of powder and the ejection of the payload work to batter, bash, bend or otherwise sunder a gun's stress-bearing components. Radial forces resulting from gas pressure will be mostly contained by the strength of the barrels, while the bolt tames those acting to pry open a breechloading gun around its hinge.

In a conventional side-by-side shotgun, the most popular bolting mechanism is nowadays James Purdey's underbolt (or "double bolt") of 1863—a spring-loaded, flat rectangular bolt that travels in slots in the action bar to engage the bites in each of the lumps of the barrels, thus locking the latter into the bar until a lever-operated cam withdraws it.

The rotational forces working to force the barrels up and open in a shotgun are actually relatively weak. In fact, in the 19th Century various gunmakers demonstrated that a gun with its bolt removed, if properly jointed, would remain closed during firing by simply holding the barrels down to the action with the hand or a tie of string.

If the Purdey design enjoys enormous reserves of strength in bolting down the barrels, it alone does little to master the destructive thrusts running along the axis of the tubes. These axial forces hammer the action face at every shot, driving the entire frame back and slamming the hinge pin into the hook upon which the barrels hinge.

Unless some form of supplemental buttressing guards the hinge, consequent wear and tear between pin and hook over time can force the two surfaces apart—leaving the shooter with a gun with "the shakes." A double gone loose will almost invariably shoot looser the more it's fired, as the gaps between hook and hinge pin and between breech and action face generate increased kinetic energy

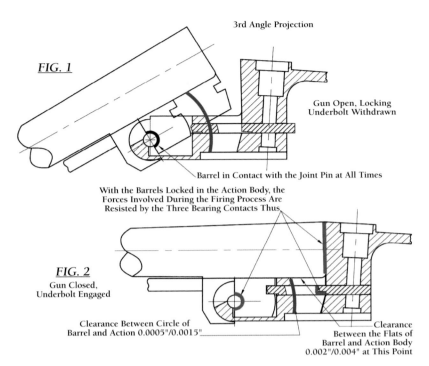

FIG. 1

Gun Open, Locking
Underbolt Withdrawn

Barrel in Contact with the Joint Pin at All Times

With the Barrels Locked in the Action Body, the
Forces Involved During the Firing Process Are
Resisted by the Three Bearing Contacts Thus

FIG. 2
Gun Closed,
Underbolt Engaged

Clearance Between Circle of
Barrel and Action 0.0005"/0.0015"

Clearance
Between the Flats of
Barrel and Action Body
0.002"/0.004" at This Point

Diagrams Showing the Bolting of a Shotgun Using the Purdey System
UNLESS OTHERWISE STATED, ALL DIMENSIONS IN INCHES ± 0.005"

*Gunmakers use the principle of jointing on three bearing surfaces
(in red) to resist the forces generated when a gun is fired. In a double
shotgun with Purdey underbolts, careful jointing on the circle (in blue)
provides a critical supplementary bolster when the gun is fired. British
gunmaker/engineer Bob Turner created these drawings to accurately
illustrate the principles and tolerances craftsmen work to.*

(Copyright Turner Richards Gunmakers)

between the colliding components—which can spiral into an ever-accelerating cycle of damage. (Over time, frictional wear from repeated opening and closing also can loosen a break-action gun, but in this discussion I will focus entirely on the consequences resulting from shooting.)

Although a common enough problem, a gun that has gone off the face is deemed to have a serious enough defect in the UK that it will not pass proof. It cannot, in fact, even be submitted to a proof house until rectified. Shooting loose is also the most common cause of failure during the proofing process. "Ideally there should be no gap at the breech face either before or after proof," said Robin Brown, of A.A. Brown & Sons, who is the Vice Chairman of the Guardians of the Birmingham Proof House. "This might be measured by our inspectors by viewing [visual inspection] or by inserting a feeler gauge. Perceptible play when the gun is bolted is also not acceptable."

Many early breechloading designs of the 1850s quickly shot themselves into rattletraps until gunmakers developed effective bolsters that reduced stress load at the hinge. One of the first answers was the top extension, which when properly designed and fitted nullifies the worst consequences of axial thrust at the action face and load-up on the hinge. But talk of top extensions will have to wait; that is the subject for the next chapter.

An action can, of course, be made so large that its sheer size and strength suffice to subdue any destructive forces of firing. But in Britain, where a gun's lightness and handling qualities are prized, the answer—with a Purdey-bolted gun, anyhow—is jointing the gun "on the circle."

The "circle" is a term that can be applied to both a general principle of jointing as well as to the specific bearing surfaces of a component. In the latter case it normally describes a circle as measured from the center of the hinge pin to a corresponding concave surface on the front of the barrel's rear lump. As the gun is closed, the circle on the rear lump mates with the "draw," which is the convex-shaped bridge in the frame located between the slots in the action flat. Conceptually, the circle also can describe similar bearing surfaces on other components—on a doll's-head top extension, for example, or on the bifurcated lumps of some over/unders.

Careful jointing on the circle fulfills three purposes: 1) It helps distribute pressure-generated stress over a greater mating-surface area of the action and barrel interface when the gun is fired; 2) it helps cam in a barrel lump for a secure fit when the bolt goes home; and 3) through the strength it lends, it allows an action to be made compact and light enough to handle nicely and exhibit grace and beauty.

It's hard to overstate how important a proper joint is to the longevity of a gun. In response to a question about which design was more durable, E.J. Churchill's Don Masters once noted: "I would not be

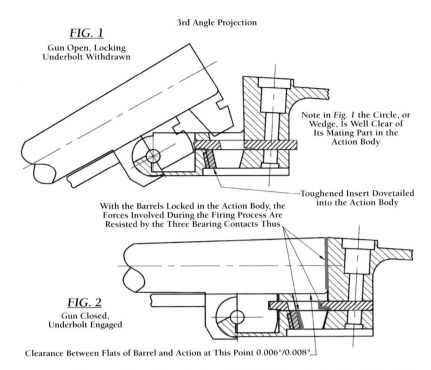

FIG. 1
Gun Open, Locking
Underbolt Withdrawn

3rd Angle Projection

Note in *Fig. 1* the Circle, or
Wedge, Is Well Clear of
Its Mating Part in the
Action Body

Toughened Insert Dovetailed
into the Action Body

With the Barrels Locked in the Action Body, the
Forces Involved During the Firing Process Are
Resisted by the Three Bearing Contacts Thus

FIG. 2
Gun Closed,
Underbolt Engaged

Clearance Between Flats of Barrel and Action at This Point 0.006"/0.008"

Diagrams Showing the Bolting of a Double Rifle Using the Purdey Underbolt
UNLESS OTHERWISE STATED, ALL DIMENSIONS IN INCHES ± 0.005"

Because of the high pressures generated when firing double rifles, gun-makers alter the bearing surfaces when jointing them. Importantly, the circle often is made wedge-shaped and becomes a primary stress-bearing surface, along with the bolt and action face (in red).

(Courtesy Turner Richards Gunmakers)

prepared to estimate the life expectancy of either a best sidelock or a best boxlock; I can only emphasize that a gun is no better than the quality of the joint."

In traditional craft gunmaking—especially best-quality gunmaking—jointing demands the highest skills of its practitioners. A craftsman must work to close tolerances in multiple planes—horizontal, vertical, lateral and radial—bringing appropriate surfaces to bear simultaneously as the gun bolts shut.

In the case of the circle these tolerances are literally as thin as smoke. In Britain a smoke lamp is used to coat metal surfaces with

Some gunmakers now use a hardened insert that is dovetailed into the "draw" to increase the bearing at the circle. This example is from recent production at Holland & Holland. For illustrative purposes it is shown attached to the circle where it bears when the gun is closed.

(Courtesy of Mike Birch)

soot to reveal hard bearings (or "high spots") where opposing surfaces touch. On the Continent engineering ink (Prussian blue) is often employed to same effect.

"Taking smoke" is the term British gunmakers use to describe how much soot is scraped away when surfaces bear. A jointer then will carefully remove visible high spots with his files—or with emery paper when the going gets delicate—and the smoking-and-filing process will be repeated until the surfaces are accurately fitted.

How close the draw and the circle bear on one another depends to some extent on the craftsman's skill but more importantly on the type of firearm being jointed. "When jointing a shotgun, I always ensure that the circle 'just takes the smoke,'" said W.W. Greener's Richard Tandy, who is considered one of the finest jointers in the British trade.

Likewise, Birmingham gunmaker/engineer Bob Turner (also a Guardian of the Birmingham Proof House) described the desired tolerances between a shotgun's circle and draw as "licking the smoke"— with just enough clearance to leave an ultra-thin gray residue on each.

"This means that tolerances are so close that any flex in the action upon firing immediately brings the draw to bear on the circle," Tandy said. "But the bearing isn't so hard that it impedes the opening or closing of the gun."

If the mating surfaces at the circle and draw were close enough to

Another variant of a hardened insert at Holland & Holland—this one pinned in to the draw rather than dovetailed. These inserts increase bearing at the circle and also facilitate jointing and rejointing.

(Courtesy of Mike Birch)

reveal high spots, the gun literally could bind up after shooting—or at least be difficult to open or close.

Actioners therefore toe a fine line between strength and ease of use, particularly with best-quality guns built with the quick-firing demands of driven shooting in mind. "If you make a shotgun where the joint is too firm on the circle," Brown said, "it will not feel good when you open and close it. Just touching the circle is fine, but hard on the circle and it will not feel good. And what do you do with a best gun but open and close it all day long? You want everything to work smoothly."

When jointing a double rifle, however, the equation changes dramatically. Here strength becomes paramount: The breech pressures generated by a .375 H&H Magnum average 62,000 psi; the typical service pressures in a 12-bore game gun, by contrast, are only around 9,000 psi (and often lower). "To allow the hinge pin to bear the stresses delivered by big-bore rifle ammunition is to court disaster," said

Turner. "The hinge pin can actually be pushed forward, bulging the knuckle. Or, the rear lump can bend or crack, or the locking bolt can shear. Sometimes it's a combination. When a poorly jointed rifle goes, it *goes* . . ."

The jointer's solution is to remove virtually all load-up from the hinge pin when the rifle is fired (relegating the pin to solely a hinge for opening the barrels). The circle instead becomes a primary stress-bearing surface, rather than a supplemental one. "When jointing rifles, it is essential that the draw has full bearing on the circle," Tandy said.

Some gunmakers change the shape of the circle to a wedge and also dovetail a toughened insert into the bottom of the draw, which increases the wedge effect and augments the bearing as the rifle closes. This insert is replaceable, and larger sizes can be fitted in to account for wear.

London's Boss & Co. used the circle-and-draw concept with its seminal over/under of 1909. Its inventors dropped the full-width hinge pin and underlumps that theretofore had made O/U actions tall and visually ungainly. Instead they built hinges into each action wall and split (or "bifurcated") the lumps, moving them to the sides of the breech assembly and action and giving the Boss gun an exceptionally sleek, low profile.

The key to this is retaining the principle of jointing on the circle: The barrel lumps are mounted on either side of the lower tube just in front of the breech, and the lumps' concave surfaces mate with the replaceable convex draws on the lumps on the action walls.

The Boss is particularly sophisticated in that the arc of its circle is eccentric to the hinge. "A Boss O/U depends heavily on the fit of the draws," Tandy said. "Its hinged trunnions are nowhere strong enough to take the stress of repeated firings. To help ensure a good fit, Boss drops the center of the circle that describes the arc of the draw, making it eccentric to the hinge. This means you get a really hard bearing when the gun is closed, but the draw moves away when the gun starts to open."

The circle is likewise critical to properly jointing many guns fitted with top extensions, and next chapter we visit actioner Keith Thomas, foreman at the Westley Richards factory, to learn more about the doll's-head extension—still in production a century and a half after its introduction and as effective as ever.

III.
Jointing & The Doll's-Head

Westley Richards foreman Keith D. Thomas
jointing a hand-detachable double rifle.

Guns and gunmakers are as subject to the comings and goings of fashion as are oceans to the pull of tides.

And tides of fashion pull in mysterious ways. Consider Birmingham's Westley Richards, today England's largest English-owned gun and riflemaker. The company's success sprouted from the ruins of its bankruptcy after the Second World War and has flourished in the past couple of decades—without a fashionable London address, without corporate backing and without gun designs deemed trendy by the herd.

Owner and Managing Director Simon Clode has coupled his un-

Gun No. 9779, a "best"-quality Westley Richards Hand-Detachable "Droplock" built in pigeon configuration in 1924, featuring the doll's-head top extension that the firm invented and made famous.
(Richard Rogers)

stinting dedication to craftsmanship with the firm's historic technical innovations for success that in many respects defies contemporary gunmaking trends.

Components are made by sister company Westley Engineering Ltd., a high-tech manufacturer of press tools. Nowadays the fashion in fine gunmaking is to make components with the latest technology to dimensions as close to finished as possible. Clode has, to the contrary, constrained the capabilities of the technology at his disposal—it takes no more than a glance at Westley's unfinished components in the white to show that its guns remain very much hand-crafted, not simply hand-finished.

There is also no mistaking a Westley gun for any other. A defining feature on the firm's traditional double guns and rifles is the doll's-head top extension. Patented by the firm in 1862 (patent No. 2506) and modified several times thereafter (in 1864 and 1871), it is an ingenious design that combines bolting for the barrels with structural support to the breech area and action.

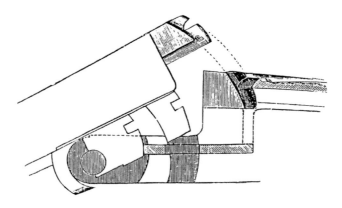

As this vintage Westley Richards catalog illustration shows, the doll's-head is jointed on the circle. In most Westley guns and rifles, the doll's-head not only is the primary bolt for locking the gun but it also absorbs much of the pressure generated in firing. The Purdey-type underbolt provides supplementary support and also serves to hold open the toplever.

The 1862 patent is one of those designs that inextricably altered the course of gunmaking. It describes a "snap action"—that is, a gun with a spring-loaded locking bolt that "snaps" home as the gun is closed, locking the barrels down. It was not the world's first snap action, but it was arguably the first to achieve great commercial success.

So named for the bulbous, circular-shaped head at the extension's tip, the doll's-head makes full use of proven engineering principles. By locking the barrels at the top of the action, the bolt and bite are located as far as possible from the hinge pin, which maximizes its gripping power.

A well-fitted doll's-head is also jointed "on the circle," and the extension's bearing surfaces behind the breech retard the tendency of this area to spring back under axial pressure when the gun is fired. This dampens the flexing of the action bar at its junction with the action face, which in worst cases can exceed the elastic limits of the metal and crack it, or more often help work the barrels off the face. Because of its strength, the doll's-head is particularly well suited to double rifles as well as big-bore shotguns or those intended for powerful cartridges.

The principles of the doll's-head inspired a host of competing top-extension designs in the decades following its introduction. Because of their mechanical advantages, top extensions became popular in the US, where stout loads are the norm. They feature prominently in bolting most classic American double guns: Parkers, L.C. Smiths, Ithacas, Foxes and Lefevers, among others.

Top extensions never caught on with gunmakers in London, however, and 19th Century pundits in the latters' orbit often complained that in general they were ugly, clumsy to use and mechanically superfluous. The most pointed criticisms came from driven-game-shooting quarters, where it was argued that extensions impeded rapid reloading. (The latter criticism never gained much truck in America, where driven shooting never was and never has been fashionable.)

Criticisms noted, the mechanical attributes of the doll's-head still outweigh any of its shortcomings, real or imagined. Clode has in fact used the design and Westley's other distinctive patents to carve out a unique footprint in today's "best"-gun market. "London may have a better name," Clode said. "I think I've got the better gun."

Guns incorporating the doll's-head in today's Westley lineup are hand-detachable "droplocks" in rifles and shotguns, fixed-lock Anson & Deeley boxlock rifles, and new sidelock double rifles introduced in 2008. (In recent years Westley's also has begun offering London-pattern sidelock shotguns *sans* the doll's-head. "People want them," Clode said, "so we make them.")

In 2008 Westley Richards moved out of its historic Bournbrook factory, occupied since 1898, and into a dedicated 20,000-square-foot, £4.5 million factory and showroom on Pritchett Street, near the heart of the Birmingham gun quarter. Built in the bones of an old enameling plant, its showroom combines an inviting contemporary design with walls festooned with African trophies and memorabilia from two centuries of gunmaking. Upstairs is the factory floor, where 14 craftsmen work along well-lit benches that radiate around a hub room where guns in process and their components are stored.

On an overcast day in November 2009, Production Manager Chris Soyza provided a tour. Scion of a Malaysian plantation owner, Soyza has an education in mechanical engineering and a long background in big-bore riflemaking—and an incurable passion for hunting elephants. He oversees the production of 30 to 40 guns and rifles each year, the majority of the doubles made with the doll's-head.

At a bench overlooking Pritchett Street, I was surprised to meet Keith Thomas, an actioner by training and now Westley's shop foreman. When our paths had last crossed he'd been in Purdey's Hammersmith factory.

Thomas, a 36-year-old Rhodesian, learned his craft at Rigby's, served a short stint at Watson Bros., and then had eight years under his apron making bolt rifles and Beesley-type sidelocks at Purdey's. Clode recruited Thomas four years ago, soon after he'd left Purdey's to work in the trade, and under the tutelage of long-time foreman Ken Halbert, Thomas learned the intricacies of jointing Westley guns and rifles. When Halbert (semi) retired, Clode made Thomas foreman.

For more than an hour Thomas generously demonstrated the handicraft that goes into building a new Westley gun—and in particular the skills required for jointing one with a doll's-head. "A Westley hand-detachable with a doll's-head is much harder to joint than a typical London sidelock," Thomas said. "To fit the barrels to the action, then the forend, and all the leverwork would take about 55 hours on a droplock, whereas the same job on a sidelock would take about 30."

One of the reasons, explained Thomas, is the droplock's design: The slots in its action for the detachable locks are large and run well up into the knuckle area, making an integral hinge pin necessary for strength. A fixed pin and the doll's-head, however, make jointing inherently more complicated. Before even beginning to fit in the barrels, an actioner must use metal templates that establish basic dimensions for the arc of the circle for both the barrel lumps and the doll's-head.

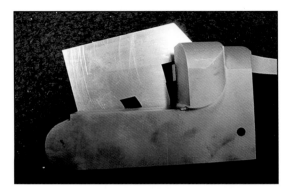

Westley actioners use a metal template to establish the radius of the circle for fitting in barrels with a doll's-head.

(Keith D. Thomas)

At Westley Richards the doll's-head is still filed up and fit in its slot by hand. The firm's machine shop is as sophisticated as any in Britain, but director Simon Clode places great premium on 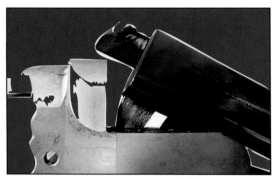 retaining traditional craftsmanship in building Westley guns. This action will be chiseled and filed to final shape by craftsmen, not machines.

(Keith D. Thomas)

A doll's-head with its bolt slot filed in but the action still in the rough.

(Keith D. Thomas)

"You use them as a guide to clean up the slots in the action and to establish the radius."

Traditionally, the circle describes an arc measured from the center of the hinge pin to a corresponding concave surface on the front of the

Right and below: A near-finished action with the doll's-head fitted and the fences and beads filed up by hand. (Keith D. Thomas)

barrel's rear lump. A modern Westley, however, effectively has two circles: that of the aforementioned rear lump and that of the doll's-head.

The most critical are the bearing surfaces on the forward shoulders of the doll's-head where they meet corresponding surfaces in the top of the action. These must hold the breech area fast against axial forces yet also be fitted so finely that the doll's-head can fall smoothly into place as the gun is closed. Jointing in barrels—by hand with smoke lamp and chisel and file—so that neither circle fights the other mechanically adds time and challenges to the process. "I quite honestly believe that if you can joint a Westley doll's-head gun," Thomas said, "you should be able to breeze through jointing any other on the planet."

Such was the strength of the doll's-head that for many years it was the only bolting device employed on Westley doubles. There was a single lump to hinge the barrel upon but no bites for an underbolt. Today the firm uses what it calls the "Type C" variant and pairs it with Purdey underbolts. On a Westley the latter's primary purpose is to hold the toplever open when the gun is being loaded, and any bolting strength the underbolt supplies is supplementary. "On a droplock the doll's-head is the primary bolt," Thomas said. "When the gun is fired, it takes most of the pressure."

It is true that for well-designed conventional guns, the Purdey system alone is entirely adequate for bolting and is especially well suited to average-weight shotguns intended to be fired with relatively low-pressure cartridges. But top extensions such as the doll's-head do one thing Purdey underbolts cannot: offer resistance to axial thrusts at the action face. On Westley's new sidelock double rifles, a stronger linkage design in the leverwork allows the Purdey underbolt to serve as the primary bolt to hold the barrels down, but the doll's-head is still fitted to contain axial thrusts as well as serve as a supplementary bolt.

Though top extensions are rightly associated with big guns made for heavy loads, the strength they lend also permits clever gunmakers to craft especially lightweight or petite actions that might otherwise be compromised in their absence. A 1915 Westley "Modern Gun" catalog notes: "Strength for strength the Westley Richards breech action can be made at least three to four ounces lighter than that of guns constructed on the sidelock system."

This isn't just sales bluster. Today, Westley's makes its hand-detachables from 8-bore down to .410 and in rifles "in every caliber up to .700 Nitro Express"—all on scaled frames in a variety of weights. The attributes of the doll's-head play no small role in fostering this diversity and in particular have helped reestablish Westley's reputation as one of the world's greatest big-bore-rifle makers.

"I think our designs and abilities and understanding in making bespoke double rifles are second to none," Clode said. "I believe ours are more practical, stronger and better suited for the purpose than any others made today."

In or out of fashion, great designs endure—and the doll's-head remains one of them.

IV.
The Hunter One-Trigger

Poor Allan Lard. His single trigger—best known in America as the Hunter One-Trigger—is arguably the most reviled in history.

So loathsome is the Lard's latter-day reputation that only a handful of American gunsmiths will now tackle its regulation or repair.

A century ago, however, it was one of the most popular single triggers on either side of the Atlantic. Britain's Westley Richards embraced it first, in the late 1890s, at the height of the firm's fame and influence, with Westley's not only adopting the "Reliable One Trigger" but also actively and avidly promoting it over standard double triggers, especially for the firm's high-quality hand-detachable "droplocks."

In autumn 1904 New York's Hunter Arms Co.—maker of the L.C. Smith—announced it had purchased Lard's American manufacturing rights after three years of "the most exhaustive possible tests," dubbing the design the "absolutely perfect Hunter One-Trigger" (or "HOT" in Elsie-speak).

According to the company's catalogs, Westley's fit at least 1,500 of its guns with the Lard trigger before superseding it with its own in-house design around 1909. L.C. Smiths, on the other hand, bore the Hunter One-Trigger until production ceased in 1950. As far as I know, no one has yet tabulated how many Smiths were fitted with HOTs, but they surely number in the thousands—thus making it one of the most commonly encountered single triggers from the Golden Age of double guns.

All of which begs a question: If Lard's triggers were so awful, why did two of the world's greatest gunmakers use so many of them?

Lard's single triggers are, in fact, ubiquitous because they were a success—they *worked* and worked well. Lard was an American with a fertile, inventive mind who took out a half-dozen or more trigger patents in the US and UK from 1898 to 1915 before turning his attentions to golf clubs and currency counters. L.C. Smith researchers have discovered numerous variations or refinements in the design but, in the words of Pennsylvania gunsmith Dewey Vicknair, one of America's specialists in HOT repairs, "If you know your way around one variant, you can understand any other."

The Lard was just one of many single-trigger designs to emerge at the end of the 19th Century. John Robertson, of London's Boss & Co., patented the first truly successful one in 1894. Dozens and dozens of competing designs followed in Britain and America; many never made it past the patent or prototype stage, while others proved popular initially, only to sputter away as their shortcomings became evident.

To defeat double-discharge, all single triggers on double guns must in some way either obviate or use the phenomenon of "involuntary pull"—that is, the subconscious, recoil-induced reflexive pull that occurs between the first deliberate trigger pull and the second deliberate pull. Depending on the design, involuntary pull can be harnessed to shift a single-trigger mechanism into contact with the second sear, or it can be blocked for long enough to prevent it from tripping the second sear until the shooter is ready to discharge barrel two. The Lard works by the latter principle, and it employs an inertia-driven pendulous bob-weight to help it do so.

The Lard's bob-weight is unusual in that it is balanced to swing forward under recoil—most operate in the opposite direction—and by containing the involuntary pull within the safety post, it prevents doubling, as well as helping maintain the lifting plate in a correct position to engage the second lock's sear after the first shot is taken. That said, a Lard is best described as a "mechanical" trigger—neither involuntary pull nor recoil-induced inertia is necessary to shift the mechanism from one sear to the other, and should a misfire occur on the first shot the second sear will still engage.

For this reason—and for its reliability—the One-Trigger was used on the dangerous-game double rifles Westley's was famous for, as well as the firm's big-bore fowlers. Westley's noted of the Lard in its Centennial catalog: "The only one-trigger with an established reputation in actual use on double rifles." (It's worth noting that at the time Westley Richards was highly innovative in its own right, and the firm's reputation was in large part built on its big-bore rifles—a reputation it would have hardly risked by installing a substandard trigger design.)

Given this, why *is* the Lard today considered a pariah among sin-

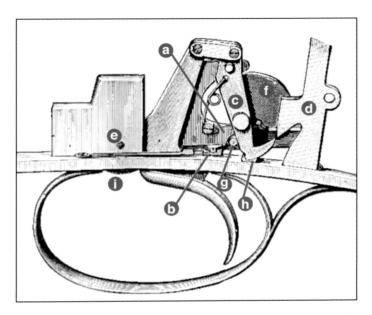

*One-Trigger parts: a) lifting plate, b) barrel selector/sear lifter,
c) safety spur lever, d) safety spur post, e) lifting plate pin, f) bob-weight,
g) bob-weight stud, h) serrated elevated stud, i) barrel-selector slide.*

---

*Despite its numerous parts, A.E. Lard's One-Trigger works on a simple
principle. When the trigger is pulled, the lifting plate (a) trips the first
lock via its sear lifter (b). Simultaneously, the hooked safety spur (c)
is elevated to engage the recess on the spur post (d), which prevents involuntary pull from further raising the lifting plate to inadvertently fire
the second barrel. Recoil drives the pendulous bob-weight (f) forward,
and its integral stud (g) rotates backward and is driven up against the
safely spur, thereby ensuring the latter is securely engaged in the post
during the process of involuntary pull. As recoil subsides and the bob-
weight returns to its former position, a slight relaxation of pressure on
the trigger allows the spur to come forward with its underside resting
on the triggerplate's serrated elevated stud (h). The lifting plate's second
sear is consequently positioned directly under the second sear, ready
to fire barrel two with the next deliberate pull. The trigger's selective
feature is activated by the shooter moving the selector slide (i) forward
or backward, which changes the height of the respective sear lifters and
determines which barrel fires first.*

gle triggers? To many gunwriters—many of whose mechanical aptitude extends barely beyond tapping keyboards (myself included)—it is undeniably fearsome to the eye. A profusion of pins, hooked and recessed components, a barrel-selector slide, bridge-like linkages, tiny springs—its sheer number of bits—all conspire to make it appear more a contraption than a construction of sound engineering. Many American gunsmiths, as noted, seem likewise intimidated.

This is a mistake, say craftsmen familiar with the design. "Usually the gunsmiths who pooh-pooh the Hunter One-Trigger are those who have the least experience with, or least understanding of, the mechanism," said HOT-repair specialist Vicknair. "The best aspects of the L.C. Smith are its rotary bolt and the Hunter trigger—and the One-Trigger is one of the best single-trigger designs around."

Abe Chaber, a Connecticut-based gunsmith with a reputation for single-trigger wizardry, broadly concurs. "When they are built correctly and have not been serviced improperly, they are very sound," he said.

Which is not to gloss over the fact that many guns fitted with Lard/Hunters today have problems—they do, and they can be difficult, frustrating and painfully dear to fix. But the majority of problems stem not from the trigger's intrinsic design; rather they are from larger design and manufacturing issues with the guns they were built in or often from simply poor gunsmithing.

Correct spatial relationships between the sears and the trigger mechanism are fundamental in keeping a Lard running reliably (as is the case with most vintage single-trigger designs). In particular, there must be proper clearances between the tails of the sears and the sear-lifters for the gun to successfully shift to the second shot: too close, and the gun can double; too far apart, and it will balk.

Unfortunately, L.C. Smiths provide plenty of opportunities for critical spatial relationships to go awry. One might fill a book chapter with what can go wrong, but stocking issues are most commonly at fault. In original Elsie manufacture, for example, relatively crude machining removed much of the wood from the head of the stock, leaving scanty bearing surfaces between the frame and lockplates and the wood. Subsequent stock cracking over time, typically behind the lockplates, and consequent shifting of component tolerances are well-known problems and can play havoc with HOT reliability.

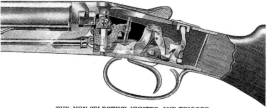

Non-Selective Hunter One-Trigger

THE NON-SELECTIVE HUNTER ONE-TRIGGER

This is the same Hunter One-Trigger we have made for years, with the selective feature eliminated. Based on the Lard patent, the Hunter One-Trigger is exceedingly simple—the parts are large and strong; it is independent of any recoil, is not frictional and will never hang when pulling the second barrel.

The trigger pull is short, clean and quick. There is no drag or creep; the speed of the mechanism far exceeds that of the firing finger, therefore, both barrels can be discharged just as fast as the trigger can be pulled.

The Non-Selective Hunter One-Trigger is set to shoot the right barrel first; then the left, which is the standard or regulation method of shooting a double gun.

We will furnish any grade of L. C. Smith gun equipped with Non-Selective Hunter One-Trigger.

*Each Hunter One-Trigger attached by us to any
L. C. Smith Hammerless Gun is guaranteed for a
period of five years to be free from all defects of
material or workmanship.*

SMITH GUN BARRELS ARE VERY HARD AND NOT EASILY DENTED

*In the 1930s, Hunter Arms introduced a simpler and
somewhat-less-expensive non-selective One-Trigger variant.*

In fact, anything that affects sear clearances—such as springy, oil-soaked wood that allows components to move, alterations to the inletting, or restocking that doesn't duplicate the original tolerances—can create reliability problems. "Overall, 90 percent of problems I see with the Hunter have something to do with the stock," Chaber said.

Lest you think I'm picking solely on Smiths, Lard triggers

*The Hunter Arms Co. actively
promoted the merits of the
One-Trigger throughout its
half-century in production.*

in hand-detachable Westleys are not immune to sear-clearance issues either. W.W. Greener gunmaker Richard Tandy—also one of England's acknowledged single-trigger experts—reports that when the lock-locating stud on the inside of a droplock's action wall becomes worn "after hundreds of thousands of rounds," the detachable lock (and its sear tail) can "flop around" under recoil, making trigger regulation "a nightmare."

Rogue gunsmithing and unskilled tinkering round out other culprits in the Hunter's fall from grace. On an Elsie, even minor mistakes can produce unintended consequences—such as over- or under-tightening the breech pins fore and aft of the trigger unit; again, this alters sear clearance. Ditto for a Smith's lockplates, the pins for which can be over-tightened to similar effect. These are issues easily enough remedied by competent hands. However, when a gunsmith unfamiliar with the trigger's operating principles has physically altered components, it takes a skilled craftsman to sort out the mess—and the remedy often isn't cheap.

For all the craft skill needed to service a Lard, this trigger is not the frail, delicate gizmo that some have claimed. The reliability of many single triggers suffers when their mechanisms become dirty or clogged with hardened oil. According to both Chaber and Vicknair, Hunters will keep ticking even when dirty. And aside from the trigger's springs, Lard components are robust and not particularly prone to wear, fatigue or damage from recoil. "Despite the number of parts," Vicknair said, "it has a simple operating design. Lard was a very, very clever man, and when someone hasn't ruined his trigger, it is absolutely reliable."

It may come as some surprise to learn that a lot of today's shooters agree with this assessment. With the assistance of Jim Stubbendieck of the L.C. Smith Collectors Association, I posted a poll on the organization's Website forum. I asked: "How reliable is your L.C. Smith fitted with the Hunter Single Trigger?" The poll remained online for three weeks, during which 100 posters responded as follows:

Perfect—41%
Very reliable—22%
Somewhat reliable—11%
Not reliable, it balks at a second shot—2%
Not reliable, it doubles—3%

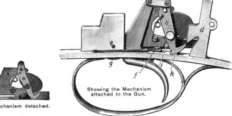
Britain's Westley Richards adopted the Lard design in the late 1890s and used it until about 1909, when it introduced its own house trigger.

Not reliable (other reason)—6%
Reliability unknown, never/rarely shoot it—15%
   Though I would not want to generalize about the poll's broader statistical validity, the responses reveal a startlingly low incidence of failure, especially given the toll that time has no doubt taken on many vintage Smiths. I thought one participant's response was particularly pertinent: "I think part of the problem is that gunsmiths only see

Pennsylvania gunsmith Dewey Vicknair is one of the few craftsmen in North America who will tackle One-Trigger regulation and repair.

[Hunter] triggers that don't work properly. It's a little like cancer doctors who only treats cancer patients—according to them, people don't die of anything else."

Judged by modern streamlined designs, the One-Trigger is indeed imperfect. But as an example of guncraft from an age when craftsmanship counted, Allan Lard's design was an admirable one—and it remains so today.

V.

The Case for Concentricity

Good barrels may not make a bad gun good, but bad barrels will assuredly ruin the best gun ever made.

British firearms auctioneer Gavin Gardiner knows a thing or two about bad barrels. During nearly three decades spent at Sotheby's and at his own auction house, Gardiner has run bore- and wall-thickness gauges through the barrels of literally tens of thousands of guns. Nowadays "thin" barrels are virtually synonymous with "bad" barrels. "Poor wall thickness can literally make a gun almost worthless," Gardiner said.

Though there is no legal definition of how thin "thin" is, experts like Gardiner and gun-trade authorities generally reckon that .020" wall thickness, measured at six to 10 inches from the muzzle, is the recommended minimum, with anything less than that considered marginal.

"A typical 'best' London sidelock that you might expect to otherwise sell for £15,000 at auction in good condition could sell for as little as £6,000 if the wall thickness is below the recommended minimum," Gardiner said. "Wall thickness has become the most critical aspect of a gun's value and can literally make or break a sale."

Whether thin barrels are actually dangerous or not depends on the condition of the gun, the location of thinning relative to pressures generated, the quality of the steel in the barrels, the loads being used, or if the barrels are exposed to hazards—a bore obstruction, for example.

But there is little question that the market perceives thin barrels as dangerous or potentially so. They are arguably more susceptible to dents and dings afield. Dents can be dangerous: If metal removal is required when raising and repairing them, it may shorten a barrel's life. In fact, any process that removes metal—honing, lapping or polishing bores, for example, or relaying ribs and re-blacking barrels—can create "light spots" in wall thickness where stress concentration has the potential to begin insidious work, possibly leading to riveling, pressure bulges or, in worst cases, bursts.

Barrels on old thoroughbred British game guns are perceived as especially vulnerable: From the starting gate many were made to be racy and lightweight—hence relatively thin—and decades of hard use and repairs, and sometimes abuse or neglect, may have cumulatively clipped away at reserves of strength the makers originally built in.

Although thin barrels give collectors and shooters cause for concern, for gunmakers the root of the problem is often *concentricity*, or lack thereof. Wall thicknesses of non-concentric barrels vary around their circumference—a little thick here, a little thin there. Concentricity is often overshadowed by the focus on wall thickness, but they are in fact two sides of the same coin.

Light spots can appear after metal removal, because wall thicknesses on many vintage guns were never concentric to begin with. Achieving *true* concentricity down all 30 or so inches of a thin-walled tube was never easy in an era of relatively primitive drilling and boring technology. Skilled barrelmakers could compensate for errors in tube machining but rarely entirely eliminate original eccentricities.

Modern artisanal gunmakers—certainly best-quality gunmakers like London's Holland & Holland—consider near-perfect concentricity utterly essential. "We are very much concerned today with concentricity," said Russell Wilkin, technical director of gunmaking at H&H. "That is our Holy Grail."

Holland's is the UK's sole sporting gunmaker to manufacture its own tubes and make its own barrels through all of the requisite steps and stages—a control that allows H&H to monitor and regulate quality at every stage of production. Holland's barrels are regarded as some of the best in the world, and barrelmakers such as Peter Higgins and Bill Blacker, who were trained at the company's Harrow Road factory, enjoy superb reputations around the trade. Germany's Hartmann & Weiss, likewise, is considered a truly great gunmaker; its barrelmaker is French, but he was schooled at Holland & Holland.

But even talented craftsmen can perform only remedial work if the tubes they build barrels from are flawed from the start. "Best barrels must begin with good tubes," Wilkin stressed.

In November 2008 production manager Paul Faraway guided me through Holland's exacting tube- and barrelmaking processes at the company's historic factory in North London. We began downstairs, where I was introduced to Dean Burman, who with six other machinists tends a bevy of CNC milling machines, lathes, grinders, reamers, spark eroders and wire cutters. With these, Holland's machinists manufacture all components for the firm's guns in-house.

Tube-making begins with bought-in solid forgings of EN24, a high-tensile nickel-chromium-molybdenum alloy steel. Though it is tempting to think that modern computer-assisted technology allows a machinist to simply chuck a forging onto a lathe, push a button and watch as a concentric tube is cranked out, this is not the case. Rather, tube-making entails a rigorously monitored nine-step process that includes three trips to CNC lathes to turn down outside diameters and

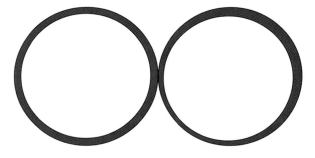

Concentric on the left, eccentric on the right
(exaggerated for illustrative purposes).

provide a basic taper and shape, with each of these steps interspersed by deep drilling, then reaming, then honing—steps that progressively enlarge the bore as the outside diameter is brought down. At regular intervals, machinists inspect the aborning tubes to ensure that their internal and external circumferences remain concentric, with the ultimate goal to accurately arrive at pre-determined dimensions.

To the din of metal-on-metal *screeing* around us, Burman walked me through a truncated tube-making tour—which starts when a solid barrel forging is given an initial turn-down on a CNC lathe. Forgings rarely arrive at the factory perfectly straight or without stress in the steel's structure. The first turn-down trues up the forging's outside diameter well enough for it to contra-spin during the next step, which is deep drilling—with the initial hole bored at a diameter just under Full choke for the intended gauge (or bore) of the barrel-to-be.

Even with state-of-the-art CAD/CAM technology, accurate, deep drilling isn't fast or easy, and the initial boring invariably "runs out" to a slight degree off the intended axis of the tube during the 40-minute process. In the bad old days, this is the stage where problems with wall concentricity sometimes crept in. However, in Holland's case the first turn-down leaves enough metal for the outside diameter to be proportionally reduced again, this time with the lathe centered off the newly drilled bore. This corrects any run-out as the tube is form-turned to establish its basic exterior shape and taper. "This is the stage where we really build in concentricity," Burman said.

The bores are next enlarged to within .005" of finished size, with a reamer pulled forward from the breech, stopping short of the muzzle. This creates a rough choke cone, which transitions to the already established one-inch (Full) choke parallel. (Final choking to customer specifications will be subsequently finished by the barrelmakers and Holland's choke regulator.)

Turning and boring operations in prior steps may have added stress to the tube that can cause it to bend or deform, so machinists carefully check it for straightness and also with a wall-thickness gauge for concentricity. Any "high spots"—that is, where tube walls are too thick relative to desired dimensions—are marked so they can be turned down during the next step.

Fine-form turning then removes high spots to the extent possible, and the tube is inspected again. The bore is then manually honed to within .002" of finished diameter, leaving just enough steel for the barrelmaker to lap out and polish as the tube is made into a barrel. At this point the tube's wall thickness should be concentric within .002" or .003".

The tube is then matched with a mate, and the breeches are machined in preparation for brazing together. The pair is assigned to a barrelmaker with relevant details—gauge, barrel length, rib type, weight and such—spelled out for the intended gun, and sent upstairs to the barrel shop.

It was quiet in the barrel shop during my visit, or at least quieter than the machine room downstairs. Files softly rasped at metal, and someone with a hammer *tap-tap-tapped* away. Potted plants hung

Marking high spots, which will be removed.

here and there in windows that craftsmen have gazed from for over a century. Mike Birch is the shop foreman and has been making barrels at H&H since 1989. Technologically, the barrel shop is perhaps the least changed of Holland's seven gunmaking departments, and a barrel man transported from 1889 immediately would recognize the tools and techniques that Birch, Warwick Dauncey and George Woodruff employ as they transform tubes into barrels. "The machine shop gives us the best tubes they can," Birch said, "and with them we make the best barrels we can."

Birch and his barrelmakers carefully check the tubes for form and correct outside diameter, then spend eight to 10 hours "striking" them—using special flat files—with long strokes down their length from breech to muzzle, working around the circumference of each tube. Striking in essence sheers away all traces of circular tooling marks left from machining, which if not taken down appear as unsightly ripples when viewed. This is more a matter of form than function; however, waves and ripples are no more welcome on the barrels of a best English gun than is a fever blister on the lip of a beauty queen.

Skilled "striking up" also perfects concentricity. Remnant high spots are identified and eliminated, with barrelmakers working to plus or minus .001" concentricity. "Personally," Birch said, "I aim for zero eccentricity."

Finally, striking up provides the last elegant touch to the sweep and taper of a set of tubes. One of the subtle joys of a best gun is peering up its barrels and seeing a beautiful, clean sweep from breech to muzzle utterly free from bumps, humps or jumps and gleaming like the surface of polished obsidian.

With striking completed, tubes are nearly ready to become barrels. Geoffrey Boothroyd once wrote: "a tube becomes a barrel when it is joined to another tube, thereby becoming a set of barrels" (aptly noting that this definition is problematic in the case of single-barreled guns). Tubes still will need to be brazed together at the breeches, have a forend loop fitted and brazed in, have ribs fitted, have the breech and lumps machined, and be chambered. Aside from lapping and final polishing, however, concentricity has been established and final wall thickness is only a whisker away.

As noted earlier, wall thickness is the flip side of concentricity—and the barrels on a modern H&H gun leave the factory with not only more concentric walls than on guns built a half-century ago but also with thicker walls. On today's Royal 12-bore side-by-side, for example, minimum thickness generally will be .032"—at least .004" or .005" greater on average than in years past and *sans* troublesome thin spots caused by barrel-wall eccentricities. The upshot is a gun with stronger barrels that are inherently more resistant to damage—and if damaged then more safely repairable.

"In nine of 10 cases the reason for scrapping old barrels today is due to thin patches following repairs," Wilkin said. "In the past when a barrel was first made, its wall thickness could be eccentric yet still be strong enough to do the job. But eccentricity may become a problem later in its life if the bore is opened up for some reason and the initially thin area becomes marginal.

Tube straightening in the factory machine shop.

"We therefore work today to very tight limits of eccentricity. This allows us to have relatively thin, lively barrels still with an immense degree of wall-thickness cover to meet accidental damage, repair and inevitable metal removal."

It's a notable accomplishment that Holland & Holland's machinists and craftsmen have been able to make barrels stronger *and* safer without increasing overall weight or detracting from the superb handling qualities that define a best British gun. That's great gun craft and the subject for discussion next chapter.

VI.

'Best' Barrelmaking

It's not especially rare to find older British or European shotguns with pristine, utterly original barrels that nonetheless have thinner walls than their apparent condition dictates.

Conventional wisdom posits that this often resulted from gunmakers striking barrels extra thin to either reduce a gun's overall weight or influence and improve its balance—or its "handling," more precisely put.

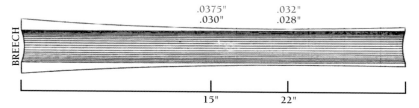

A typical barrel profile of a Holland & Holland Royal 12-bore side-by-side has changed over time. The lower set of wall-thickness dimensions (in blue) show nominal wall thickness at 15 inches and 22 inches from the breech of a barrel, circa 1900. The corresponding dimensions above them (in red) show nominal wall thickness circa 2009. Not indicated are the accompanying wall thickness reductions at the breech on today's guns, which can vary to fit each gun's action. The effect of removing wall thickness from the breech area and moving it farther up means that barrels can weigh no more than they did a century ago yet be thicker and stronger at the areas most susceptible to damage or metal removal.

While this was sometimes the case, Russell Wilkin, technical director of gunmaking at Holland & Holland, offers a more prosaic explanation: "Poor tube-making," he said. "Someone in the maker's barrel shop did not pick up on inherent flaws in the tubes before starting work."

The barrel shop remains among the most traditional at Holland &
Holland, with most tools and techniques recognizable from a century
ago. Here, tubes are being struck up by hand. (Courtesy of Mike Birch)

In part it was this problem that led Holland & Holland to bring all of its tube- and barrelmaking operations in-house when engineering conglomerate Vickers-Armstrongs, Ltd., stopped supplying tubes to the English gun trade in the early 1960s. Holland's faced the choice of either finding another supplier or making its own.

"The tubes Vickers had been making were just awful," Wilkin recalled. "Typical problems were eccentricity, dreadful exterior shape and very poor dimension tolerances brought about by the machine operator only working to the correct diameters at the points along the tubes that he knew the 'inspector' would check. Our barrelmakers had to spend an entire day—a hard slog—just 'stripping and striking.'"

Rather than face the vagaries of another bought-in product, Holland's purchased the Vickers machinery in 1965, brought it to its Harrow Road factory, and since has made its own tubes in its machine room, thus gaining full control over the entire barrel-manufacturing cycle. In Chapter V, "The Case for Concentricity," I discussed the steps that H&H uses to ensure near-perfect concentricity in its tube-making: a multi-step operation that combines craft skills with aerospace-age machining technology.

I left off in the barrel shop on the factory's second floor, where I watched as three craftsmen—foreman Mike Birch, Warwick Dauncey and George Woodruff—turned tubes into barrels. In contrast to the machine room, Holland's barrel shop remains one of the factory's most traditional.

It takes a minimum of four or five years to train good barrelmakers, Wilkin said—"forever" in today's job environment—and their skills only improve with seasoning. Holland's barrelmakers work to a set of prescribed dimensions for wall thickness and outside diameters when building barrels, but their craft is founded on hand-skills needed to wield a bevy of specialized files and with eyes trained and tuned by experience to catch the tiniest imperfections or variations from form. With them, Birch, Woodruff and Dauncey produce barrels that to the casual observer appear virtually identical to those from a century ago.

Yet there have been changes—some obvious, some subtle—and not only with the composition of barrel steel, which has improved dramatically since the First World War. One obvious change is the use of only chopper-lump tubes—or demiblock tubes in the case of over/unders. Dovetail construction, associated with lower grades of guns, has disappeared from H&H production, and the modern monoblock has yet to appear at Harrow Road.

A more subtle change has been in a typical barrel's profile—that is, its exterior shape and wall thicknesses from breech to muzzle. The ubiquitous 12-bore side-by-side serves as an example. On today's Holland Royal, the profile is more parallel down its length than in the past—thinner at the breech, where there are immense reserves of strength, and slightly thicker about halfway up and extending to the muzzles.

"So many old guns have had their lives shortened through the years by damage or metal removal in the critical area 12 to 24 inches down the barrels," Wilkin explained. "One of the very first things we did in the '60s when we brought tube-making in-house was to 'pinch' some metal off the breech and, in essence, move it down the tubes."

Whereas a typical Holland 12-bore barrel circa 1900 might have a nominal .030" wall thickness measured 15 inches from the breech

Barrelmaker George Woodruff striking a rib.

face, today's barrel would mike .0375" at the same location. This correspondingly will produce minimum wall thicknesses of .032" farther up at a barrel's thinnest spot, rather than .028" (or thereabouts) typically seen in the past. As noted in the preceding chapter, when combined with today's tough modern steels and Holland's stringent emphasis on concentricity, this creates stronger barrels that are inherently more resistant to damage—and if damaged, then more safely repairable.

"Because metal has been redistributed down the length rather than added," Wilkin said, "overall barrel weight has not increased, nor has the weight of the gun." Considered in isolation, metal redistribution such as this will move the balance forward—or, more accurately, increase moment of inertia (MOI). However, the redistribution effect is subtle and can also be counterbalanced elsewhere.

"Weight added to the stock can be positioned forward toward the action or just below the butt end," Wilkin said. "Varying the barrel length also has a much greater effect on handling than moving a few thou of material 12 inches up the barrels."

Though I have discussed *typical* barrels and *nominal* wall thicknesses, it still is possible for Holland's to make thinner or thicker barrels, depending on the purpose of the gun or customer requirements. Customization is, after all, the essence of a bespoke "best" gun. For a 12-bore Royal side-by-side, for example, H&H uses three tube configurations to build barrels upon: a standard game tube, a heavier pigeon version, and tubes that dimension-wise fall between game and pigeon weights. Typically, the latter are used for "fitters-in" (replacement barrels), due to variations in the sizes of vintage actions, their breech faces and their accompanying forends.

"If we are looking to reduce the weight of a barrel assembly or looking to match replacement barrels," Wilkin said, "a barrelmaker will 'strip' material with files, then strike up, always keeping an eye on wall thickness and concentricity." Holland's barrelmakers can "strip & strike" down to .027" or .028" if requested, and they can even go to .025" for 12-bore two-inch guns.

"I should emphasize that stripping of a tube to produce desired variations to the form must take place at the start of the process before the tubes are joined together," Wilkin said. "Once joined, the full circumference of the tubes becomes inaccessible."

After the tubes have been struck (and stripped, if necessary) to perfect form and concentricity, the barrelmakers braze (hard-solder) them together at the breech lumps in a muffle furnace at 600° C with a cupro/silver eutectic alloy to ensure a precise melting point, thus creating the basic barrel assembly. The forend loop is then hand-fitted and brazed in place, the tubes cleaned off, and the breech ends hand-filed to blend with the profile of the barrels. After blending, the barrels' breech rings will be just smaller than the face of the action, leaving enough metal surplus on the latter for an actioner to file and shape the gun's fences.

During my visit, I watched Birch and Woodruff "smoking in" ribs in preparation for soft-soldering—or "tinning"—them on. First they blacked a rib with smoke from a paraffin lamp, and then they fitted the rib to the barrels, examining it carefully upon lifting for any bright "high spots" revealed by excessive metal-to-metal contact during the dry fitting. High spots were then dutifully filed off. It is a process repeated as often as needed to perfect the junction between rib and barrels, as well as to perfect their sweep and taper—and the overall

Barrel-shop foreman Mike Birch tinning on ribs.

aesthetic relationship between components when joined. It is a job that clearly cannot be rushed. "We spend a lot of time filing the ribs," Birch said. "Maybe 14 to 15 hours, all done by eye and hand."

Holland's still uses the time-tested method of soft-soldering to join ribs to barrels. The undersides of the ribs and the corresponding surfaces of the tubes where they will be secured are first painted with an aggressive flux and tin mixture, then heated to tin-coat all of the components, and then thoroughly cleaned. The ribs are attached and wired on at four or five locations down the tubes, with a small wedge placed under each twist of wire atop the ribs to help compress bearing edges together. A clip at the muzzles keeps the tubes straight and parallel. The barrel assembly is then placed on parallel steadies to lend support as pure pine rosin flux is dribbled into the crevices between rib and barrels as the barrelmaker plays a 240° C "soft" flame from a gas torch over the assembly, moving it constantly to keep the tin from burning. The rosin melts (it smells like turpentine), causing the tin to run, thereby creating a seal that will withstand decades of hard shooting.

Nowadays there are any number of ways to lay ribs on double guns, including silver-soldering and even using lasers, but the low

Mike Birch lapping a bore.

temperatures involved in Holland's traditional process not only prevent any distortion between rib and barrels but also are benign enough
to obviate any heat-related compositional changes that might weaken
the steel. Should a rib eventually spring through repeated shock, it
can be easily re-laid, and the tinning used protects the barrels against
rust and corrosion should any water leach in past a lifted rib.

Holland's barrelmakers no longer use "packing pieces"—the small
supports traditionally placed at intervals between the tubes to keep
the axes of the barrels in the same relative position and to complement the strength of the brazing at the breech. I asked Wilkin about
their absence.

"You don't need them if you know what you are doing," he said.
"At Holland's we set great store in machining the mating faces of the
tubes to give the correct breech centers and to bring the barrel muzzles to a touch. By careful wiring and the use of wedges, we hold the
barrels true in tinning.

"Many old guns show marks in their bores where they have been
lapped, revealing packing-piece 'hollows' where the packing expanded
from the heat of friction during lapping, creating a slight bump, which
was lapped off. When the metal contracted on cooling, it would leave

George Woodruff smoothing barrels. (Courtesy of Mike Birch)

a witness in the bore—much like shaving a pimple off. Without packing pieces, this does not become a potential problem."

With the ribs on, the barrel set is then painstakingly cleaned of burnt rosin and excess tin with files shaped to fit crevices, and then the barrels are papered down. The chokes—at this point still at .040" nominal Full constriction—are then reamed to the customer's nominal specifications. The bores are lapped and then mirror polished on an old lathe with a revolving rod tipped with a Turk's head of emery-paper strips. The processes remove only a thou or two from the bores, but the task is time-consuming—taking about five hours.

The ultimate goal is, in Wilkin's words, for each barrel to be "absolutely true." These steps—the final lapping and polishing—"true up" the bore. "Passing the reamer down the bore to modify the choke can leave superficial blemishes," Wilkin said. "Final truing up removes any slight imperfections or tiny variations in bore diameters.

"I doubt this has any effect on the shooting of the gun, but it is nice to look up a pair of barrels and see a lovely shape up the outside and a bright true bore—it just reeks of quality and attention to detail and skill, and everything that goes with it."

Aesthetics aside, Holland's emphasis on form—being graceful and "true" in every respect—implies underlying functional perfection: barrels that are absolutely straight; convergence angles that are properly machined; chambers, forcing cones and chokes that are properly reamed and polished and utterly concentric to the axes of the bores. It will take Holland's barrelmakers more than 60 hours of skilled guncraft per set to achieve this. The product of those 60 hours will last the lucky owner—assuming proper care—beyond his lifetime.

At this point the barrelmaker's tasks are almost finished. Barrels are sent back downstairs for the breechblock to be machined for barrel lumps and extractor beds, then they're issued to the action shop for jointing in, then they're chambered, and then they're sent to proof.

When the gun is mechanically complete, the barrels will be sent from the finishing shop back to the barrel shop for a final polishing with 1,000-grit emery paper prior to blacking. Steven Cranston—Holland's long-serving in-house barrel regulator—will pattern and regulate the chokes at the firm's Northwood Range and Shooting Grounds. Holland's choke design and Cranston's magic regulating them—the latter some of the most specialized and arcane skills in guncraft—are subjects in the next chapter.

VII.
Hand-Regulating Chokes

When Gough Thomas commissioned a bespoke "best" gun from Henry Atkin, Ltd., in 1947, he was particularly picky about its chokes and the cartridges they were regulated to. From surviving correspondence between Atkin's and Thomas, we learn that after the gun's initial delivery, the latter sent it back to have remedied several unspecified "barrel defects."

Since the late 19th Century, Holland & Holland has been famous for its shotgun-choke and double-rifle regulation.

In a letter accompanying the gun's return to Britain's most renowned shotgun authority, Atkin's wrote: "We have since shot the gun for pattern and it has not altered one pellet from its original trial at the 'plate.' We plated it with the load as stipulated by yourself, viz. 33 grains of 'E.C.' and $1^{1}/_{16}$ oz of No. 6 shot, and the patterns were . . . ." Atkin's then listed the pellet counts at the plate for five shots per left and right barrels, which in this case placed an average 58 percent of the specified load in a 30-inch circle at 40 yards. Thomas had ordered both barrels with "Half Choke" (throwing roughly 60-percent patterns), which approximates America's Modified choke. Though Thomas's comments are quite detailed, nowhere are "points" (or measurements) of choke constriction mentioned—only performance expressed as a pellet-strike percentage using his pet load.

As a trained engineer and ballistic expert, Thomas was no doubt fussier than most, but his request—hand-regulating chokes for specified performance with a chosen cartridge—had long been standard procedure when ordering a bespoke gun.

This state of affairs hardly exists nowadays, thanks to a confluence of changes in cartridges and choke manufacturing over the past half-century. Not only have there been vast physical alterations in shotshells—plastic hulls, wads and pellet protectors; better powders; increased use of buffering; and new nontoxic shot—but now there also are a bewildering variety of loads readily available to shooters. Moreover, screw-in chokes are increasingly ubiquitous, even in best-gun circles. Notes Purdey Chairman Nigel Beaumont: "We are fitting removable chokes to a great many of our guns now. This is approaching 50 percent, and it will keep rising." Many fine-gun makers in Britain and elsewhere no longer even regulate chokes; they are simply bored to a desired constriction in a fixed or screw-in configuration, and it is left to the owner to find the shotshell-and-choke combination that best suits an intended purpose. This makes old-fashioned choke regulation, if not a dying art, a craft of gunmaking fast receding in the tides of technological change.

But not at Holland & Holland. The London firm is one of a handful of gunmakers that still regulates its chokes by hand—and Holland's is perhaps unique in that it employs a full-time barrel and choke regulator at its Northwood Range and Shooting Grounds to perform solely that function. I visited the grounds to meet regulator Steven Cranston as well as Russell Wilkin, Holland's director of technical gunmaking.

It is worth noting that H&H made its reputation not only on the mechanical and aesthetic excellence of its guns and rifles, but also on how perfectly they were regulated. William Froome, Holland's director of gunmaking in the late 19th Century, was noted during his day as being Britain's most-skilled rifle regulator, and the firm owes him much credit for cementing it as one of the world's greatest gunmakers.

Today Cranston wears Froome's mantle and is heir to his legacy. A 28-year veteran of Holland's, Cranston—tall, loquacious and with

Barrelmaker Steven Cranston carries on Holland & Holland's long tradition of hand-regulating chokes at the firm's Northwood Range and Shooting Grounds. (Courtesy of Mike Birch)

a head topped with a shock of close-cropped hair going white—was trained as a barrelmaker for four years before moving to the shooting grounds to specialize in regulating. Given the importance of riflemaking at Holland's, much of Cranston's craft centers on bolt- and double-rifle regulation, but he also fine-tunes the chokes of every Holland smoothbore at his dedicated workshop on the grounds.

As noted in the prior two chapters on Holland's tube- and barrelmaking, rough chokes are established (to Full constriction) in the machining process and later are reamed out by barrelmakers to desired nominal points of constriction as the tubes are made into a set of barrels. Proper barrel convergence is built in early by meticulous machining of the breeches to predetermined angles, and careful assembly assures it during the barrelmaking process.

Cranston gets the gun when it has been made fully functional but is still in the white. It is his task to plate it, count pellet strikes within a 30-inch circle and determine if the chokes not only give desired percentages matching its nominal choke borings but also produce game-getting patterns—in Cranston's words "nice, consistent, even patterns."

Almost invariably the chokes will need some tweaking, and Cranston achieves this by altering the angle and shape of the choke cone. His tool of choice is an old lathe with a revolving rod tipped by a modified bore-lapping lead—split at its head to accommodate a wedge than can be tapped in or out to change the lead's angle and the force brought to bear on portions of the cone. Cranston coats the lead with an oil-emery paste, holds the barrels in his hands, inserts the spinning lead from the breech end, quickly runs it up the barrel to minimize contact with the bore, and then goes to work on the choke cones.

Here is where Cranston's mastery of the "black arts" of traditional guncraft comes into play. The talkative regulator was momentarily at a loss for words when I asked him to describe his technique. "It's all by feel," he said finally. "That and by experience. When I touch the cone, I can feel the shape of it and the way the lead bites."

H&H regulator Steven Cranston uses a modified bore-lapping lead—split at its head to accommodate a wedge—to alter the angle and shape of the choke cone.

Cranston will work the lead in and out against the cone, varying the pressure and sometimes spinning the barrels as he works. "Then I'll put a cleaning rod through it and check the cone formation," he explained. "Depending on what I see, I might tinker around a bit— maybe tap the wedge in a bit, maybe pull it out, and touch the cone again."

Then it's back to the plate to check patterns. Plating and honing are processes repeated as often as needed, with an average of about 25 shots taken at the plates per barrel. "During regulation, I'm just changing the shape of the choke cone," Cranston said. "I like to keep angles in the cone as soft as possible; for one reason I don't know what sort of loads the owner will put through it in the future."

Cranston's ultimate goals are to ensure that the gun prints its patterns to point of aim and that its chokes produce patterns as well as the laws of physics governing pellet distribution allow.

Conventional British chokes traditionally have been made to a conical-parallel design—that is, with the choke cone transitioning from the bore to a parallel section of a certain constriction and length. Within the broad parameters of this design, UK gunmakers have arrived at any number of variations: in the length and angle of the cone as well as in the length of the parallel section, with each individual firm having its own ideas as to ideal form.

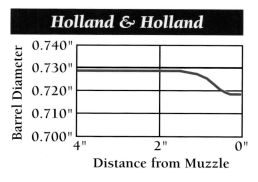

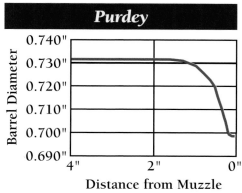

British ballistician Dr. Derek Allsop developed an electronic probe to record choke profiles. Though his examples above are of different constrictions, they point out the contrasting choke-design philosophies of two famous firms. (Courtesy of Dr. Derek Allsop)

Dr. Derek Allsop, one of England's foremost contemporary ballisticians, developed an electronic probe used to measure choke profiles in guns of differing makes (see charts on the previous page). He noted the following of his measurements in guns from London's two leading firms: "Purdey and Holland & Holland have totally different philosophies to achieve their choke pattern. Purdey deliberately gives its choke profiles a sharp angle with a short parallel at the muzzle, whereas Holland & Holland bores its chokes with a shallow angle and longer parallel muzzle section. There is no doubt these well-known gunmakers achieve excellent patterns but by using totally different approaches." (This example could be expanded upon almost ad infinitum, given the variety of choke configurations in use today.)

Cranston discussed Holland's preferred design: "With a game gun, we like about a one-inch parallel at the muzzle—three-quarters of an inch minimum—and a soft slope to the cone and a straight tidy bore from the breech forward. There should be no recesses in the bore, and we try to keep everything as tight and straight as possible." A long parallel potentially serves a couple of purposes: It can help protect the critical cone area from dents or damage that could occur were it located at the muzzle, and—according to one traditional theory, anyway—it helps stabilize the shot column after it passes through the cone before exiting.

Ideally, chokes should be regulated with a customer's preferred cartridge—per the Gough Thomas example—but this is hardly the case anymore. "It's very rare now," Cranston said. "Only one or two customers a year ask us to regulate using their own cartridges."

When a customer doesn't specify, Cranston regulates using a traditional load for the particular gauge (or bore) of the gun. In the case of the ubiquitous 12-bore, this is a proprietary 67mm $1^1/_{16}$-oz load of English No. 6s with a fiber wad made for H&H by England's Hull Cartridge Co.

This long has been the standard payload and shot size for regulating guns in the UK, and fiber remains popular in Britain because many estates where driven shooting takes place require biodegradable wads.

"We try—we *try*—to get what we perceive as the perfect choke formation," Cranston said. "In doing so I will regulate for a certain cartridge, get it right, then if the owner wants, he can play around and change cartridges for different applications."

For best results, Cranston emphasized, this requires the owner to invest time at the plate or at the pattern board. "You've still got to do your homework," he said. "If you don't like the patterns with what you are using, then you change the cartridge and find something that works."

Given potential performance variability from changing shells, does the sort of old-fashioned choke regulation as practiced by Cranston still matter? As noted earlier, many fine-gun makers no longer think so.

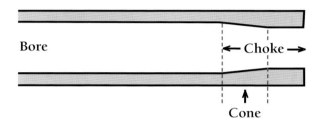

Bore

← Choke →

Cone

Chokes in Britain have traditionally been made to a conical-parallel design—with the choke cone transitioning from the bore to a parallel section of a certain constriction and length. These can vary from maker to maker.

British 12-bore game guns have tradition-ally been regulated with $1^1/_{16}$ oz of English No. 6s—289 pellets. At right are choke classifications based on pellet counts of this load within a 30-inch circle at 40 yards.

CHOKE CLASSIFICATION BASED ON PATTERN PERCENTAGE		
Choke	Pellets	Percentage
Cylinder	116	40%
Improved Cylinder	145	50%
Half	173	60%
Full	202	70%

It's a question, however, that really should be considered on a couple of levels. At the most fundamental, Holland's entire barrelmaking process—including Cranston's careful choke regulation—does assure that the chamber, forcing cone, bore, choke cone and parallel are all concentric with one another and that both barrels will print where pointed when fed appropriate loads. Should the gun be used with cartridges to which it was specifically regulated, the shooter can enjoy *full confidence* that it will perform—within the constraints of the laws of physics and the vagaries of cartridge manufacture—exactly as promised.

And confidence is of not inconsiderable importance in the art of shooting—promoting in the gunner what Gough Thomas called "relaxed preparedness" when faced with challenging birds. If the shooter has complete confidence in his choke-and-cartridge combination, that in itself often promotes better shooting.

In that regard, the answer will be evident in a bigger bulge in your game bag.

VIII.
Toys No More:
The New Purdey .410s

For eons creatures of prodigious size haunted the imaginations of pre-scientific man. From Cyclops of Ancient Greece to Goliath of the Old Testament, giants were real and frightening things. This forever changed in 1638 with Galileo Galilei's explanation of nature's scaling laws. In *Dialogues Concerning Two New Sciences*, the Italian scientist, among other things, debunked the giants of yore using mathematics to show why they did not exist.

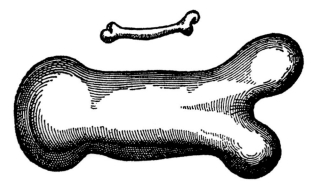

Galileo's bones help illustrate the problems encountered when stress-bearing objects—including gun components—are scaled up or down.

Galileo used an illustration of two bones—one from a smaller animal and the other from a larger one, the hypothetical latter being three times taller (see illustration above). The taller animal's bones would need to be much more massive than the smaller animal's, Galileo showed, because a bone's strength is determined by the area of its cross-section. Area is two-dimensional—length x width—so if a bone were three times longer than the smaller and still of the same shape, the area of its cross-section would increase nine times (3x3). Weight, on the other hand, is three dimensional, so with the larger animal would increase a whopping 27 times (3x3x3)—effectively crushing said bones unless they miraculously were made of a much stronger material or were scaled up to grotesque proportions.

In an inverse way Galileo's bones provide one clue as to why properly scaled .410s always have been as rare as the femurs of giants. Scaling mechanisms dramatically up—or down—in size is rarely simple or straightforward, and historically it's been no easy task for gunmakers to downsize designs originally made as 12-bores to diminutive .410s. As size shrinks to .410 dimensions, tumblers become lighter, sears and bridles thinner, springs more stressed, and the effects of friction increasingly important. The geometry of cocking and ejection changes, and components become Lilliputian and more difficult to machine and work with. The more complex the gun, the more difficult the scaling process.

In recent years, however, CAD/CAM (computer-aided design/computer-aided manufacturing) and CNC (computer numerical control) have given gunmakers engineering abilities as powerful as the giants of legend. By fusing modern technology with old-fashioned craftsmanship, London's James Purdey & Sons today is producing exquisitely scaled .410 versions of the doubles that helped make the firm famous.

In 2007 I visited the firm's factory in Hammersmith to watch how the new .410s were being made and to interview the men responsible for making them. The visit was an eye-opener, and I left with newfound appreciation for not only the skills of Purdey's bench-trained craftsmen but also the talents of the firm's high-tech machinists and the critical roles the latter now play in designing and building today's "best" guns.

Properly scaled best Purdey .410s evolved in the 21st Century, but their genesis harkens back a hundred years or more. In his marvelously researched book *American & British .410 Shotguns*, author Ronald S. Gabriel recounts the evolution of the cartridge and double guns built for it on both sides of the Atlantic. During the late Victorian and Edwardian eras, writes Gabriel, the .410 in Britain typically was embraced by two extremes of society: on the one hand by either poachers with cheap Belgian folding-barrel single-shots or gamekeepers with "vermin destroyers," and conversely by gentlemen employing them

A scaled-frame Purdey .410 over/under. (Clair Kofoed)

for self-protection as cane guns or using them to collect specimens for taxidermy. The .410 also was thought of as a starter gun for "boys" or "ladies." What it wasn't considered was a proper game gun and seemingly never a best gun. Most shooting authorities of the time ignored the .410 completely; W.W. Greener, in his enormously influential *The Gun*, simply stated, ". . . the 28 bore is the smallest caliber of any practical use as a game gun."

Nonetheless, Purdey's did produce a handful of good-quality .410s in the pre-war period. The earliest Purdey .410s seem to be either mid-grade "E-Quality" back-action hammerguns built before the First World War on actions supplied from Birmingham or later conversions from rook rifles. Gabriel notes that it was not until after the First World War that the first publicly documented best-quality bar-action hammerless Purdey .410 was made. In 1927 the renowned Harry Lawrence built gun No. 23398 for a "Mr. Johnson" in the US. (Lawrence was at the time an actioner but would go on to become the firm's managing director in 1951.) This may well have been one of the first best-quality .410 sidelocks built by the London trade, and it marked a shift in British .410 production.

Whereas earlier mid-grade British .410s had been built mostly for the domestic or colonial markets, best sidelocks built to that bore were almost always destined for America. In the years between the wars the .410 was becoming popular with skeet shooters in the US, and in the early '30s Winchester introduced the 3" .410 cartridge with its respectable 3/4-oz shot load. American wingshooters also had discovered that in expert hands—at appropriate ranges and with appropriate chokes and better loads—the modern .410 was adequate for thin-skinned upland game such as bobwhite quail, woodcock and rail. In the decades of affluence following the Second World War, American collectors also "discovered" the .410 and helped stoke a small-but-growing market for best British smallbores.

As examples of Harry Lawrence's gunmaking genius and traditional craft skills, vintage best-grade Beesley-action Purdey .410s are superb. Because of their rarity and Purdey's prestige, they are among the most collectible—and priciest—of the British smallbores on the secondhand market. That said, they are not perfect, either mechanically or aesthetically. The original best Purdey sidelock .410 largely evolved during an era of contraction in the British gun trade, and the guns exemplify some of the "make-do" attributes of the time.

According to ex-Purdey stocker David Trevallion—who helped build at least one best .410 in the late '50s and has restocked several since—ejection on some older guns can be problematic, especially with 3" hulls, which induce considerable friction with the chamber when thrown.

Moreover, older Beesley-action .410s clearly suffer from scaling issues vis-à-vis ideal proportions. Though the gun was reduced across its bar, the .410's locks are virtually as tall as a 28-bore's and its action is deep, the latter necessitated by the need to accommodate the tumbler's throw as well as to maintain the correct geometry for the cocking and self-opening features of the Beesley/Purdey system. When paired with slender .410 tubes, these dimensions give it a somewhat gawky, unbalanced look. "We have always considered the end shapes and sizes of our older .410s to be 'inelegant,'" said Purdey Chairman Nigel Beaumont. "They were not as good to look at as they could have been."

Fast-forward to the late 1990s and Ian Clarke, Purdey's machine-shop manager. Clarke began his career in the aviation industry with Westland Helicopters before migrating in the early '90s to machining precision parts for the motor-racing industry. He entered the fine-gun

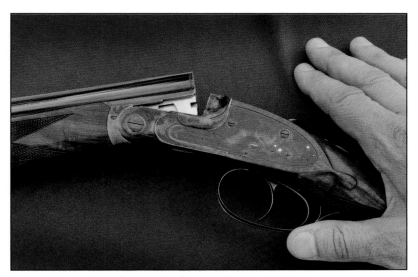

*Built in the Purdey factory, this scaled-frame .410
bears the name of James Woodward.* (Clair Kofoed)

world in '93 with John Shirley, at the time an important high-tech machinist to the best British trade. At Shirley's Clarke trained in CAD/CAM and CNC manufacturing, including wire/spark-erosion technology. In 1996 Holland & Holland hired him, and two years later he was offered his current position as machine-shop manager at Purdey's.

When Clarke joined the firm, Purdey's was in the throes of modernizing its factory and gun-production process under the supervision of then works director Beaumont. (As recently retired Chairman Richard Purdey put it: "Dragging the 19th Century into the 21st.") Thanks to substantial capital investment from new parent company Vendome PLC (now the Richemont Group), Purdey's was able to completely revamp its machine shop. It now boasts three other fully trained machinists—Andy Wood, Barry Brown and James Moody—who along with Clarke program and operate three CNC spark-eroders, two CNC wire-eroders, three CNC millers, one CNC surface grinder and one CAD digitizer as well as three manual milling machines.

A modern in-house machine shop has helped Purdey's in a couple of important ways. For one, integrating CAD/CAM and CNC technology has been crucial in keeping the firm competitive in a market that is truly global—both in terms of customers and competitors. Ad-

Machine-shop manager Ian Clarke (left) and Chairman
Nigel Beaumont launched the scaled-frame project for the Purdey
over/under in the late 1990s. (Courtesy of James Purdey & Sons)

vanced manufacturing technology helps strip out some labor costs
that can be done more efficiently by machines. Also, apart from raw
materials—bought-in walnut blanks, action forgings and bars of steel,
and barrel blanks—all components of a gun now can be made in-
house to Purdey's designs and exacting standards, assuring consistent
quality control. And as Italian pioneer Ivo Fabbri has shown, CNC
capabilities—judiciously employed—can make a best gun mechanically even better. For example, the modern steels used in best CNC
manufacture—specifically low-carbon vacuum-degassed steels—have
better grain structure and are free from the flow holes and hydrogen
bubbles that can cause structural weaknesses or cosmetic flaws. Surfaces that should be made perfectly square will indeed be so, what
should be absolutely flat is flat, and what should be round is round.
Components can be standardized, facilitating not only manufacture
and functional reliability but also repairs in the future. By themselves,
better components made of better materials can make for a more durable, more reliable gun.

Clarke's first task at Purdey's was to digitize its 12- and 20-bore
Woodward over/unders on CAD software to facilitate standardized
component production by CNC methods. "I was handed 30-year-old
rough sketches that quite frankly were more trouble than they were

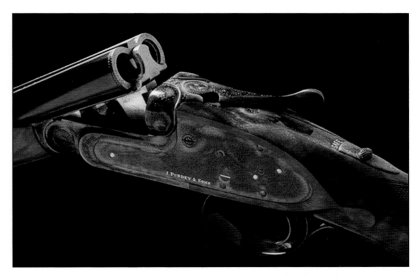

*A new scaled-frame .410 side-by-side built on the
Beesley/Purdey action.* (Courtesy of James Purdey & Sons)

worth," Clarke said. "So I set about analyzing some finished guns, then got directly involved with the craftsmen and listened to their ideas about how to produce a superior action."

This also allowed him to tweak some aspects of the Woodward design, which was patented in 1913. "With the 12- and 20-bores, it had always been considered that the actions were too bulky and square-looking," Clarke said. "So we moved the ejector-rod holes up the wall of the action and worked out minimum diameters to allow more roundness and shaping on the underside of the action."

Soon after, Beaumont broached the idea of new .410s using the Woodward and Beesley designs for the O/U and side-by-side, respectively, but scaling them down to create sleeker, more attractive guns. Clarke's work on the bigger-bore Woodwards—which emphasized extensive consultation and close cooperation with Purdey's bench-trained craftsmen—provided the framework for making the new baby-frame .410s.

"I scaled down all the parts of our 20-bore O/U by 21 percent on our CAD software," Clarke said. "This gave us the basic .410 action size we wanted. I then had to reengineer all the parts in order to maintain required function and strength—for example, determining the correct size and grip of the action bolt [which secures the barrels to the action when the gun is closed] was critical."

Early on Clarke also had to consider the effect of scaling down the action on the size and shape of the stock. "After all, a customer's hands and body are not going to be proportionally scaled down too," Clarke said. "The stock had to be large enough to retain strength and serve its purposes whilst retaining a scaled appearance appropriate to the action." For expert assistance, Clarke turned to Dick Bayley, the senior craftsman in Purdey's stocking shop.

At this point all parts were cut out as templates on the CNC wire-eroder, and then arranged to form a two-dimensional gun. Templates provide machinists and craftsmen with physical examples that can be used to help improve and modify the actual components.

Clarke then turned his reengineering efforts to the lockwork—in this case the back-action locks of the Woodward design. He said, "If I'd sit a craftsman down in front of a CAD drawing on my computer and say, 'Here's my .410 tumbler. Is it going to break?' He'd look at it and say, 'I haven't got a clue.' But when I'd wire one out and he could handle it, he'd say, 'Oh, that will break here,' or, 'It's too thin there.'

"Scaling a gun is very much a collaborative process. You have to be on the craftsmen's side and listen to what they say. After all, they are the original sources of knowledge, and it's their experience that will tell you if something will work."

A prototype lock was made and then assembled and tested by finisher and lockmaker Keith Ackerman. After a few small refinements, Clarke and Ackerman produced a perfected version.

The ejectorwork was scaled down in a similar manner. Woodward-type ejectorwork uses V springs framed in the forend that are compressed as the gun opens before being tripped on the over-center principle to eject the fired cartridges. It's a powerful system—Beaumont calls it the "king of O/U ejectors"—but Clarke initially was unsure if it would work effectively in a version scaled so small. "Senior ejector-man Nick Robinson and I sat down one morning and went through it all," Clarke said. "Initially, he wasn't confident it would work, and I was a bit unsure, but in the end we made it work perfectly."

Actioner Ian Brunt assembled the first prototype gun and assisted with shaping the action, and Clarke consulted with senior finisher Bob Nicholls during and after every assembly stage. "Bob needed to

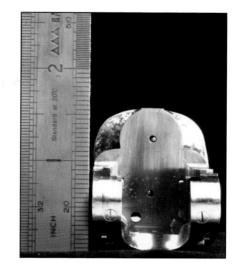

The ruler gives a good indication of the reduced size and scale of a new .410 action.
(Courtesy of James Purdey & Sons)

be kept informed, as he would ultimately bring the gun to life," Clarke said.

Work began on scaling the .410 Beesley side-by-side in 2002 and followed much the same process. In certain respects, however, the Beesley proved a more problematic gun to scale because of its fully integrated design, which uses the mainspring to not only power the tumblers but also to "spring open" the gun. "You can't just shrink a Beesley's spring down proportionately," Clarke said. "The geometry would be all wrong, and it gets too weak to do everything its needs to."

Moreover, a certain depth is required through the bar of the action to accommodate the lifters and rods that help open and cock the gun and to ensure proper geometry to work in conjunction with the mainspring and lock-lifter cams on the lockplate. Clarke also had to consider the ejector rods, which run down the bar of the action and through the underbolt as well as through the knuckle. Finally, the over-center ejectors, housed in the forend, needed to be robust enough to effectively throw the 3" .410 cartridges. In plain language the Beesley has a lot of mechanical goings-on in a confined space, and for this reason all Purdey/Beesley guns, regardless of bore, have the same knuckle radius: 10.5mm. Though this keeps the .410 a little tall through the action bar relative to its bore size, Clarke was able to reduce the overall scale of the action by about 12 percent from prior versions and the lockwork by as much as 20 percent.

The first new scaled Beesley gun was finished in 2004; the first scaled .410 Woodward in 2005. Clarke is particularly pleased with the scale of the latter. "Every single part is completely scaled down," he said, holding a .410 O/U action in the palm of his hand. "This is a true scaled gun that has had blood, sweat and tears in its making."

Marvels of modern technology aside, it bears stressing that what distinguished a Purdey in the past is present still—that is, handcraftsmanship of the highest quality. CNC has indeed taken the grunt work out of making components, but it has not replaced the time-honored bench skills that make a Purdey a "Purdey." As of spring 2010, 24 craftsmen still work with hand tools and smoke lamps to create what arguably remains the world's most prestigious guns. As yet there is

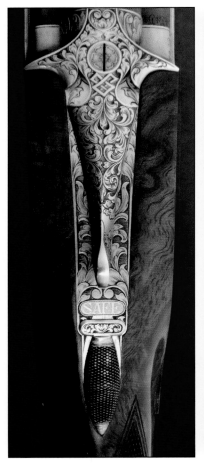

*These views—side, top and bottom (above and facing page)—show
the beautiful lines and proportions of the new .410. In particular,
the trigger guard must be large enough to accommodate a shooter's
finger yet not so large as to ruin the gun's petite appearance.*
(Courtesy of James Purdey & Sons)

no machine-made substitute for the attention to detail that goes into
meeting the subtle requirements of a bespoke order, nor are there
automated alternatives that can better the meticulous hand-regulating
and exquisite hand-finishing that are hallmarks of Purdey guns.

Today the firm's .410s can be had bearing either the Purdey or
Woodward names as side-by-sides or O/Us, and though the aesthetics will conform to each respective house style, the mechanics will be
the same irregardless. In each configuration actions can be ordered
with traditional square, round or ultra-round frames. Single or double
triggers are available, and all guns are chambered and proofed for
modern 3" cartridges.

Though more perfectly scaled, most new Purdeys are paradoxi-
cally made heavier than comparable sidelock .410s of the past. "We
could have made them even smaller and lighter," Beaumont said, "but
you've got to maintain enough weight to have a shootable gun. A 3½-
to four-pound trigger pull on a gun so light is the majority of its dead

weight. Just the action of pulling the trigger will move the gun, which doesn't help your shooting."

Today Woodward-type over/unders with no additional weighting will be about 5 pounds 3 ounces; Beesley side-bys will be 4 pounds 12 ounces. "Most clients now want them heavier," Beaumont said. "We think you need a .410 at $5\frac{1}{2}$ pounds to 5 pounds 10 ounces. They feel great at that weight and shoot well too. We can make them six pounds plus, if asked."

Smallbore enthusiast and longtime Purdey customer Joe Toot was one of the first purchasers of a new scaled .410 O/U—or "Under & Over" in Woodward parlance. His Woodward, delivered in the summer of 2006, tips the scales at 5 pounds 11 ounces with 29-inch barrels, with the weight concentrated between the hands as Toot specified. This was achieved, per friend and British-gun expert Cyril Adams' advice, by weighting the portion of the top rib closest to the action with a high-density metal. Beaumont suggested adding a few ounces by placing high-density metal under the fins on the barrels, which also helped keep the weight between Toot's hands.

An accomplished shot, Toot and his Woodward were soon on their way to Argentina, where the gun was put through its paces on doves. "Perfect function the entire time," Toot said. "I've never had a miscue with firing or ejection." He since has shot it extensively at wild quail, woodcock and ruffed grouse—his best shot, he says, was a grouse taken in upstate New York "which fell dead at 46 paces." Toot asked Ohio-based barrel specialist Ken Eyster to tune the barrels—ordered Full & Full—to deliver 90 percent of a $\frac{1}{2}$-oz load of No. $7\frac{1}{2}$s evenly spread within the killing portion of the pattern at 30 yards. This places a premium on marksmanship, but Toot says it delivers big-bore lethality when he places the pattern where it should be. "I think these are among the most exciting guns to come from the great London makers in modern times," he said.

The British .410 once was regarded as a gun for boys, but today's Purdeys are toys no more.

IX.
The Art of Finishing:
David H. Sinnerton

Visit any of the world's major sporting-arms expositions these days, and you'll note many gunmakers building very fine double shot-guns to very high standards. In general, innovation and quality in the double-gun market haven't been this high for more than a half-century and arguably since before the First World War. The confluence of new manufacturing technology and Old World craftsmanship—leavened with a heaping measure of global prosperity—has made the late 20th and early 21st centuries a new Golden Age for fine gunmaking.

Yet, I'd argue that despite elevated quality levels and novel designs, only a handful of today's makers truly deserve the accolade "best gun-maker." There are real differences between even very fine guns and "best" guns—some readily visible, others quite subtle. Fine guns must always be made of high-quality materials, be soundly designed and re-liable, possess excellent weight distribution and good balance, and be stocked in quality walnut with a layout that provides not only beauty but also structural strength. A best gun, by contrast, must possess the same utilitarian attributes yet also elegant, harmonious proportions— a certain purity of lines, in other words—and be *finished* perfectly inside and out.

Aesthetically, best-quality finishing means seamless metal-to-met-al and wood-to-metal fit, beautifully fitted and slotted pins, perfect checkering, graceful drop points and a lustrous stock finish. Trigger pulls should be crisp, the ejectors precisely timed, the leverwork and cocking smooth, and the travel of the safety firm yet silky. Internally, the components of a best gun should be polished to a mirror finish to prevent rust and should be fitted and regulated to work in harmony with each other. Most important, components must be hardened and tempered properly, as a gun lacking these qualities will soon wear out no matter how flawless its exterior appears. A best gun should be as a diamond: beautiful in its many facets and forever lasting.

Though technology now duplicates much of the skilled handwork once associated with best guns, the specialized task of finishing still remains the domain of the master craftsman. England's David Harold Sinnerton is one such craftsman.

Trained at Purdey's, Sinnerton is regarded as one of Britain's finest independent finishers. From the late 1980s he has worked "in the trade" for most of London's best makers. So sought after are his skills that retail clients of other makers have asked for Sinnerton specifically to finish their guns. And since 2001, guns are available not only finished by but also built by—and bearing the name of—D.H. Sinnerton.

In March 2006 I visited Sinnerton at his workshop for a first-ever look at his new guns. At the time he was living near the village of Colgate, in Sussex, some 15 miles south of London's austral outskirts. His workshop—a spacious converted annex—was beside the house shared with his wife, Louise. His shop was well lit, with a full-length bench fronting one wall. In a corner was a rack of shotguns in various stages of repair or manufacture. Along the wall above the bench hung the tools of Sinnerton's trade—meticulously arranged, more clinically Continental in their organization than the jumble one finds in many British workshops.

Sinnerton was born in London in 1959 to Harold and Maud Sinnerton and grew up shooting in the rural Sussex countryside. "I got interested in guns through my Dad, really," he told me during my workshop tour. "We mostly went for pigeons and the like, but we'd go to Scotland a few times for rough shooting too."

His first shotgun was a single-barrel .410; his second a plain 20-bore boxlock non-ejector. "There was no maker's name on either," he recalled. Ironically, the next guns to pass through his hands would bear the name of one of Britain's most illustrious gunmakers.

In the fall of 1975, at the age of 15, Sinnerton decided to make a career of his childhood passion: He applied for a job at James Purdey & Sons. "I probably wrote to a couple of others," Sinnerton said, "but I knew of Purdey's as being one of the best."

Sinnerton interviewed with Chris Gadsby, a longtime Purdey craftsman who'd by then become factory manager. "I remember being shown a new 12-bore side-by-side engraved with gold by Ken Hunt," Sinnerton said. "It is something I've never forgotten."

David Sinnerton at the bench in his workshop in Sussex.

A good impression he made, and Sinnerton joined Purdey's in August 1976. He was apprenticed to Robert (Bob) Nicholls—still a finisher at Purdey's and even today regarded as one of the factory's best craftsmen. "Bob was quite a young gaffer at the time," Sinnerton recalled, "and I was his first apprentice." A "gaffer," in Purdey parlance, is an experienced craftsman charged with training an apprentice.

Had he always wanted to become a finisher? "No," Sinnerton said. "Luck of the day, really. There was simply a vacancy in the finishing shop at the time." Before ever putting a file to the steel of a gun, Sinnerton had to first learn to make his own tools—turnscrews in bunches and clamps for holding springs and various internal components. Following what was then the British guild system's traditional five-year training period, young Sinnerton presented a gun he'd finished to viewers from the Worshipful Company of Gunmakers at the London Proof House. The work was approved, Sinnerton was an apprentice no longer, and the young man joined the Worshipful Company as a Freeman of the City of London—and the Purdey factory as a craftsman proper.

In 1976 there were seven major stages that each Purdey gun passed through on its way to completion—barrelmaking, lockmaking, ejectorwork, actioning, stocking, engraving and finishing—and craftsmen at each stage worked according to the firm's idiosyncratic manufacturing process known as the "Purdey Way."

This started with the barrels, when the barrelmaker struck up the tubes, brazed them together at the lumps, tinned in the ribs, drilled and lapped the bores, machined the lumps, and then passed everything on to the actioner. The actioner machined the action; cut or filed out the necessary slots and cavities; fitted the bolt and barrels to the action; fit in disk-set strikers, locks, the hinge pin and the leverwork; made and fitted the forend iron; and then jointed the barrels to the action, which he then shaped with files and chisels. The gun then passed to the ejector shop, where the ejectors as well as the cocking and self-opening mechanisms were made and installed. The gun then was sent to the London Proof House, and after proof it was returned to the stocker. At Purdey's, stockers not only stocked the gun by hand but also did much of the metalwork, including making and fitting the triggerplate, hanging the triggers, making the pins and much of the work associated with the forend.

With the gun stocked, it was ready for its first visit to the finisher. Purdey guns long have been noted for their exquisite finishing, and it is requisite that a good finisher possesses a complete understanding of all aspects of the gun and how it functions.

Sinnerton's initial task was to prepare the metal components for the engraver. He installed and slotted the pins, and then polished the action and components until their surfaces "looked like mirrors." This process took three days. After the gun returned from the engraver, Sinnerton re-polished or refit anything that might have been marred. The gun then went out for hardening and was returned to him. Sinnerton first checked the action and all components for any distortions that may have been caused by heat during the hardening process. This meant not only assembling the locks and internal components but also fitting the action and lockwork to the stock. "Sometimes," Sinnerton said, "you'd have to set [bend] parts of it to get a perfect fit again on the stock."

Then he let in the barrels and bedded them in on the face of the action, using a smoke lamp to ensure that the jointing remained perfect.

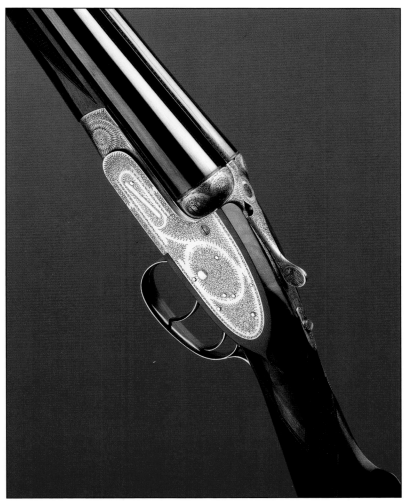

The first gun to bear Sinnerton's name: a 12-bore made for the craftsman's father and completed in 1992. Built on a Purdey/Beesley-type action, it was engraved by Charles Lee. (David Grant)

The next step was to bed in all of the internal components to make sure everything still worked perfectly. (To "bed in," or "free up," refers to the process of subtly shaping, filing or polishing each part to ensure a good fit—not too tight and not too loose.) After this the mechanics of the gun—the locks and self-opening mechanism, the ejectors, the safety, the toplever, the triggers and the springs—were regulated.

With everything working harmoniously, Sinnerton then hardened and tempered all of the internal parts.

Sinnerton's attentions then turned to wood. He prepared and sanded the stock with five grades of paper, the finest saved for last. Then came two to three months of oil-finishing using Purdey's famous "slacum" formula. While this was taking place, Sinnerton completed his final finish on the metalwork, which entailed another three days of polishing components. During this time the barrels were sent off for blacking. After they returned and the stock and forend were finished, the gun was reassembled, with careful attention paid to making sure everything still worked perfectly. Then several hundred rounds were put through the gun to ensure it worked and patterned properly. Last it was sent to the factory manager for his (and chairman Richard Beau-

A recently completed 28-bore over/under built by Sinnerton and associated craftsmen on a true Boss-type action. A single gun from a trio, it was engraved in Italy by Creative Art. (David Grant)

mont's) viewing and approval. After 750 hours of highly skilled hand labor—of which 85 to 100 hours were the finisher's—a new Purdey gun entered the ledger books and was delivered into the hands of a patient and proud customer.

As fine a finisher as he became, Sinnerton never was satisfied working solely within the confines of his prescribed specialty. "When I was at Purdey's, the finisher would not work on the ejectorwork for an over/under," he said. "But I would say to the ejector man, 'I'll do it for you if you teach me how.' That's how I learned ejectors, even though the ejector man still got paid for the work."

Thereafter he learned the art of setting stocks as well as techniques such as charcoal blacking, all outside the normal purview of a Purdey

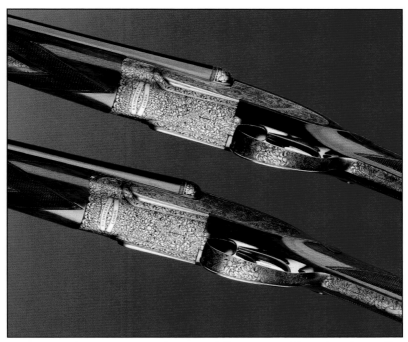

These 20-bores are not only beautifully engraved but also show all the hallmarks of Sinnerton's skills as a finisher and gunmaker.
(David Grant)

finisher. "It wasn't as if I had an idea of leaving at the time," Sinnerton said. "I just wanted to learn."

But in 1988, after 12 years at Purdey's, Sinnerton did depart, leaving under amicable terms to become a freelance finisher (or out-worker) to the trade. "It was not over money," he said, "and I'm not a recluse. I get along with everyone. I decided it just wasn't me to work on a factory floor forever."

Sinnerton's first workshop was modest: his bedroom in a flat in Wallington, in Surrey. "When I left Purdey's, I had absolutely no idea how much work was out there for me," he said. "I had five jobs lined up for one gunmaker and, given the wages I was earning at the time, I knew this gave me a cushion of about two months' work."

He's never been idle since. Trade clients have included the cream of British gunmaking—Purdey's, Boss & Co. and Peter V. Nelson, among others—as well as restoration and repair work for retail buyers and the trade. "I stayed busy even in the recession in the late '80s," Sinnerton said. In part, he credits his thorough gunmaking education for his success. "The best thing about coming from Purdey's was that I had been trained to the very highest standards. Also, Purdeys are more complicated than some other designs, so that helped prepare me to tackle difficult projects."

Some of those more difficult projects included repairing single triggers on best British guns. Traditional single triggers are ingeniously made from a mechanical standpoint, and the best of them are reliable—but all are susceptible to inferior repair work. Once "buggered," they typically are difficult to set right. "I got to be known a bit for fixing single triggers," Sinnerton said. "If there was a Boss or Purdey with a broken trigger, people would often send it to me.

"Purdey and Boss single triggers are great designs. Unfortunately, a lot of them on older guns have been spoilt by poor gunsmithing. I learned to fix them through experience and, especially, by taking my time with them."

A work ethic so Puritan did not initially bear heavy financial fruit. "In the early days I was a bit afraid to charge enough," Sinnerton said, "so I lost loads of money working on them. You'd never believe the number of hours or days you can spend trying to get a single trigger working after someone's buggered it up."

He still clings to this uncompromising philosophy when finishing a gun. "I don't care if getting it right takes me an extra day or an extra week," Sinnerton said. "I won't be getting any more money; I'll be losing money, in fact. But it's finished when it's finished, and that's the bottom line."

Setting no time limits is also at the core of Sinnerton's success. He admits to sometimes spending 12 hours a day at his bench. "Nothing about finishing is difficult," he said modestly of his skills. "It's just a matter of paying attention to detail, having patience and not counting how many hours it takes to get it right."

It was during those long uncounted hours that Sinnerton built his first gun—and for the man who helped make him a gunmaker: his father, Harold. Employing a 12-bore Purdey/Beesley-type action, Sinnerton worked on the gun for five years in his spare time. Engraved with fine rose & scroll by Charles Lee (also ex-Purdey's), it was completed in 1992.

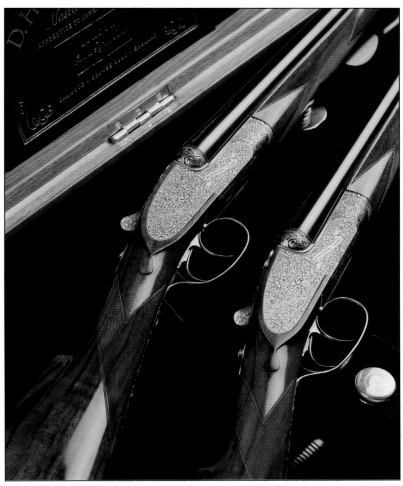

A recent pair of D.H. Sinnerton 20-bore sidelocks built on Holland-type actions and engraved with bold scroll by Wesley Tallett.
(David Grant)

Nearly a decade would pass before Sinnerton felt ready to build another gun with his name engraved on it. "When you finish or work on a variety of guns by different makers, you get to understand how they work," he said. "You are always learning in this business, but today I know a lot more than I did when I was 30. Having worked on some of the best guns made in this country for almost three decades, I felt I had learned enough to build them as well as anyone."

The Art of Finishing: David H. Sinnerton 79

His retail customers also were beginning to ask for them. His first order came in 2001 from an English businessman who approached him with a request for a pair of 20-bores. Built on Holland-type actions and engraved with bold scroll by Wesley Tallett, the guns were completed in October '04, just in time for the client's shooting season.

Since then Sinnerton has taken numerous orders for a diverse range of guns, including smallbore Boss-style over/unders and even a pair of 10-bore Purdey/Beesley-style side-by-side self-openers.

It might come as no surprise that Sinnerton is a traditionalist when it comes to gunmaking and builds only the classic London designs—Purdey/Beesley- and Holland-style side-by-sides, or Boss- or Purdey/Woodward-type over/unders. He argues there is little room for improvement. "These guns are right to begin with," he said. "I've seen a couple of makers try to 'improve' these designs, but by the time they've finished building them, they've discovered why the inventors didn't do that sort of thing to begin with."

Sinnerton uses only British-made components in his guns—in many cases from traditional suppliers to the trade. As a gunmaker, Sinnerton now has a hand in many tasks other than those he initially was trained in, including helping build locks and ejectorwork, filing up the actions, and stocking and checkering. As is typical with other small independent makers, Sinnerton uses talented specialist outworkers when needed. Most of these craftsmen prefer to work in anonymity, so he divulged no names; but he did elaborate on how he picks those who assist him.

"I haven't got one set team as such," Sinnerton said. "I use more than one stocker, more than one barrelmaker, more than one actioner. I use the best people for a particular job." For example, the craftsmen helping Sinnerton build a Purdey/Beesley-type side-by-side might be different than those assisting him with a Boss-type O/U.

Though traditional, his guns do possess a few of Sinnerton's own stylistic signatures. For example, he likes the look of the Boss-style top strap (short with high shoulders) on his side-by-sides, and he employs them even on Holland- or Purdey/Beesley-type actions. The striker disks in the face of the action have elegant slots instead of round holes for the tool that is used to remove them. Why? "I just like the look of it," he said.

As with any new British best built by elite craftsmen, there are no bargains, but suffice to say that Sinnerton guns are about two-thirds the price charged by West End firms with higher overheads.

Sinnerton hasn't forsaken finishing for the trade, either; his goal is to build just a handful of guns annually for appreciative clients, not to enter a race with established makers to build guns in volume. Working for demanding gunmakers, he admitted, also helps keep his skills sharp. "Purdey's and Peter Nelson have been great to finish guns for," he said. "Working for them keeps my standards right up there and makes me know what I have to achieve with my own guns."

Those achievements—in Sinnerton's case—have come to a craftsman who finishes last.

X.
British Color Case Hardening

C ase hardening is sometimes called a "black art."
It is not.

Case hardening is a scientific—if low-tech—process that has been practiced for many centuries. It is a method of giving low-carbon steel a glass-hard surface to prevent wear and corrosion while also preserving the metal's tough ductile core, which provides strength and the ability to absorb shock and stress.

Historically, this has been achieved by packing the steel into a carburizing agent—that is, into animal bone meal, wood charcoal, leather, horn or another high-carbon material—then heating the "pack" to a critical temperature so that carbon transfers to the metal and is then set in the latter's surface layers by a quench in liquid, usually water or oil. Though there are many formulas for the carbon pack and heat treatment (depending on the purpose of the object being hardened), all follow proven metallurgical principles.

Where black art and alchemy spill into the science of metallurgy occurs in the craft of color case hardening fine guns. Naturally, there are similarities between case hardening for industrial applications and for firearms—the processes must always ensure that the end products are durable and wear-resistant—but there are critical differences too. Distortions in metal caused by heat that might be acceptable in some industrial applications of grosser scale would be no more welcome in the mechanism of a fine gun than they would be in a Swiss watch. And the term "color case hardening" highlights an essential difference in the process from that of industrial case hardening: In the former, producing gemlike colors to tease the eye is a coterminous goal with proper hardening.

The set of skills needed to harden a gun while simultaneously showcasing attractively arranged colors, all with minimal metal distortion, have been hard earned enough to make most masters of the process very secretive about their techniques—so furtive, in fact, that

Gunmaker Robin Brown, of A.A. Brown & Sons, is one of
the few craftsmen in Britain who color-hardens his own guns.
(Matthew Brown/Orange Media Photography)

they lend the process an air of mystery, even magic, especially in Britain. Author Rich Grozik, in his book *Game Gun*, writes: ". . . to this day English casehardening evokes images of occult-like rituals, gurgling caldrons, and cryptic formulas applied to gun steel behind closed doors." Grozik goes on to mention rumors of old-time practitioners using human bones and urine to achieve extra-lustrous colors.

This secrecy noted, there is little to suggest witchcraft or worse at the factory of British gunmaker A.A. Brown & Sons, where I visited owner Robin Brown in November 2008 to discuss his color casehardening techniques.

Robin, now 63, is the fourth generation of Browns to make guns in and around Birmingham, and he has practiced color case hardening going on a half-century. Brown's is one of the few English gunmakers to not only make its own guns but also harden them in-house. (Most British gunmakers today send traditional color-case work to commercial hardening specialist Richard St. Ledger, on Price Street in the truncated remains of Birmingham's old Gun Quarter.)

Robin is an old friend, and in the nearly 20 years I've known him he has been unfailingly generous in sharing a lifetime's knowledge learned on the bench as one of England's finest gunmakers—including revealing his very traditional techniques for color case hardening. "I came into the trade in an era when you walked into a craftsman's workshop he would drop a cloth over his vise so you couldn't see what he was working on," Robin recalled as we sat in Brown's small factory in Alvechurch, south of Birmingham. "I've never liked that sort of secrecy. I think it sad to see skills developed over generations get lost."

In the era after the Second World War there were two principal color hardeners to the Birmingham trade: Billy Woodward and the Century Polishing & Hardening Co. Both were metal polishers and hardeners, the polishing of components being a critical last step before the gun was engraved prior to hardening. Woodward went on to train renowned Ray St. Ledger, father of aforementioned Richard. Robin Brown, on the other hand, was tutored by Ted Stokes, an elderly craftsman who had spent most of his career at Century Polishing. "Ted was probably in his late sixties when Century went down as the Birmingham trade contracted," Brown recalled. "We hired him to polish components and harden for us two days a week."

In stark contrast to much of the British trade, A.A. Brown & Sons was expanding when Robin joined the firm in 1961 as a 15-year-old apprentice. Under the leadership of Robin's uncle, Albert, and father, Sidney, and by dint of will and skill, the Browns pursued a growth strategy of bringing as many gunmaking processes as possible under one roof—machining, lockmaking and hardening being notable examples. By the early '60s, Brown's had become one of Birmingham's most important gunmakers to the post-war trade and employed nine full-time craftsmen, building some 200 to 250 guns per year, many for companies such as Holland & Holland, Churchill's and Westley Richards. Although Robin also was apprenticed as a stocker, Stokes

*Robin Brown, age 17, two years into his apprenticeship
with his family's gunmaking firm. He is holding a
Brown-made, scaled-frame smallbore sidelock.*

took him under his wing. By the late '60s, Robin was working closely with Stokes hardening guns.

Traditional color case hardening consists of four major steps: bone-meal preparation, the arrangement of the components in the carbon pack, the heat cycle and the quench. "The first thing Ted taught me was to prepare the bone meal," Robin explained. "It wasn't ready to use when you bought it; you had to condition it first."

Conditioning meant heating the meal in a furnace to about 500° C to burn off excess fat, grease and other contaminants invariably present in the meal of the day. As the meal was being heated, Robin was taught to rake it continuously, ensuring that the fat was burned off and also preventing it from scorching, which would de-carbonize the material. He remembers the odor—"an abattoir smell"—but stresses the importance of the process. "If there was any fat or grease left in the meal when you hardened, it would cause ugly flaking on the surface.

"Whenever we got in a fresh batch of meal, we'd first experiment by color hardening different pieces of metal to make sure we were going to get the results we wanted. We never knew exactly where the meal came from or the sorts of contaminants we'd find in it.

"The level of flaking we'd see in those experiments told us how much meal prep we needed to do before hardening actual gun components. The quality of the meal back then was not predictable and was the grayest area of the whole process."

This has changed for the better, as these days Robin is able to obtain the same bone charcoal that Scotch distilleries use to filter whisky. "There is much less grease in it," Robin said. "Consequently, preparation is now easier and quicker."

Unlike some American color-case recipes that call for additional carburizing agents such as wood charcoal and leather, Stokes' recipe employed bone charcoal alone. "Pure bone meal, just animal bone," Brown said. "Nothing exotic was added, I'm afraid—no magic powder, no old shoes, no human bone."

And urine?

"Certainly not. We always had good results with animal bone alone."

Color case hardening is one of the last stages of craft gunmaking—at this point the gun is mechanically complete and fully engraved. Components traditionally hardened are the action (or frame), various pins (screws), the triggerplate, the triggers, the forend tip and decorative furniture and, in the case of a sidelock, the lockplates and lock bridles. Some English gunmakers have used a higher-carbon steel for their forend irons that obviates the need for case hardening, but Brown's typically used the same mild (or low-carbon) steel for their forends as for their frames and consequently case hardened these, too.

After the gun was disassembled, components had to be thoroughly degreased. "Cleanliness is *everything* in color case hardening," Robin said. "Just the oil from your fingertips left on the metal would cause flaking if it wasn't removed before hardening.

"In those days Ted and I boiled off the components in soda water to remove any traces of grease, then rinsed them again in clean boiling water to get rid of the traces of soda."

Next came the process of "packing the pots"—carefully arranging the components in layers of prepared bone meal in their "pots," which at the time were rectangular cast-iron boxes with loose-fitting lids. There were two sizes: for one gun or a pair.

Stokes taught Robin not only how correctly positioning the components in the meal influenced proper carbon absorption and conse-

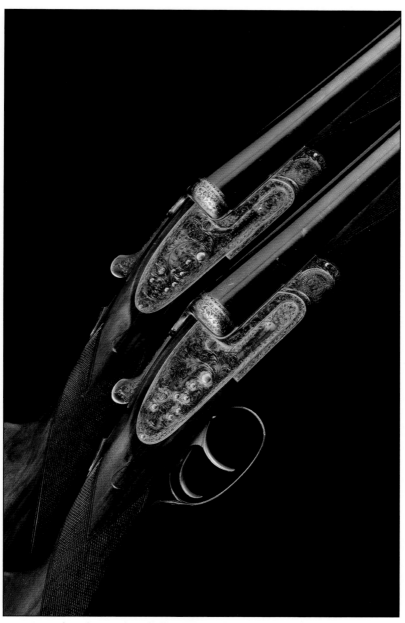

A pair of 12-bore Churchill Imperials made for the London firm by A.A. Brown & Sons, in Birmingham, in 1963. Craftsman Ted Stokes color-hardened the guns assisted by then-apprentice Robin Brown. The original finish remains pristine. (Courtesy of Gavin Gardiner, Ltd.)

quent hardening for each piece, but also how specific arrangements could minimize distortion and affect coloration. "You didn't just jumble the bits in," Robin said.

The action, for example, was always put in the center surrounded by a maximum amount of meal, and to encourage additional carburization it also was placed in the upper portion of the pot. "The top of the pots got hotter than the bottom, so you packed them in such a way that each piece was getting the correct heat." No major parts were allowed to touch each other, although Stokes sometimes wired specially shaped blocks of steel to the backs of lockplates and triggerplates to enhance colors—especially blues. "The slower a piece cools, the more blue it will have," Robin said, "so wiring metal in effect gave these pieces greater thickness, which helped retain heat."

Temperature and time at heat along with the nature of the carburizing material determine the depth of carbon penetration into mild steel—and thereby the latter's surface hardness once quenched. Higher temperatures and longer heating times make components harder but also increase the risk of metal distorting or becoming too brittle. Traditional color case hardening always has been a balancing act between aesthetics and achieving correct hardness.

Heated metal glows at different colors depending on its temperature, and Stokes had learned his craft in the first decades of the 20th Century, when many gun-trade practices were still more akin to medieval blacksmithing than the scientific processes of a mature Industrial Age. The act of balancing was more difficult then.

"Ted learned to harden before gas furnaces were used in the trade and before any means for accurately measuring temperature were available," Robin said. "He would harden by putting the pot directly into a fire. Temperature control was done purely by eye—by looking at the color of the pot. He had to move the pot around the fire to keep it at the critical temperature. And the ambient light of the day would make a difference in how the pot looked as it glowed. On a cloudy day he'd have to adjust to how it should look on a bright day.

"The skills of these men were immense then. Most of the guns they color hardened came out perfectly, but I remember stories of occasional mistakes." By the time Stokes was teaching Robin during the '60s, Brown's was located in Westley Richards' factory complex in Bournbrook and had access to Westley's pyrometer-equipped gas

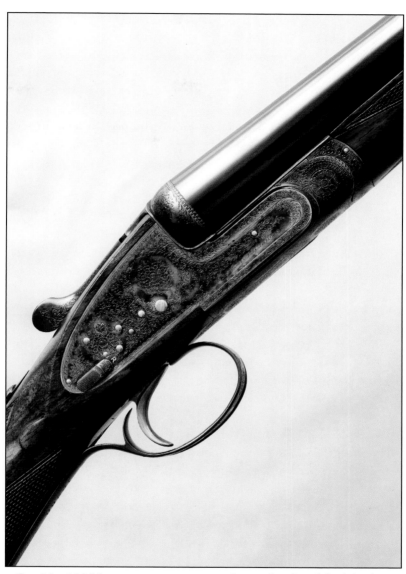

Gun No. 19288, an easy-opening Westley Richards sidelock built in 1966 by Brown's when the latter's workshops were sited in Westley's Bournbrook factory. Made for J.P. Morgan Jr. (a descendent of the J.P. Morgan Jr. discussed in Chapter XXII), the gun was fitted with a Brown-variant, Baker-type single trigger with a rare barrel-selector slide located on the lockplate. Robin Brown and Ted Stokes color-hardened it, and its finish remains in original condition. (Richard Rogers)

furnaces, making temperature control easier and more accurate than observing an open fire.

Although the gas-fired furnaces at Westley Richards in those days had automatic temperature settings, they lacked real precision. "We'd set them for the temperature we wanted," Robin said, "but in reality the range of heat was drifting up and down on either side of our setting. I found the high peaks caused more distortion."

Careful packing of components, as noted earlier, helped minimize these dangers, but experience has since taught Robin that *exact* temperature control is equally critical for quality results.

Robin walked me to the machine-tool room that houses Brown's furnace—a natural-gas-fired muffle furnace custom made in 1974. Today Robin eschews auto-controls; instead he manually sets for a certain temperature—between 750° C and 775° C, depending on the characteristics of the bone charcoal on hand—and carefully monitors the pyrometer to ensure "absolutely stable" temperatures. "You can't go off and brew a pot of tea and forget about it," he said.

The heat cycle lasts about three hours from when Robin places the pot in the pre-heated furnace to the time when he removes it. During the final 20 minutes, Robin drops the temperature by 10° C. "I found this decreases distortion," he said. Before tipping the contents into the quench, Robin rests the pot outside the furnace an additional two minutes. "The steadying of the bone-meal temperature prior to tip seems to 'bind' the parcel of gun parts and bone meal during the drop from pot to water," Robin explained. "That way the tip seems less explosive and more predictable."

If a gun's hardness—and subsequent durability—is influenced by heat, then the quench helps dictate its beauty. Case colors—comprised basically of iron oxide—are formed as a chemical reaction during rapid cooling as red-hot metal and surrounding bone meal interact with water. Preventing components from "flashing"—that is, from coming into contact with open air during their fall from the pot to the liquid—was (and remains) critical. A "flashed" component would be hard but also gray and devoid of desired colors due to oxidation.

A good "tip" was key to preventing this. "The tipping technique was partly black art," Robin said. "You had to tip in such a way that everything remained in an envelope of bone charcoal as it passed into the water."

Robin demonstrated a practice tip: Using a long set of tongs to lift a pot from the factory furnace, he walked out back to where a tub of water would have stood had this been a genuine operation. With his lead hand grasping the underside of the tongs and rear hand nestled over the top, he flicked the pot upside down with a swift, deft turn, and then quickly scuttled backward like a scalded crab. "There would be a mini-explosion of hot bone meal hitting water—sparks flying up in the air, and a great *whoosh* of steam and burnt-off bone meal," Robin said. "Under modern safety rules, if you were to subject an employee to this process today you'd have to dress him as if he were going into a volcano."

"We never did that," Robin added, "and I still have one or two scars to prove it."

You occasionally will see discussions of some practitioners adding ingredients—secret or otherwise—to the quench to enliven colors, or guidelines for holding water at a certain optimum temperature to affect same. Robin's approach is decidedly elemental: "We just use cool water, fresh out of the tap."

Standard procedure does recommend oxygenating quench water for better colors, a procedure Robin follows. "We use a hose to create turbulence, which increases oxygen content," he said. "But I personally don't think you should have air bubbles floating in the water at the time of the tip. There is an increased risk of flashing, I think, and you get colors that just don't look 'right' on a traditional English gun—too many bright pinks and oranges."

Three-quarters down the tub a sieve would have caught the components as they sank through the water and cooled, with the leftover meal settling to the bottom.

"We'd then remove the parts and examine them with interest," Robin said, "gasping if the colors were especially good, cursing if not . . . ."

Components were then put back into the pot—still hot from the furnace—to dry, and afterward they were quickly lacquered and oiled to resist any rust. Then it was on to the finisher for reassembly and final regulation and freeing any parts with minor distortion.

Although Robin has modified—even modernized—many of the techniques he learned from Stokes, he recalls his mentor with great fondness. "Ted was a very kind man, absolutely charming," Robin said. "His color hardening was an art and a real craft, and he passed all of it on to me at a time when a lot of people in the trade were very precious about what they knew and didn't want to share their skills.

"For all of that, Ted never made much money. What he earned he drank away. That seemed to be his life in his last years; his wife had died, but he still had a dog he loved. He didn't aspire to anything other than to come in to our factory and mix with the craftsmen, do his job and then go have a few pints with his friends after work. One

Colors on Brown Guns

In recent years talented practitioners—such as America's Doug Turnbull and the late Dr. Oscar Gaddy and his disciples—have evolved a number of techniques that have been immensely consequential to the development of, and reproducibility of, colors and color patterns. These include any number of jigs, blocks, shields and mechanical fixtures that either retain heat or keep the carbon material close to the metal as it is quenched. The most vivid colors seem to come when components cool more slowly as they quench and also when the carbon pack remains enveloped around the metal as it falls through the quench.

Robin Brown's methods remain almost alchemical by contrast and rely on his skill in "packing the pot"—that is, his placement of components within the carbon pack and pot—to achieve desired colors and hardness. "The way in which I arrange the components affects the amount of heat they receive, how much carbon is absorbed and how fast the bone meal is washed away in the quench," he said. Since being tutored by Ted Stokes, Robin has eschewed

Facing page: A recently made 20-bore Supreme De Luxe before and after color hardening. It showcases some of Robin Brown's aesthetic preferences: The darker colors are concentrated nearer the center, with the lighter tones radiating to the edges. This highlights the engraving (by Keith Thomas) while also framing the lighter edges against the browns of the stock. Note the evolution of the action shape from Brown's earlier days of making guns for the trade.

day he was walking up the steps of his local pub, and he just fell down dead, with his little dog at his side.

"And that," Brown said, trailing off, "was the end of Ted Stokes . . . ."

Life is a fleeting thing, and one lived as obscurely as Ted Stokes' seems but a nanosecond measured against the infinity of time. Yet great guncraft is timeless—and in the thousands of guns he hardened and in the techniques he passed along, the legacy and skills of Ted Stokes live on.

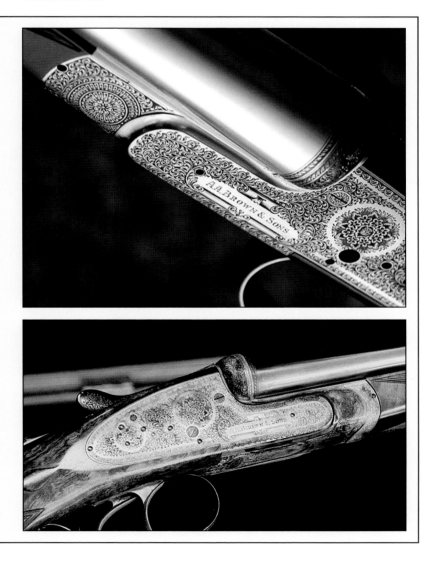

wiring extra metal to components to increase coloration. "I found this can increase distortion."

The latitude of permissible techniques and materials (as well as personal tricks of the trade) means that almost every hardener has a signature coloring style—or *styles* in the case of commercial hardeners like Turnbull, who works with a wide variety of guns of different makes, models and designs and from many countries. Robin's methods, by contrast, have evolved for essentially one gun—the Supreme De Luxe, Brown's easy-opening best sidelock of modified Holland & Holland design—although he also re-hardens sidelocks and boxlocks from other British makers when he restores them.

Robin smiles as he speaks of the "joy of colors" on a gun he has correctly colored, and for him correctness follows certain principles of pattern, placement and color. On Supreme De Luxe lockplates, for example, the darker colors—the blues and related permutations—will be nearer the centers, with grays, browns and tans radiating outward, the lightest shades predominating at the edges. A form of framing, this highlights the bolder colors and sets them off against the chocolate hues of the stock.

Aesthetics are, of course, only half the equation in color case hardening; the carbon skin and its protective qualities will matter to the shooter long after colors have faded. Colors on a gun a century old may have rubbed off through use, but a properly hardened case will keep the metal largely unsullied by wear.

The case itself seems surprisingly thin. Robin estimates that his are about .002" deep. "This is plenty thick to prevent wear," he said. "If you go much deeper, I've found you run the risk of metal distortion." Brown's guns, it should be noted, are rarely built as "closet queens"—or collectors' pieces—but instead are commissioned by a clientele that tends to shoot them hard and incessantly at driven game year after year. I have seen any number of Supreme De Luxes with their stocks in tatters but their metalwork invariably as pristine as the blade of Excalibur.

British sculptor Eric Gill was quoted as saying, "Art is skill. That is the first meaning of the word." That art—and those guncraft skills—are exemplified in Robin Brown's color case hardening.

XI.
Gianfranco Pedersoli:
Italian Super-Engraver

Italy's Gianfranco Pedersoli has helped transform modern gun embellishment with his artistic vision and bulino techniques.

Every day from the third-floor window of his home and studio in Gardone, Val Trompia, Gianfranco Pedersoli gazes at a scene that scarcely has changed in decades. The mountain out back still climbs into the Italian sky as it always has; just across the road, his boyhood home remains much as it was in his youth.

Yet from a vise perched on a bench at window's edge, Pedersoli has created engraving that has not only helped transform the embellishment of "best" guns worldwide but also helped alter the nature of gunmaking itself.

Pedersoli, now 64, is not tall, but he is still trim, and his head is topped with a tousle of hair that, had it not gone silver, belongs on a man 20 years his junior. His brown eyes sparkle when he greets you— "they are almost 'naughty' but in a good way," said Italian gun-trade translator Elena Micheli-Lamboy. Daniela, Pedersoli's wife of 37 years, is quick to offer visitors coffee and sweets; Pedersoli himself shakes his head and declines both.

"For me, no smoking, no alcohol, no coffee," he says. "OK, sometimes coffee, but not much." It could make his hands unsteady.

Unsteady hands could never produce what is clamped in the vise behind him. Spinning his chair to the window, he faces a sidelock over/under action. He takes a graver in his right hand and a jeweler's loupe in his left. Like a boxer ducking a jab, he hunches over the vise, brings the loupe to his eye and attacks the action with a series of quick, staccato flicks of his graver. *Pop-pop-pop*—the sound of steel on steel is audible. Under the graver's tip, a partridge bursts into flight from a swirl of scroll and foliage. *Pop-pop-pop* . . . .

Pedersoli removes the action from the vise and passes it to me. My hands tremble just to take it. Even under the loupe I can barely discern the countless tiny dots and lines that comprise the partridge and scrolls.

How many incisions will he cut before the engraving is complete? He pauses for a moment. "Millions," he replies. "For sure, millions!"

Bulino is a tool, and shorthand for the technique perfected by Pedersoli and by Italy's other great gun engravers. In Italian, "bulino" means "graver," the sharpened instrument engravers use to cut micro lines and dots in the metal's surface. Using hand pressure alone, the engraver varies the depth and number of incisions to influence how light interacts with the metal: The more dots and lines and the closer and deeper they are, the darker the shading effect; the farther apart and shallower, the lighter the gray tones. In talented hands, bulino produces images of near-photographic realism. In hands such as Pedersoli's you almost can hear the wingbeats in one of his flushing pheasants; in his portrait of a goddess you can feel the breeze through the gauzy folds of Diana's chemise.

A full-blown commission can take the engraver as many as 1,000

The engraving on this Piotti is a masterpiece of subtle light and shading—and it exhibits the varied motifs typical of Pedersoli.
(S.P. Fjestad/Blue Book Publications)

hours to finish. It will cost as much as or more than the $100,000 gun it adorns.

In Northern Italy today there are dozens upon dozens of highly talented, highly skilled engravers plying their trade. Only a handful, however, can claim the title *Maestro Incisore*—Master Engraver. Pedersoli's rank amongst this élite belongs on the first couple of fingers of that hand.

Superb Italian engraving is of course nothing new in a nation where art flourishes as verdantly as olive groves and vineyards. Since the Middle Ages, weapons have been made north of Brescia in Gardone, and there long have been artisans to embellish them. In the modern era, however, engravers of sporting shotguns have worked under an ideal that the British established in the early 19th Century: A fine gun is foremost a tool and only distantly second an aesthetic object. Even on best guns engraving costs were normally 10 to 20 percent of a gun's total price. Until the 1970s many Italian engravers rarely signed their work, were barely known outside their country and usually worked on conventional scroll, floral and ornamental motifs dictated by centuries of tradition.

Pedersoli learned his craft from one of these old-style masters—Giulio Timpini, who took the 14-year-old Pedersoli under his wing

On this Fabbri, circa 1993, Pedersoli mixed geometric elements with more traditional ornamental designs. Despite the disparate designs, the overall effect is harmonious. (S.P. Fjestad/Blue Book Publications)

for 4^1/$_2$ years after recognizing the latter's artistic talents. Always fond of drawing and art, Pedersoli soon mastered the traditional hammer & chisel technique—*punta e martello*—that dominated at the time. In 1970 Timpini became the head of Beretta's engraving department and took his young protégé in tow. But five years at Beretta engraving rote patterns left Pedersoli yearning for more.

Befriending two men—engraver Firmo Fracassi and gunmaker Mario Abbiatico—in the mid-'70s changed Pedersoli's life. Fracassi (along with Angelo Galeazzi) was a pioneer and innovator in the emerging bulino engraving style, whereas Abbiatico, co-founder of gunmaker Abbiatico & Salvinelli (FAMARS), had a knack for not only recognizing budding engraving talents but also convincing rich Amer-

Floral elements are used to frame a full pheasant game scene. Note Pedersoli's skill in using the engraving to complement the lines of the gun. (S.P. Fjestad/Blue Book Publications)

Pedersoli's application of gold frames the woodcock game scene without overpowering it.

(S.P. Fjestad/Blue Book Publications)

ican patrons to take a chance on these talents and to commission "high-art" engraving where money was literally of no object. Pedersoli learned from Fracassi's and Galeazzi's bulino styles and embraced Abbiatico's commissions. Freed from the strictures of the past and from budgetary restraints, Pedersoli and other talented colleagues took techniques and embellishment styles to new levels. Thus dawned the Age of the Italian Engraver.

Pedersoli eventually left Beretta to work full-time for FAMARS until Abbiatico's untimely death in the early '80s. His skills developed and reputation assured, Pedersoli then began a high-profile freelance career that remains highly influential to this day.

Barry Lee Hands, a talented Montana-based engraver, is a student of engraving history and has met and interviewed many of the world's finest practitioners, including Pedersoli. "Today Pedersoli's influence is seen in the production on new best guns everywhere," Hands said. "He was one of the first to pull together fantasy and baroque styles with his use of traditional patterns of ornament with more modern themes and figures. The neo-classic movement in postmodern engraving, in which he was a leader, was taken even further by engravers such as Manrico Torcoli and engraving houses such as Cesare Giovannelli and Creative Art."

Pedersoli now considers himself "retired"—but this really means he is cutting back on work, not quitting. Reflecting on his life, he says his engraving has been marked by three major stylistic periods: landscapes and small ornamental motifs from 1980 to '85; floral patterns from '85 to '94; and grotesques from '94 to '98. Today he concentrates on ornamental scroll and lavish game scenes.

Though many in Italy have attempted to imitate his style, there is no mistaking a Pedersoli engraving, regardless of its period. All are characterized by intertwined motifs that are often disparate in individual subject matter yet harmoniously blended into a composition that is greater than the sum of its parts. That nothing ever seems incongruous is the mark of Pedersoli's genius.

Pedersoli's aesthetic vision no doubt reflects the Italian love of *Spoletto*—or visual spectacle—and his stated intent is to generate emotions in the viewer. His mastery with shading and highlighting sets the mood for each piece. "Light is everything in my engraving," Pedersoli noted. "The light and movement you see creates feelings, which is the purpose of engraving.

"Italian engraving is all about beauty, balance, light and details."

It is also about old-fashioned handwork. Unlike American engravers who routinely employ machine-assisted tools, Italians work almost exclusively with hand tools. Beside Pedersoli's vise are only a few gravers, a sharpener for them, a hammer, a couple of chisels and a loupe or two. "The bulino is like an extension of an Italian engraver's hand," Pedersoli said.

He works by natural light—hence his workstation at the window—and engraves eight to nine hours per day; after dinner he will sketch and trace. About 85 percent of his engraving is performed with the hand-held gravers, the remainder with hammer & chisel. His dexterity with a graver is astounding; so too the intensity with which he works. Barry Hands writes of him engraving with a bulino tool "so quickly that it sounded like he was using a machine."

Ultimately, though, it is what is in Pedersoli's head rather than the tools in his hands that have garnered his reputation. "I think imagination is more important than technique," Pedersoli said. "Imagination and creativity are really the keys to great engraving."

The rise of superstar Italian engravers such as Pedersoli and Fracassi has transformed not only engraving but also gunmaking in the past three decades. It is evident in the designs of the guns themselves: So-called pinless sidelocks are now the norm on many best-quality guns. "Our guns have been designed and built to make the engraver's work easier," noted Tullio Fabbri, of Italy's most esteemed maker of best-quality over/unders. "This is demonstrated by the elimination of the pins and external screws that otherwise would restrict an engraver's imagination."

The maker's reputation and name itself, formerly sacrosanct in establishing a firearm's value, sometimes play second fiddle to the engraver's name signed on the gun. No longer primarily a tool for killing, a best gun today often serves equally as a canvas for an artist whose medium happens to be steel.

A covey of quail emerges from ovals framed by myriad flowers topped with songbirds. Pedersoli was an early innovator in integrating diverse motifs into his engraving.
(S.P. Fjestad/Blue Book Publications)

Good engravers have become plentiful as demand for their talents has increased. When Pedersoli was a boy, there were no schools in the Val Trompia training engravers; today there are two. Moreover, the bulino techniques perfected in Italy have spilt over national borders, and there are now stunning practitioners in the US, Austria, Germany, France and Belgium.

Even the once-staid British—whose august classicism dominated engraving for so long—today embrace exuberant techniques that would make any Colonel Blimp blanch. Philip Coggan belongs in the vanguard of the renaissance that swept British engraving in the early 1980s. "I became aware of Pedersoli around 1983," Coggan said. "I had just started to engrave, and I was told there was an Italian engraving book I should see. When I bought it, I couldn't believe the engraving therein—I'd never seen anything like it. The engravers that really stood out for me were Fracassi and Pedersoli."

Although Coggan—today renowned for his gold inlays—developed his own tools and techniques largely by experimentation, he credits Pedersoli for inspiration: "Pedersoli was just one of a handful of engravers who gave me enthusiasm for my future work."

In an age when the engraver's skills often overshadow the gunmaker's, Pedersoli, by contrast, always respects his medium—his compositions always complement the guns. "Gianfranco's work carries with it the highest sensitivity to form and function, with impeccable layout and design," Hands said. "There's always an innate sense of decorum and balance that enhances the lines of metal and wood and never exceeds the bounds of taste and artistic integrity."

Tony Galazan, founder of Connecticut Shotgun Manufacturing Co., is one of the few non-Italian gunmakers who Pedersoli has worked with. "Pedersoli is a true artist," Galazan said. "He understands the proper flow that the engraving needs to follow with the gun."

Pedersoli is picky about the gunmakers he engraves for—Fabbri, Piotti, F.lli Rizzini, Beretta and Galazan are prominent in the select group. The makers must take special care when finishing the guns so none of the engraving is worn off. "The guns never lay on sharp edges," Galazan said.

Each Pedersoli engraving is unique, another characteristic that distinguishes Pedersoli from more commercial engravers. "I never execute the same engraving on two guns," he said. "I don't agree with repetitive engraving." He also normally works on only one gun at a time, preferring to focus his imagination on the sole task at hand.

Is he an artist or artisan? Centuries ago art critics would have

*This F.lli Rizzini, circa 1998, was
one of the first guns Pedersoli engraved
with gargoyles and grotesques.*
(S.P. Fjestad/Blue Book Publications)

lumped in engraving with other crafts. As the boundaries between art and craft blurred in the 20th Century, however, the critics' easy categorizations no longer stood on such solid ground, especially in the case of pathfinders such as Pedersoli.

The engraver himself broaches no doubt on the subject: "There is no question in my mind that engraving is an art just like painting or sculpting, but the recognition is not there yet. What I can do in metal is no different than what a master painter can do on canvas."

Perhaps this is why he rarely collaborates with other engravers. In the past Pedersoli has worked with Fracassi and Torcoli—who are his friends—on individual guns, but, he said, "The integrated nature of my engraving makes it difficult to work with others."

Elena Micheli-Lamboy describes Pedersoli as a "gentle soul," and this, I think, is reflected in his best work: scenes that evoke a certain state of innocence and the shimmering wonder of nature where the

hunter and death seem far, far away. Does he ever feel a tension between this sort of engraving and the practical purposes of a gun?

"The gun is just a canvas," Pedersoli said. "It could be a plate or
a piece of jewelry and it would not make any difference. Most of my
customers feel the same way."

How the world of guns has changed.

XII.
Last Gasp in Liège

Rain was falling as the train I rode pulled into Gare de Guillemins. It still was falling a week later when I left the Liège station for Brussels. The sun had shone only once during my stay, when leaden skies cracked open above Citadel Hill, where I stood in the mist looking over the city and the River Meuse that meanders through it.

When the author visited Liège in 1997 (top), he found its artisanal gun trade collapsing and almost gone. The circa-1913 postcard (above) shows the city when it was the undisputed gunmaking capital of the world.

Sullen weather reflected the gloom hanging over Liège's economy during my visit in autumn 1997. In the 1970s the city had begun to spiral down the drain of de-industrialization. The gun trade Liège was famous for had not escaped. At the time of my visit, the biggest and most famous arms maker, Fabrique Nationale, had been bleeding money for years and recently had been sold by its French owners to Belgium's Walloon Government. Because FN owned Browning and the Winchester brand, the takeover had been covered widely in America's sporting press.

By contrast, the fate of the traditional Liège trade—the independent artisanal gunmakers that for centuries exported millions of guns to every corner of the globe—had been ignored. To learn more, I hopped a plane to Belgium to check the pulse of what then appeared a mostly moribund trade and one whose future seemed tenuous at best.

Liège's gun trade is ancient. From the Middle Ages on, the city's craftsmen were famous for their metalworking skills. Ruled for centuries by prince-bishops as an independent principality, Liège cleverly played its hand as a neutral, particularly during the religious wars of the 16th Century. This fostered an arms trade to which any warring nation could turn. By the time the city was incorporated into the modern state of Belgium, in 1830, its gunmakers were poised to challenge Birmingham for the right to claim the title "small arms arsenal of the world."

If the first half of the 19th Century belonged to Birmingham, Liège caught up in the 1860s, passed the former's output in the mid-'70s and, after the '80s, never looked back. At its zenith, just before the First World War, Liège's trade numbered more than 200 firms and perhaps 14,000 workers producing about 1.5 million firearms per year.

As with Birmingham, most of the production was military weapons and trade guns, the latter cheap muskets destined for natives in the colonies of Imperial Europe. But Liège also built sporting guns, the best of them crafted with the style, grace and elegance to challenge England's finest.

That's largely because they were English guns—or at least copies of them. Although sporting guns built in the early 19th Century reflect the rococo influences and ornamentation of the great French gunmaker Noel Boutet, the Belgians were quick to adopt British patents and aesthetics in the 1870s and '80s as London and Birmingham began to perfect hammerless designs. "While the Liègeois may invent hardly a thing," noted M. Mangeot, a 19th Century Belgian gunmaker, "they can on the other hand imitate anything—very quickly, very well and very cheaply."

*The traditional Liège gun trade was an archetype of cottage industry.
In this 1914 photo (above) two engravers work from their kitchen.
The other image dates from the same era. Its description reads:
"Arms-worker's hut … with cracks in the walls. The family of 10 lives
in one room, which serves as workshop, kitchen and bedroom."*
(Courtesy of Claude Gaier)

It was this ability to build guns so cheaply that bedeviled Birmingham. "The Belgian manufacturer will deliver . . . finished [guns] for almost the same price as the Birmingham manufacturer will have to pay for English material out of which to make them," lamented Charles and William O. Greener (writing under pseudonyms Artifex and Opifex), of England's W.W. Greener, in 1907.

Local supplies of coal and iron were one secret to Liège's competitiveness; another was the cottage-industry nature of its decentralized gun trade. Think of the system as a pyramid: a vast network of home-based outworkers at the bottom, subcontractors and middlemen above them, and at the top the "gunmakers"—merchants and entrepreneurs who placed their names on guns they may or may not have assembled and finished.

Although gunmaking in other city centers was structured similarly, Liège was able to produce guns so cheaply because most outworkers lived and worked outside the city, in rural villages nearby. In tiny cottages they toiled 12 hours a day on subcontracted parts, and in their spare time they tended chickens, pigs and gardens. Wives and children helped deliver parts to subcontractors for assembly. Components, in turn, were assembled into guns, which were finished by subcontractors and sometimes even by the "gunmakers" themselves if they were higher-grade guns.

With few factories to build or maintain, most Liègeois gunmakers had little overhead, and home-based craftsmen not only survived on cheaper wages but also were more isolated and easily exploited. Socialist reformers at the turn of the century described Belgium as "a worker's hell and capitalist's paradise."

Craftsmen in different villages surrounding Liège became known for their expertise in producing different components. Those in the Val de Vesdre, for example, were barrelmakers; those in Vottem were stockers; in Rhees they were trigger-guard makers; and in Herstal they were actioners. But guild-style organization tended to retard mechanization and modernization (with notable exceptions being FN and barrelmaking factories). A delegation of Birmingham makers visiting Liège in 1902, for example, was shocked to discover craftsmen in one workshop using a running dog inside a circular cage to power their lathes.

Cottage industry also promoted anonymity, and it's not uncom-

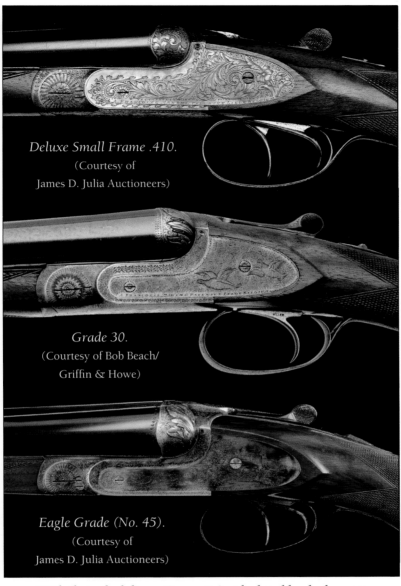

Deluxe Small Frame .410.
(Courtesy of
James D. Julia Auctioneers)

Grade 30.
(Courtesy of Bob Beach/
Griffin & Howe)

Eagle Grade (No. 45).
(Courtesy of
James D. Julia Auctioneers)

With their sleek lines, Francotte's sideplated boxlocks were prettier than many English boxlocks—and as well built as any—and they were an affordable alternative with American sportsmen seeking European guns. Made especially for the US market, these sideplated guns were popular imports from the late 19th Century until the middle of the 20th.

mon to encounter Liège-made guns with no address or maker's name on them. Vast numbers were exported to France, Russia and the US and then marked with the seller's name, not the maker's. Some were built as forgeries to be marked with prestigious English names. At the top of their game, however, the best makers—among them Aug. Francotte, Dumoulin Bros., Lebeau-Courally, A. Cordy, Jules Bury, Thonon, E. Masquelier, J. Defourny and A. Forgeron—turned out double guns as good as any.

Although 20th Century mechanization may have inevitably doomed this anachronistic, labor-intensive trade, the First World War began the bloodletting: More than half of the city's makers disappeared after 1914. Still, the interwar years saw Liège turn out some shotguns of exceptional quality and innovation—notably over/unders by A. Cordy, Francotte and Lebeau-Courally. Liège suffered again in the Second World War, but the trade still had enough life to partially rebound through the early '60s.

But a trade founded on an abundance of skilled workers could function only when there were enough craftsmen competing to keep prices low. Better wages and working conditions in other industries stifled recruitment of new craftsmen, and that, combined with Belgium's postwar socialist society, sent labor costs—as well as prices for new guns—soaring in the '60s. The industrialized world's cheapest labor force had become its dearest. Worldwide inflation in the '70s and a recession in the early '80s delivered the coup de grâce. Bereft of new blood and crippled by rising costs, most of the Liège trade simply withered away like an uprooted rose, leaving only its guns to mark its passing.

By the late '90s there were just a handful of survivors—the few firms fit enough to compete with the best makers of Britain and Brescia. One of them was Auguste Francotte et Cie, at the time Liège's oldest surviving gunmaker. The company's reputation was succinctly summarized in 1910 by another Belgian gunmaker who remarked: "I believe in the Liègeois arms industry almighty and in the Francotte firm, its eldest son."

The first gunmaking Francotte was Barthelemy, a Liège-born musician at the court of Louis XVI. Fleeing the guillotine in revolutionary Paris, Francotte abandoned music and returned to Liège in the 1790s to try his hand at gunmaking. But it was Auguste (probably

This Francotte 12-bore heavy game gun with single trigger exhibits the superb engraving that Belgian artisans were capable of. (Courtesy of James D. Julia Auctioneers)

Barthelemy's son) who is credited with founding the firm in 1805.

In the first three-quarters of the 19th Century, Francotte built both military weapons and sporting guns in a vast range of models and grades. Unlike many Liègeois makers, Francotte actually had a factory—or, more accurately, an assembly plant—but the company also would have relied on an army of outworkers, using the most talented to build high-grade sporting guns.

The adoption of repeating rifles by the world's militaries in the 1880s marked a turning point in Francotte's history—indeed, in Liège's. Along with 11 other prominent gunmakers, Francotte helped found Fabrique Nationale D'Armes de Guerre (FN) in 1888, and in the latter's factories military arms would be built increasingly by machinery. The sporting-gun trade, like that of Britain's, largely remained the domain of craftsmen, and in this endeavor Francotte still excelled. The company's place among the world's shotgun makers was not unlike that of top Birmingham makers such as W.W. Greener or Westley Richards—making everything from yeoman-grade guns to those of "best" quality and in a stunning variety of configurations.

Francotte's output was prodigious: Although there are no production records for early military arms, it's likely that the firm produced more than a million, perhaps twice that. As for graded sporting guns, Francotte is believed to have built at least 100,000 from the 1880s on. Even today Francotte remains the best-known Belgian name in the US, thanks to thousands of shotguns imported by Von Lengerke & Detmold, Inc. (VL&D, 1889 to 1929), and later by Abercrombie & Fitch (A&F, 1929 to 1971). Francotte offered customers double guns that were more refined than their American counterparts yet less expensive than British guns—and often every bit as good.

If there's a signature Francotte shotgun in America, it's the *système Anson & Deeley à contre-platines*—the sideplated boxlock. VL&D and A&F sold these guns in 10 gauge through .410 and in a variety of numbered grades: No. 45 [Eagle] at the top, with models such as No. 30, No. 25, No. 20, No. 14 and the Knockabout following in descending order of fit and finish. These guns were specially configured for the US market.

In a November 14, 1896, *Sporting Life* article on the increasing popularity of Francottes in America, Will K. Park noted: "Mr. Von Lengerke visited the [Francotte] works and had them model their guns to suit the American tastes and the beauty of these guns shows how well he succeeded. All guns imported to VL&D have the Anson & Deeley lock . . . and a cross bolt; Purdy [sic] side breech clips, doll's head extensions, covered bolts, safety intercepting sears, complete sidelocks [sic], plate, etc., according to quality and costs.

"Judging from the number of these guns now being used we think that the Francotte guns are the most popular of any imported make." According to researcher Bob Beach of Griffin & Howe—which owns the relevant records—there were about 4,550 Francottes imported by VL&D and A&F between 1901 and 1970. There were undoubtedly hundreds more imported before 1901, and other importers brought in Francottes after 1970.

Francotte remained active after the Second World War, building 300 to 400 guns per year until the 1960s. Although a Francotte still sat on the firm's board of directors in the '90s, the family sold the company in 1972—sales were slowing and there were no sons in-

The late Ivan De Stoop, of Auguste Francotte et Cie.

terested in taking the reins. The company was purchased by an individual who then enlisted the financial backing of SIPEF, a multinational agro-business corporation. After a couple of years SIPEF bought out the owner and assumed full management.

During my 1997 visit, Francotte was based in a quiet Herstal neighborhood in a spacious, if nondescript, postwar factory. I met managing director Ivan C. De Stoop as he huddled over a tattered Francotte order book in the showroom. "Look at these initials," he said, pointing out the particulars from an over/under built in 1937. "L.C.—a gun engraved by Lyson Corombelle. Lyson and her father, Hyppolite, were two of Belgium's greatest engravers."

De Stoop, the scion of a prominent Belgian family, spoke English with the polish of an old boy from Eton. He had managed Francotte for SIPEF since 1984, and he lamented the difficult times and changing markets. "In the mid-'80s, when the dollar was very high, we were still selling 80 or 90 guns a year in the US," he explained. "Today I'm selling three or four."

Like other Belgian firms making guns by traditional methods, Francotte had been priced out of the middle market—its stock and trade in America. De Stoop escorted me to the gunroom and picked out a side-plated boxlock. "This is a gun we were selling back in the '80s for $6,000 to $8,000," he said. "The gun now begins at $15,000—not because our prices went up that much but because the dollar has gone down."

Through the '90s, Francotte remained prestigious on the Continent, especially in France, Greece, Spain and Portugal. As the US market wilted, De Stoop was able to shift some sales, particularly of double rifles, to European buyers. "Today we build 25 to 30 guns [per year], mostly sidelocks and a few boxlocks," he said.

De Stoop was hoping to regain a market that once had been enormously important for the firm. "I'm looking east," he told me. "There's interest coming from Russia and former Iron Curtain countries, which before 1917 were huge markets for Francotte guns. If the dollar strengthened considerably, we'd still get a lot of interest from the States."

Because rumors haunted the Francotte name in the US, there was something I had to ask: "Can you explain the matter of Spanish guns being sold as Francottes?"

At this De Stoop's voice became somber. "A sad, sad moment in our firm's history," he admitted. "This occurred for only a couple of years in the mid-'70s, when the firm first changed hands. The man who initially purchased the company decided to supplement profits by buying Spanish guns and marking them as Francottes. It was a terrible mistake on his part, and he didn't last long. There were not many of these sold, none directly to the US. And we destroy these forgeries when we come across them.

"I must stress that this happened only with a few guns, for a short period of time in the '70s, and that many legitimate Francottes were made at the same time. And it has nothing to do with current management; it's past history."

De Stoop took me to the factory floor. There were holes worn through the linoleum in front of each vise where for decades craftsmen had stood with file and hammer and chisel. During my visit, Francotte still had four craftsmen in-house, another three full-timers who worked exclusively from their homes, and five outworkers employed on a contract basis.

Though the firm was clearly past its prime, Francotte still enjoyed a reputation for having the best barrel shop in Liège. "We consider the barrel the soul of the Francotte gun," explained De Stoop. "They must be perfect from the get-go; the rest you can always fix." It is a badly kept secret in the trade that some of Britain's best makers often turned to Francotte to obtain big-bore double-rifle barrels.

Though hardly cheap, Francottes were at the time of my visit still less expensive than the guns of English competitors, closer in price to Piottis, or Bertuzzis or equivalent guns from other boutique Italian makers. "We're making greater use of CNC technology to rough out components," De Stoop said. "It helps keep us competitive. But all Francottes are still assembled, regulated and finished by hand—pre-

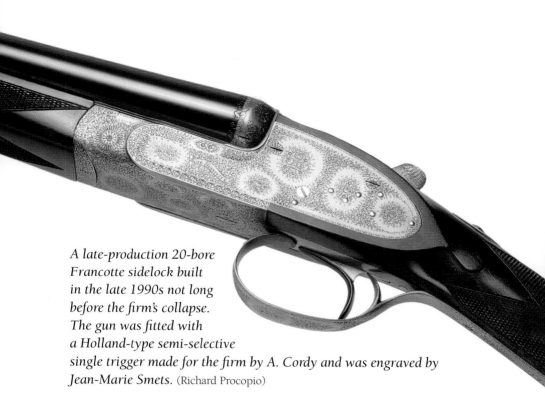

*A late-production 20-bore
Francotte sidelock built
in the late 1990s not long
before the firm's collapse.
The gun was fitted with
a Holland-type semi-selective
single trigger made for the firm by A. Cordy and was engraved by
Jean-Marie Smets.* (Richard Procopio)

cisely the approach Holland & Holland and Purdey's employ today."

As I left the city in a rain-streaked rail car a few days later, I was sobered—even depressed—by what I had seen. There was still a pulse at a few shops like Francotte, Marcel Thys and Lebeau-Courally—but it was beating slowly and ever more faintly. Winter had descended on Liège, and for most of its makers there would be no spring. Thys would fail soon after my visit, while Lebeau has changed hands since and has managed to survive. Unknown to me, De Stoop was not a well man when I saw him, and he succumbed to cancer in 2000.

Not long after my visit, Francotte changed hands and attempted to team up with Holland's Tom Derksen, president and founder of Holland's Verenigde Gewermakers ("United Gunmakers"). An accomplished engineer, Derksen had built VGM during the '80s and '90s into one of the most technologically advanced sporting-gun makers in Northern Europe. A "gunmaker's gunmaker," VGM had supplied components and near-finished actions to a variety of makers, including some in Britain.

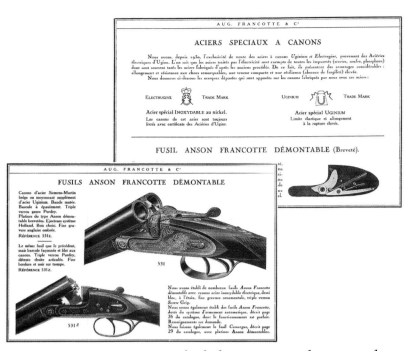

In the late 1990s Francotte had plans to reintroduce a number of its unique vintage designs, such as the Anson Francotte Démontable—essentially a simplified sidelock with boxlock-inspired lockwork mounted on its plates.

The idea was to couple Francotte's world-class marque and traditional workforce with VGM's technology-driven manufacturing capabilities. Not only would the firm continue to build boxlock and sidelock rifles and shotguns as well as Boss-type sidelock over/unders, but there also were plans to revive a number of brilliant-if-short-lived Francotte designs originally introduced in the 1930s but cut short by the Second World War.

These included some superb Francotte-designed over/unders as well as the Anson Francotte Démontable, essentially Anson-style lockwork on a sideplate that could be disassembled and reassembled by hand—a simplified sidelock sans intercepting sears. There were also plans to reengineer the SuperBritte, Belgium's famous side-opening over/under, and to build it anew under the Francotte name.

Unfortunately, the venture collapsed in 2001, with the Francotte factory shuttered and its workforce dismissed. It was an ignominious end to one of the world's most influential and longest-operating craft gunmakers. Derksen's own company went bankrupt in 2003. According to Belgian gun expert Luc Vander Borght, who worked for Francotte from 1977 to '85, the original Francotte name is now owned by a Dutch investor and is today dormant.

Sic transit gloria mundi: "Thus passes the glory of the world"—and that too of the Liège gun trade.

XIII.
The SuperBritte

It is not recorded whether Théophile Britte started work on his over/under design just before or after the Great Depression, but it's clear that Black Friday and its aftermath proved little deterrent to the industrious Belgian gunmaker. Théophile's vision was to craft the lightest and shallowest-frame over/under game gun ever made, and he wasn't about to let a global financial catastrophe stop him.

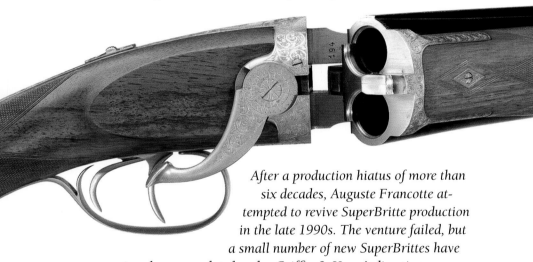

After a production hiatus of more than six decades, Auguste Francotte attempted to revive SuperBritte production in the late 1990s. The venture failed, but a small number of new SuperBrittes have since been completed under Griffin & Howe's direction.

The economy aside, Liège in the late 1920s and early '30s was fertile ground for a talented gunmaker to harrow. In 1930 Fabrique Nationale began producing John Browning's great Superposed gun, and top makers like Auguste Francotte, Lebeau-Courally and A. Cordy were introducing elegant new sidelock O/Us. Many others were making O/Us on Dieudonné Saive's boxlock patent. Each was an excellent design in itself, but all shared a common trait: high action walls, thanks to the underbolt fastening systems they all employed.

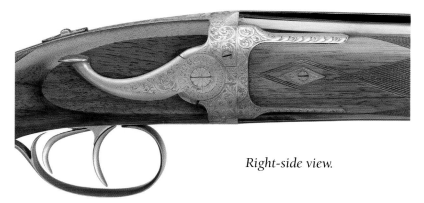

Right-side view.

Britte wanted his gun to be vastly different, combining the low profile and handling characteristics of a side-by-side with the recoil and sighting advantages of an over/under. In late 1931 he brought his design to fruition, successfully patenting it. In an advertisement touting the new SuperBritte to the gun trade, he called it "The latest revelation for 1932!"

And it *was* a revelation—light and shallow, much more so than not only its competitors in Liège but also those from London. That's because it opened to the side, completely unlike any of the conventional actions of the day. Soon Britte's company was making the SuperBritte in 12, 16 and 20 gauge, and the guns began appearing in shops across Europe. But only four years later the SuperBritte essentially vanished.

Left-side view.

Until 1999 . . . .

At The Vintage Cup that year, Dutch gunmaker Tom Derksen—who recently had been hired by Auguste Francotte's owners—unveiled the first SuperBritte finished in decades. Although my time behind the SuperBritte's triggers was short, it was long enough to conclude that the gun was everything Théophile Britte had designed it to be.

A new SuperBritte bearing the Francotte name was not entirely unusual, considering the history of Etablissements Britte SA, the gun's original maker. In 1896 Théophile and his brother, Lambert, started doing business as Britte Fréres (Britte Brothers). The pair were not only superb craftsmen but also progressive.

Their firm invested heavily in the most modern equipment of its era and had a large factory and a highly skilled in-house work-force. The company specialized in making *armes en blanc* (guns in the white) to be sold to and finished by other makers in Belgium, France and Germany. A search through factory records reveals that Belgian customers included the crème of Liège: Francotte, Lebeau Courally, Christoff, Defourny and many others.

In 1923 Britte Fréres was incorporated as Etablissements Britte

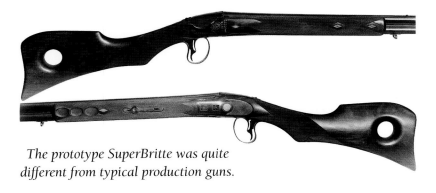

The prototype SuperBritte was quite different from typical production guns.

SA, with additional capital coming from three important new part-ners: Charles and Ernest Masquelier and Jules Bury. The Masquelier brothers were well-respected gun dealers in Liège, and Bury was a gunmaker whose best work was held in the same esteem as that of Francotte or Lebeau. At the peak of its sporting-arms production, Britte employed 300 craftsmen and made thousands of barrels, ac-tions and guns annually, though only rarely will a gun surface today bearing the Britte name.

By agreement between the partners, the majority of SuperBrittes were sold under the Bury or Masquelier names, although Belgian gun expert Luc Vander Borght reports he has seen an early SuperBritte bearing the name of America's Savage Arms Co. Gough Thomas's *Gun Book* pictures one built as a Lebeau-Courally. Undoubtedly, there were other SuperBrittes sold in the white and finished off by others.

Théophile Britte (front row, center) with brother Lambert (at Théophile's left) and other craftsmen at Britte Fréres, circa 1897.

It's interesting to speculate how much of Théophile's vision was his own and whether he found inspiration elsewhere. Britain's W.W. Greener had patented a side-opening O/U in 1873, but it seems only one was built, a prototype. Edinburgh's John Dickson had made a small number of side-opening O/Us based on its round-action patents—the first of them around 1888. For its part, the Britte company claimed its antecedent was an obscure 18th Century Italian single-barrel side-opening design. But if the SuperBritte's inspiration remains shrouded in history, Théophile's consummated design was nothing short of brilliant.

Driven largely by British ideals of what a game gun should look like and be, fine gunmakers in the first several decades of the 20th Century expended huge amounts of creative energy attempting to make over/unders as light and shallow as they could. To bolt the gun, however, most clung to underbolt fasteners as used on side-by-sides, which inherently made for high-wall O/U actions. All stuck with the traditional break-open, barrel-drop design. Britain's Boss & Co and James Woodward made enduring improvements with their brilliant shallow-action designs, but like the chained prisoners in Plato's allegory of the cave, most of their competitors were too shackled by convention to look beyond the design constraints cast by the side-by-side. Théophile, on the other hand, looked at the potentials of both designs and bent them to his will.

At first glance, the SuperBritte resembles a side-by turned on its right side, with a rib at the top and triggers underneath. The ejectors are housed in the left side of the two-part forend, and the gun opens on the right via a sidelever.

Unlike most Liège gunmakers, Britte had a large factory filled with then-modern equipment.

At the time of its introduction, the SuperBritte was the shallowest-frame over/under ever put into regular production. It may still be. A 12-gauge stands only 56mm (2.20") high, compared to 63mm (2.480") for a Boss—the benchmark by which all shallow-frame O/Us are judged. A typical 12-gauge Browning Superposed action is, by contrast, 68mm (2.680") high.

Without the typical O/U's U-shaped action, the SuperBritte can be made exceptionally light: A 12-gauge weighs but 6 pounds 9 ounces; a 20 will weigh 6 pounds. Nonetheless, it is also enormously strong, thanks to its design. When the gun is fired, the rigid structure of superposed barrels flexes less than that of a side-by-side—and even less so in the absence of the usual horizontal pivot point at the hinge (it's vertical in the SuperBritte's case).

For strength, the barrels and action lock up in three places: via two barrel lumps that protrude through the left side of the action and by a side-fastener that provides not only vertical strength but also lateral stability. The design is strong enough that Britte originally made 9.3x74R

double rifles on the action—and on the smaller-frame version at that.

Unlike the Scott-type toplever used on most side-by-sides and O/Us—which simply allows a gun to open—the SuperBritte's sidelever not only unlatches the gun but also cocks the locks via a double cam as it is depressed. Firing pins are separate from the vertically mounted tumblers, which are powered by short but powerful coil springs. The gun is, therefore, exceptionally easy to open and close. Were the lever on top, it would perhaps be stiff, but because it's on the side it's easy to operate using natural leverage. Also impressive is how the gun pivots in hand when the barrels

An early '30s-era advertisement.

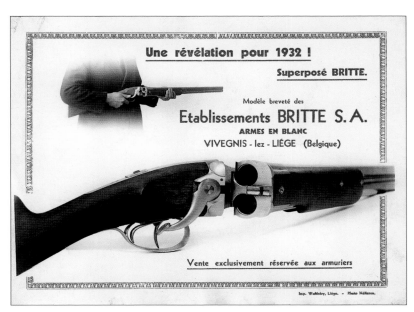

The Second World War cut short what might have been a promising future for Britte's novel design.

open to become a "side-by-side" for easy reloading, and then seems to right itself again when you close it.

When I was shooting it at Vintage Cup '99, the biggest glitch I encountered was entirely mental: When I pushed the sidelever down, I tried to open the gun the same way—by pulling the barrels down. At which point Derksen would smile and say, "To the side."

For a game shooter, a light, shallow-frame O/U possesses more than Platonic virtues. One of the advantages an over/under enjoys over a side-by-side is the reduction of perceived recoil, particularly from the lower barrel. That's because an O/U's lower barrel is more in line with the comb and center of the butt, so recoil is delivered in a straighter line, generating less torque than a side-by-side of comparable weight. Ditto for the upper barrel, though to a lesser extent. The shallower the action, the "straighter" the recoil from both barrels.

The 12-gauge SuperBritte I examined also had side-by-side-like game-gun balance and weight distribution. It handled beautifully. Obviously, this isn't unique to a SuperBritte: Many best British and Italian O/Us share these qualities, as do quite a number of far-less-expensive examples. Where the SuperBritte theoretically excels is in the relationship it promotes between the hands and the barrels.

For starters, the gun's two-piece forend is actually made of two shallow forends, each to a side, with the bottom of the lower barrel exposed. Britte's original sales literature touted the "thermal" benefits of this arrangement (allowing both barrels to cool equally), but more important to instinctual wingshooting is that the lower barrel is in contact with the leading hand—just as it would be on a properly gripped side-by-side with a splinter forend. Moreover, the upper tube also is cupped deep within the leading hand. Paired with the Super-Britte's shallow action and a straight-grip stock, the shooter's hands remain on the same plane relative to the bore axes—thus fulfilling one of the requisites for instinctive wingshooting.

For the most part, SuperBritte guns have proven not only reliable but also durable. Vander Borght told me, "I have seen SuperBrittes that have been shot constantly since they were made, and they have never been back to a workshop.

"I know of an original double-rifle SuperBritte in 9.3x74R in use by the third generation of hunters, and I doubt it has ever been refurbished. They will need rejointing after years of heavy use, just like

Whether Scotland's side-opening over/unders from John Dickson (above) served as a precedent is unknown, but Britte claimed his gun was inspired by an 18th Century Italian design. Nevertheless, this ultra-rare Dickson displays conceptual similarities.

(Courtesy of Gavin Gardiner, Ltd.)

any other break-open design, but this is easily accomplished, thanks to the replaceable hinge pin."

With all of these attributes, the SuperBritte should have enjoyed a long production run. Unfortunately, Théophile had invented the right gun at a very wrong time. By 1936 the Depression was digging deep into sporting-arms sales, and the whiff of another world war was in the air. Etablissements Britte decided to halt almost all sporting-gun production in favor of broader industrial diversification. Soon the company was making everything from machine guns and cannon foundries to metal desks and chairs. In retrospect, it proved a propitious decision. Today a prosperous Britte SA remains in business, still on the cutting edge of manufacturing technology, its diversified client base including leading companies in the aerospace, defense and automotive industries. The artisanal Liège gun trade, on the other hand, is almost dead nowadays.

Though it officially had forsaken sporting arms, the firm still built a few SuperBrittes after the Second World War at the behest of Louis Dessart, grandson of Théophile, who had become company owner in 1949. Dessart was not only a superb businessman but evidently a compassionate man as well. Long after the company had abandoned shotguns and hunting rifles, Dessart kept 20 or so gunmaking craftsmen on board and, occasionally, had them build guns from a retained inventory of parts to be presented as gifts to Britte's corporate clients. About 25 SuperBrittes and approximately 100 sidelocks and A&D boxlocks were built postwar.

From company records, it appears the last SuperBritte was assembled, finished and sent to the Belgian proof house in 1962. In total, only about 250 SuperBrittes were ever finished by the firm. For all intents and purposes the SuperBritte would have died then and there, a fascinating but mostly forgotten footnote in the annals of gunmaking history.

As the 20th Century ended, however, there appeared an opportunity for the SuperBritte to rise again. Luc Vander Borght reported that in 1999 Louis Dessart—who had sold his interest in Britte SA—contacted him for help in selling off Dessart's entire inventory of components and guns, which included 17 finished SuperBrittes and 10 in the white. Vander Borght said that he first contacted Tom Derksen, who he reported had been hired to lead Auguste Francotte. The firm

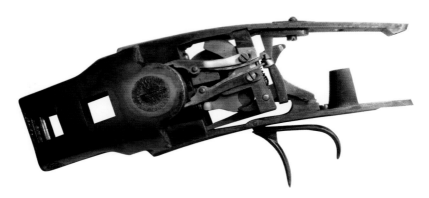

Left view of a SuperBritte action bearing the Lebeau-Courally name, shown sans stock. (Courtesy of Claudio Opacak)

subsequently made plans to revive production of SuperBrittes under the Francotte name, initially using the Britte guns and components, and then later manufacture its own. Unfortunately, these plans did not go much beyond the marketing phase.

The SuperBritte I shot at Vintage Cup '99 was one of a handful finished out with the Francotte name on an existing Britte action. (These included a double rifle [9.3x74R] built on a 16-gauge action sold to Swiss gun dealer Ernest Mayor, of Geneva.) When Francotte went belly up in 2001, it appeared the SuperBritte had again drifted into limbo.

Fortunately, Vander Borght was able to team up with America's Griffin & Howe to build out the remaining unsold Britte guns by Dutch craftsman Roelof Lucas and then sell them in the United States. Griffin & Howe—successor to longtime Francotte importer Abercrombie & Fitch—has also since obtained the SuperBritte and Jules Bury brand names.

As of spring 2010, G&H has sold almost all of the SuperBrittes it purchased. A few barreled actions remain in stock, with quotations for finishing them based upon the grade of wood and engraving desired. When they are gone, the final chapter in the SuperBritte saga likely will have been written—the end for a superposed made sideways.

XIV.
The Spanish Way

It was in Germany that I first got an inkling of how the Spanish build their guns. I was with Dan Moore, of US gun dealer William Larkin Moore, when we walked up to the Arrieta booth at the 2008 IWA Show, in Nuremburg. In the booth two men were engrossed in an animated discussion. When they spotted Dan, they stood and greeted him like a long-lost friend. I was introduced to Juan Carlos Arrieta, co-manager at the Spanish gunmaking firm Arrieta and the grandson of the firm's founder, Avelino Arrieta. With him was Alberto Garate—the ebullient manager of Pedro Arrizabalaga.

"Me, Arrizabalaga," Alberto said, thumping his chest and then pointing to Juan Carlos. "He, Arrieta." Alberto cocked his hands and squared off in front of his counterpart. Juan Carlos responded in kind. They stood facing each other momentarily, circling their fists like pugilists of old.

And then they smiled and embraced in the sort of brotherly hug one would find utterly unfathomable between rival gunmakers from, say, Great Britain.

After some friendly banter in broken English—Moore is a dealer for the guns of both makers—Dan and I wandered off to see the rest of Europe's version of the SHOT Show. When we passed the Arrieta booth a couple of hours later, Juan Carlos and Alberto were still there, yapping away and laughing, this time over a baguette, slices of cheese and cured ham and a bottle of *vino tinto*.

With that vignette in mind, I left IWA just a little puzzled, given the Basque reputation for prickly independence and what I had understood to be their inability to work together, much less get along.

A couple of days later Dan and I caught up with Juan Carlos and Alberto again—this time in northern Spain at their respective factories in Elgoibar and Eibar. Our translator for our three-day tour of the Basque gun trade was Maria Maguresi, daughter of Ramon Maguresi, partner in and actioner at Pedro Arrizabalaga. Manolo Santos, marketing director for Arrieta, had arranged her services. The first stop on our tour was Armas Garbi.

So much for my misperceptions of insular gunmakers going about their businesses each to their own ways.

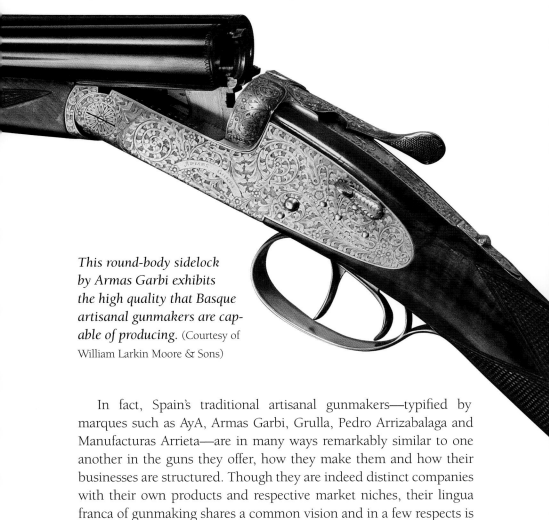

This round-body sidelock by Armas Garbi exhibits the high quality that Basque artisanal gunmakers are capable of producing. (Courtesy of William Larkin Moore & Sons)

In fact, Spain's traditional artisanal gunmakers—typified by marques such as AyA, Armas Garbi, Grulla, Pedro Arrizabalaga and Manufacturas Arrieta—are in many ways remarkably similar to one another in the guns they offer, how they make them and how their businesses are structured. Though they are indeed distinct companies with their own products and respective market niches, their lingua franca of gunmaking shares a common vision and in a few respects is as cooperative as it is competitive.

For these reasons—and for others I'll discuss—Spanish gunmakers remain uniquely positioned to offer something other craft gunmakers the world over cannot: a handcrafted double shotgun of very high quality at a reasonable price relative to their international competition. In a nod to the medieval pilgrims' route across northern Spain, I will dub this the Spanish Way or, more accurately, the Basque Way. (I ought mind my categorizations: As *The Times* journalist George Steer once admonished, "There are few things the patient Basque won't tolerate, and one is the suggestion he is Spanish.")

Basque country: the harbor at San Sebastian.

At the end of the first decade of the 21st Century, the very notion of a handcrafted double—much less an *affordable* example— tacks bow on into the headwinds of history. From the priciest Purdeys to the cheapest Turkish imports, the computer-assisted revolution in gun design and manufacturing is in flood tide. Though there is often still considerable handwork involved in building fine guns—and particularly "best" guns—from a strict manufacturing standpoint, a lot of traditional craftsmanship is increasingly optional (and regarded by some as superfluous). Today it is increasingly concentrated in the assembly, fitting & finishing, and embellishment stages.

Artisanal Basque gunmakers remain exceptions to this trend. A huge part of a fine gun's expense always has come down to bench time—or paying for it. The paradox of Spanish gunmaking is that it still relies on labor-intensive, traditional craftsmanship, yet it produces the world's most accessibly priced quality sidelocks.

As I discovered over three days at Arrieta, Arrizabalaga and Garbi, the Basque Way is indeed a paradox, but it is no accident. The directors of these firms remain convinced that there is and always will be a market for traditional handcrafted doubles built to order at reasonable

Basque gunmakers are competitive with one another but also often cooperative. Juan Carlos Arrieta (right) with close friend Alberto Garate, manager of Pedro Arrizabalaga, at the latter's small factory.

prices. Their trade—that is, its production techniques and industrial organization—is specifically structured to deliver just that.

To understand how the trade achieves this, one ought first examine the guns being built. Today Basque artisans basically make one: a Holland & Holland-pattern sidelock side-by-side with Southgate-type ejectors. Yes, this in an exaggeration. Indeed there are exceptions: AyA and Ugartechea, for example, both build popular Anson & Deeley boxlocks, with AyA also producing a range of over/unders of both modern and traditional design. Kemen, located in Elgoibar, is noted for its Perazzi-like over/unders with detachable trigger groups that are built by modern manufacturing methods. There are a couple of new hammergun models floating around, too. By and large, though, these are blind alleys off the Spanish Way.

The straight & narrow remains the Holland-type sidelock. Arrieta, Garbi, Grulla and Arrizabalaga build nothing but, and this gun remains an AyA mainstay. Among sidelocks, the Holland is a forgiving design capable of giving almost infinite service and good reliability, even when built to varying standards (which has been the case in Spain).

Building one standard gun has allowed these makers to be more efficient. Craftsmen can concentrate on producing one primary design across a range of grades and qualities, from entry level to "Spanish best." Even less-expensive Basque sidelocks boast standard features that in other countries are pricey upgrades: automatic safeties, articulated triggers, disk-set strikers, hand-detachable locks and a variety of rib configurations. Chopper-lump barrels are ubiquitous on Spanish sidelocks of all grades. In Britain and Italy, by contrast, such barrels normally are reserved for only best guns. Bespoke options, such as barrel lengths, weight (within a range), balance, chokes, trigger pulls and stock specifications remain the choice of the customer.

How do Basque makers provide deluxe features for Everyman's asking? Common aspects of the production process provide one clue. Gunmakers, for example, typically purchase components in volume from outside suppliers. In the storerooms of each of the companies I visited, I saw bin after bin of components that looked remarkably similar to those at other firms. (I did not visit AyA—the largest of the artisan Basque makers—but it is my understanding that the company builds and supplies at least some of its competitors' components.)

Not only do Spain's gunmakers share many of the same component suppliers, but they also make extensive use of investment castings—forend irons, trigger guards, triggers, safeties, toplevers and various inner bits. Important exceptions are the actions and barrels (both forgings). Investment castings are generally less expensive to begin with than components machined or filed up from raw forgings, and they also require less-extensive (and expensive) bench time to file up, fit and finish from the raw. (That said, Spanish components require more handwork to file and fit than counterparts CNC'd to near-finished dimensions.)

Basque sidelocks also often will share many of the same components, regardless of grade. It is mostly additional hand labor that makes the costs climb. For example, a Garbi Model 101 (retailing for $9,800 circa 2009) takes about 100 hours of hand labor to finish. Garbi's easy-opening Model 103-B ($19,800) takes 260 hours, and the firm's top-of-the-line De Luxe ($30,000 plus) takes 440 hours. Notes Jesus Barrenechea, senior partner at Garbi: "The percentage of the gun's final price reflected in labor costs is 80 percent, and the percentage in material costs is 20 percent."

Though Spanish sidelocks typically make wide use of generic components, they should not be thought identical. Each company has its own distinctive house style, and as prices increase, so does the overall quality of fit, finish, engraving and aesthetics. Moreover, artisanal Basque makers take great pride in building intrinsic standards of reliability and durability into their guns, regardless of final cost.

There are a couple of important caveats to my statements above. One is that Basque barrel tubes normally are made of a nickel-steel alloy, with the higher-grade guns often being fitted with barrels of chrome-nickel steel, the latter being somewhat stronger (and more expensive).

Basque gunmakers often buy common components in the rough from trade suppliers, yet each of the five principal makers builds guns to a respective house style.

Basque makers also fit several styles of locks, usually a couple of variants of the Holland type. A prominent variant is the so-called five-pin lock, which uses a tiny coil-spring plunger to actuate its interceptor (intercepting sear). A second is the seven-pin lock, which employs the traditional leaf spring for its interceptor. The latter is often—though not invariably—associated with higher-grade guns. For example, Arrieta employs five-pin locks on its Model 500-series guns and seven-pin locks on its pricier easy-opening Model 800-series.

The Basque region is Spain's most industrialized and, like Brescia in northern Italy, it still supports an infrastructure that allows gunmakers to outsource not only components but also jobs to specialists on a more cost-effective basis than it would be to tackle them in-house. There are, for example, companies where action forgings are sent to be rough machined, a lockmaker, a barrelmaker, polishers, barrel blackers, metal hardeners and stock-blank suppliers. There are also individual outworkers—craftsmen on their own working for the trade or on contract to particular gunmakers. It remains a classic example of the guild system that once characterized gunmaking centers such as Liège and Birmingham.

After spending most of the day at Garbi, we were driven by Jesus Barrenechea to visit a couple of outside specialists to the trade. First up were *picadors* (checkerers) Jose Antonio Bastida and Mari Jose Sanchez. The walls of their workshop, a darkened cave-like room with a low-slung ceiling in a concrete factory building, were festooned with stocks—for boxlocks, over/unders and sidelocks. A sole tiny window was covered with a blanket. Here Bastida and Sanchez work under the glare of open lamps for eight to 10 hours a day, their only task to checker stocks by hand—about 800 to 1,000 per year. It was all rather Dickensian in a Basque sort of way, and as I left their hobbit hole I felt I'd been transported back a century or more.

Next was a visit to one of the more notable examples of the cooperative approach Basque makers use in certain aspects of gun production. Barrena Bostak is a barrel-boring cooperative set up by AyA, Arrieta, Garbi, Arrizabalaga and Grulla. This is where all five gunmakers send barrels to have chambers and chokes reamed and bores honed.

It is not only Eibar's volume-production techniques and industrial organization that keep Spanish guns relatively affordable. Basque gunmakers do not subsidize showrooms in expensive capital cities. Nor have they corporate owners in far-off lands. Basque artisans themselves are the owners—or at least they have substantial ownership stakes—and their unadorned factories are their showrooms.

Numerous observers have commented on the incredible work ethic of Eibar's craftsmen, and after seeing them with files and chisels in hand, I can only second that they work very hard and very fast. They are also very experienced: Of Arrizabalaga's six-man workforce, three have more than 40 years each on the bench, one has 26 and the remaining two have eight. This is not much different from what I saw at Arrieta and Garbi.

Dan Moore, whose father's company has imported guns from seven Spanish makers and 10 Italian firms over the years, contrasted Basque makers to those in Italy. "Italian gunmakers are like artists," Moore said. "Flamboyant, sometimes temperamental, working to their own schedule. The Basques are like farmers: They say, 'We have a job to do, we are happy to do it, we are proud of it, and we do it on time, all day, every day.'"

*Traditional hand tools and handwork characterize
the work methods of Basque gunmakers.*

In the UK I've seen English craftsmen climbing in and out of Jaguars, Aston Martins, Range Rovers and even Lamborghinis; in Gardone I've seen Italian craftsmen driving Mercedes and BMWs. In

Spain when the company managers took us to lunch, we crammed into smallish Renault or Citroen sedans. Anecdotal evidence, yes, but the examples above support the thought that Basque gunmakers accept lower standards of material prosperity than their counterparts in England or Italy. Yet the region is by no means poor—it enjoys the highest per capita disposable household income in Spain.

Which in a manner of sorts brings me to the future of Spanish gunmaking. Today's economic times are turbulent worldwide, but the Basque Way has survived this before. Owners admit that a weak US dollar is a perennial worry, but more so is the shortage of young craftsmen signing on as elders retire. There are easier ways to make a living, and many are more lucrative.

Yet each of the factories I visited had young men (and some women) on the bench, though they were clearly outnumbered by their older peers. According to Arrieta importer Jack Jansma, of Wingshooting Adventures, the *Asociacion Armera*, which represents the interests of the Basque makers, has set up an apprentice program to aid all the gunmakers—yet another example of their cooperative philosophy.

I made a point to ask gunmakers at each company if they planned to follow global trends and transition to computer-aided design and manufacture. The response, to a man, was an emphatic, "No!"

Artisanal gunmakers dislike change in general, the Basques particularly so. Yet a trade based on hand labor coupled with an aging workforce one day will face dolorous consequences to its bottom line. This already has affected—and will continue to affect—the viability of some of the lower-priced models that carry the slimmest profit margins, especially for the smaller-volume makers who do not enjoy forgiving economies of scale. In recent years, for example, Garbi dropped its entry-level Model 100; Grulla likewise discontinued its starter Model 209.

At the moment, continuing to move upmarket seems the sole path forward. Wealthy Europeans have embraced Basque sidelocks in higher-priced versions. But as Terry Wieland notes in his book *Spanish Best*, most Americans still associate Spanish guns with utility- or field-grade guns and generally not as those of collectible quality. This clearly presents a dilemma, given the importance of the US market.

The precise course of history can never be predicted—financial realities, for example, may one day impose a grudging adoption of

Basque gunmakers use volume production methods to help keep their guns affordable—but the guns are in no sense mass-produced.

more modern gunmaking technology. This certainly is available in Eibar and its environs. Or the Basque Way as a whole may eventually trundle up the path of boutique Italian and British makers—that is, producing a limited number of guns priced accordingly, cost be damned. Basque bench skills at their best are as good as any, but to compete in the rarified best-gun market, I believe the artisans of Eibar may need to embrace (and encourage) the sort of transformational "high art" engraving techniques that make today's best guns as much objets d'art as tools for getting game. There are signs that this is beginning to happen; stay tuned . . . .

Most important, though, the future depends on the market's continued appreciation for—and willingness to pay for—traditional handcraftsmanship. Old-fashioned gunmaking still defines the Basque Way, and it still remains a bargain.

XV.
Manufacturas Arrieta

In the mid-1990s, when I was reviewing guns for *Shooting Sportsman*, I got to play with everything from chronically misfiring junk out of central Asia to the best of the best from England and Italy. Nowadays I struggle to recall the details of most, but I remember one I wish I'd made my own.

It was hardly the most expensive side-by-side I reviewed, nor in absolute terms was it the finest, but I still regret not buying an Arrieta 2-inch 12-gauge Light Game Gun.

The 2-inchers were the brainchild of longtime Arrieta importer Jack Jansma of Wingshooting Adventures, who asked the Basque gunmaker to replicate as closely as possible the dynamics and handling characteristics of vintage British 2-inch guns—which at the time were enjoying an upswing in popularity with American upland hunters.

Two-inch 12-gauge game guns mostly had been made in Britain in the '30s, and there were never many to begin with. They are invariably light—almost all weigh less than six pounds—and they are praised for their low recoil and for the quality of patterns they throw. The combination of lightness and lethality make them ideal guns for grouse, woodcock, quail and other thin-skinned upland game shot at close to moderate ranges.

Sensing an unfilled niche, Jansma began discussing the concept with Arrieta in 1992 and brought the limited-edition guns to market in 1995.

The example I reviewed in '97 was just the right blend of luxury and practicality—nothing too fancy, but everything about it exuding quality. It was a case-colored, rounded-action, Holland-type sidelock with hand-detachable locks, 27-inch barrels, Southgate-type ejectors, a straight grip, a splinter forend and double triggers. Fit and finish were excellent for a gun that retailed for less than $5,000, and the working components were smooth to operate and reliable. The gun weighed 5 pounds 15 ounces and was lively in the hands but not whippy.

Manufacturas Arrieta: a gunmaker's gunmaker. Arrieta recently made these William Powells for the Birmingham firm's Continental range. In addition to its retail line, Arrieta also makes guns for other makers and shops throughout Europe and Britain to badge under their respective names. (David Grant)

The engraving was well executed and based on an old Lebeau-Courally pattern: cutaway scroll on the fences, ornamental scroll ovals on the lockplates and underside, with the locks framed by scroll borders. As I wrote in my review: "It's pretty enough to be proud of yet not so ornate you'd be afraid to take it through an alder run."

Not only was it handsome, but it also proved deadly in Georgia's

The Arrieta factory inside and out: little changed in decades, either in appearance or methods of manufacture.
(Richard Rawlingson)

quail woods. With it, I almost could convince myself that I was a passable wingshot. I thought long and hard about buying the gun—or commissioning one like it—but for reasons lost to me now I didn't. It is the gun that got away, and the space in my gun rack where it ought to be haunts me still.

A decade later, in March 2007, I was able to see where Arrietas are made while on a tour of Basque gunmakers with Dan Moore, of American fine-gun dealer and Spanish-gun importer William Larkin Moore. We sandwiched our visit to Arrieta between trips to Armas Garbi and Pedro Arrizabalaga. The latter two makers, smaller than Arrieta, have concentrated their production solely on high-quality guns that retail in America for $12,000 to $30,000. Arrieta competes in this range, too, but the firm still offers new handcrafted sidelocks to bespoke configu-

Arrieta gunmakers generation three:
Juan Carlos (left) and Asier Arrieta.

rations for less than $5,000. In an age of gunmaking dominated by machine work, Arrieta's ability to achieve this is remarkable.

Arrieta's small factory sits perched on a steep slope overlooking the Mela River and the heart of Elgoibar across it. The mustached, burly man with a balding pate who greets you at the entrance is Juan Carlos Arrieta, and as he leads you into the factory you face a long bench arrayed with vises and covered in hand tools and gun components. About a dozen craftsmen stand at stations along the bench facing frosted panes that allow natural light to penetrate. Off to the right in the corner is the stock-finishing station; to the left and in a separate small room are house engravers Eduardo Aramburu and his son, Aitor.

The premises appear exactly as they do in older factory photographs; many of the craftsmen are the same, their hair only whiter. When British gunwriter Richard Rawlingson visited recently, he remarked to manager Manuel "Manolo" Santos that little seemed to have changed since his last visit. "I've been here 40 years," Santos replied, "and nothing has changed at all!"

In an English gun factory you'll find benches manned by a few old hands and lots of young faces. In Basque gun country it's just the opposite: The young are vastly outnumbered.

Arrieta's in-house engravers: Eduardo Aramburu (right) and his son, Aitor. (Richard Rawlingson)

Three generations of Arrietas have guided the family-owned firm, beginning with Avelino Arrieta, who entered the Basque gun trade as a teen during the First World War. He worked for other makers mostly until 1940, when he founded the firm that bears his name, bringing in his two sons, Jose and Victor. Jose's son, Juan Carlos, joined in 1972; Victor's son, Asier, started in 1989. Avelino passed away in 1979, and Jose and Victor have since retired. Today Juan Carlos heads up final finishing and quality control; Asier runs the stock-finishing shop. Manolo Santos joined as an apprentice in 1962, and the firm was officially incorporated as Manufacturas Arrieta in 1973.

Today Arrieta builds one shotgun type: the Holland-pattern sidelock. Standard guns begin with the basic scroll-engraved Model 557 (suggested retail $4,950) and ascend in price through

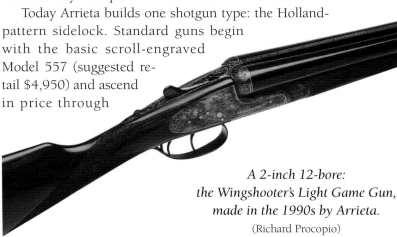

A 2-inch 12-bore: the Wingshooter's Light Game Gun, made in the 1990s by Arrieta. (Richard Procopio)

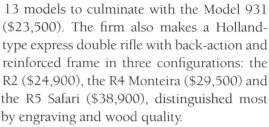

13 models to culminate with the Model 931 ($23,500). The firm also makes a Holland-type express double rifle with back-action and reinforced frame in three configurations: the R2 ($24,900), the R4 Monteira ($29,500) and the R5 Safari ($38,900), distinguished most by engraving and wood quality.

Arrieta also builds a host of models special to its trade clients and importers in the US and Europe. In America both Orvis and Griffin & Howe have house models badged under company monikers, while in Britain E.J. Churchill and William Powell are notable clients. Arrieta has a stable of some of the best—and most adventurous—engravers in Basque country who work both in-house and from home, and their talents allow the firm to offer a series of engraving patterns unique to each client.

Two decades ago Jansma helped initiate the advertising campaign that helped Arrieta establish its name in the US. He recalls that initially most orders were for 12s and 16s, but he has seen a definite trend toward smallbores—20s, 28s and .410s. In America the 557 and 578 ($6,100) remain popular, coming in price-wise on either side of AyA's popular No. 2. In Europe the trend is increasingly toward more-expensive guns, and in England many well-known driven-game shooters are buying easy-opening Arrietas to save wear and tear on the century-old Hol-

A Zenith model made for Powell's by Arrieta. It features bold acanthus scroll and is fitted with a Holland-type easy-opener.
(David Grant)

lands and Purdeys their grandfathers passed down to them.

As I discussed in the chapter "The Spanish Way," the guns from each of Spain's artisanal makers share many of the same parts suppliers and components in the white, and production methods are remarkably similar from firm to firm. That said, each company has a distinct house style, which Dan Moore discussed at length as we drove around Eibar and Elgoibar. "Every maker has its own look," Moore said. "Arrizabalaga is perhaps the most English-looking, followed by Garbi. Arrieta has unique shapes." In particular, Arrieta's forends are very slender, noticeably tapering down from the knuckle toward the muzzle. The lockplates are filed to make them appear perhaps sleeker than some, and the drop points on the stocks are elongated. The nose

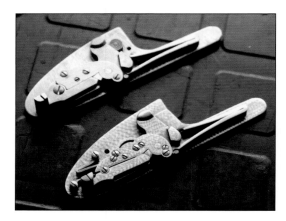

Arrieta uses two bar-action-lock styles: a seven-pin lock with leaf spring for the interceptor (bottom) and a five-pin version (top) that employs a hidden coil spring for the interceptor.
(Richard Rawlingson)

of the comb rising from the grip is not as steep as, say, that on a Garbi. Stylistic differences are not necessarily better than others, only different, which helps define each gunmaker's identity.

As prices increase, a few design differences do show up in the Arrieta line. For example, the Model 600 series (beginning at $8,490) and most of the 800 series (beginning at $10,250) are fitted with Holland-type easy-openers and have traditional seven-pin locks—versus the five-pin versions on 500-series guns. (An exception is the 871, a non-assisted-opening rounded-action with five-pin locks starting at $7,250.)

The two extra pins on seven-pin locks are needed to fit traditional leaf springs and intercepting sears, and thus to inlet they require more stocking time (adding to cost). Functionally, however, they operate

Traditional handcraftsmanship is still the order of the day at Arrieta.
(Richard Rawlingson)

the same as the five-pin versions, which use tiny coil springs to activate the interceptors. "Although many clients prefer the seven-pin locks," Santos said, "there is no difference in reliability."

Although better-quality engraving is a giveaway on the more-expensive guns, it is matched by better hand-finishing—some of which is obvious, some not. Externally, as prices increase, the action bars and fences are more gracefully filed, the barrels are better polished, and wood-to-metal fit is closer. Internally, everything should work just that much smoother—from the shift of the safety to the cocking of the locks and ejectors. That said, Arrieta's artisans put great store in building in fundamental function and reliability, regardless of price.

The company's particular genius is its ability to take the basic Holland design and transfigure it to suit different markets, diverse customers and many types of shooting. Jansma's 2-inch Light Game Gun provides a perfect example for filling a niche in the American market; in Britain one of Arrieta's latest offerings is the Linhope, a heavy-frame, easy-opening model built for William Powell for high-pheasant shooting. The two models couldn't be farther apart in application, but each is done equally well. (Although the Light Game Gun is no longer made, per se, 2-inch barrels are available on any 12-gauge model at no extra cost.)

About 20 percent of Arrieta's annual production is sold in Spain; the remainder is exported. According to Santos, approximately 40 percent goes to America, 25 to 30 percent to Britain (now the company's fastest-growing market), and the remainder to France, Denmark, Germany and other Continental countries.

Basque culture is conservative and sometimes inward-looking, and in the past some Spanish gunmakers have not always been adept at matching the expectations that foreign customers might have for their products. Much of Arrieta's export success owes not only to the skills of its craftsmen but also to the ability of Santos to keep both retail and trade customers happy. "He sees the big picture," Jansma said.

For more than two decades, Arrieta has made guns for Britain's William Powell, first for its Heritage line and now for its re-badged Continental line. "In 1988 we met with a number of Spanish gunmakers and were not impressed with either their quality or integrity," said former director Peter Powell, who now works for the firm as a consultant. "Manuel Santos proved to be an honest, reliable and thoroughly nice man to deal with. He strives to constantly improve his guns, and he listens to what his customers want. Arrieta have been first-class in delivering what we have asked for, and they always back up their product 100 percent." (About 20 percent of Arrieta's current production is sold bearing the names of other makers, such as Powell and Churchill.)

Vigorous exports have allowed Arrieta to maintain volume— until recently it has made 400 to 450 guns per year—and in volume the firm finds greater economies of scale and lower per-gun production costs. This has allowed the firm to maintain production of entry-level models like the 557, 570 and 578. However, the near-collapse of the global economy in 2008 and America's Great Recession have ravaged many fine gunmakers worldwide, and Spain's gunmakers are no exception. "The economic situation has been very bad for all artisanal makers," admitted Santos.

Sales are down across the board in Spain, but Arrieta hasn't short-changed its production methods or quality. "We continue making guns like classic artisans," Santos said, "and only by the old system of handwork."

*New Arrietas built for the English market are an increasingly
popular option among driven-game shooters wishing to
"rest" their vintage British guns.* (Richard Rawlingson)

Committed—some might say stubbornly so—to traditional craft
manufacture, Arrieta finds ways to introduce new models based on
finish and engraving to fill niches. The latest to appear in the US is the
Model 06 ($17,200), a finely finished rounded-action with Boss-style
rose & scroll engraving. According to Jansma, the gun was modeled
after a 20-gauge Boss that was sent to the factory.

Michael McIntosh, who preceded me as *Shooting Sportsman*'s Gun Review Editor, wrote in 1988 that Arrietas were some of the world's great values in fine double guns. A lot has changed in the world since then, but the wisdom of his words has stood the test of time.

Guns

XVI.
The Greener G-Gun

*W.W. Greener was one of Britain's seminal
gunmakers of the late 19th Century.*

In 1892 William Wellington Greener began preparing for the Chicago World's Columbian Exposition. To showcase his world-fair exhibit, the gunmaker would construct an elaborate vaulted pavilion. To fill it, his craftsmen would build more than 110 shotguns and rifles. Virtually all of Greener's line would be on display in a multitude of models—Sovereigns, Facile Princeps, Foresters, Dominions, Treble Wedge-Fast hammerguns, express double rifles, trap guns, pigeon guns, miniature guns and more. But the real showstoppers would be eight "special exhibition-quality guns," all sharing the same design but each uniquely—and lavishly—engraved. They were "G-Guns," hammerless ejectors built by W.W. Greener's finest craftsmen.

At the time Greener was arguably the world's most famous maker of quality sporting arms. He billed his 37,000-square-foot Prize Works factory, at St. Mary's Row in Birmingham, as the "largest and most complete sporting gun factory in the world" and each year turned out more than 1,000 hand-built shotguns and rifles. Unlike most of his London-based contemporaries, Greener had retail operations and agents in many of the world's greatest cities: New York, London, Paris, Berlin, Zurich, St. Petersburg, Montreal, even Buenos Aires.

The Columbian Exposition proved hugely successful, attracting millions of visitors during its six months of operation. It was a coming-out party of sorts, a celebration of America's growing industrial might, and the world had been invited to showcase its best products for America's increasingly affluent consumers.

With its vast number of shooters, the US market was particularly important to Greener, hence his splashy exhibit. His New York agent, Henry J. Squires, already was adept at keeping Greener guns in the hands of some of the greatest American wingshots of the day, notably Doc Carver, trick shot extraordinaire; J.A.R. Elliot, 10-time American Field champion; and Captain Brewer, ace pigeon shot. One year after the Columbian Exposition Greener was able to brag that "nine of the first 11 shots used Greener guns" at the 1894 US Grand Nationals.

No doubt part of Greener's worldwide sales success was because of W.W.'s formidable marketing skills. His seminal work, *The Gun and Its Development*, already had gone through numerous editions in English, French and Russian, with other works such as *The Breechloader* and *Modern Shotguns* in print in Spanish, French and Italian. In them Greener never passed up an opportunity to promote his firm's proprietary designs. But there was more to success than clever self-promotion: Greener and his family were legitimate gunmaking geniuses, with talents in virtually every aspect of production. Though Greener's today remains best known for choke-boring, a technical development W.W. popularized (though did not invent), Greener employees were also prolific inventors—with designs like the crossbolt and the inertia single trigger remaining enormously influential in contemporary gunmaking.

By the time of the Columbian Expo, the firm was probably at the peak of its powers—and Greener wasn't afraid to let others know it. He was always opinionated, at times dictatorial and arrogant, and he ut-

*Greener was proudest of his Grade G Guns. The exhibition-grade
12-gauge Self Acting Ejector (left) was built specially for the 1893
Columbian Exposition. The presentation-grade 8-bore, built on Greener's
Unique design, is one of only three of its gauge ever made on that action.*

(David Grant)

The Greener G-Gun   153

terly despised giving credit for much of anything to gunmaking rivals.

Yet in many respects the very force of his persona today overshadows Greener's accomplishments. Because of the braggadocio and biases in his writing, it is sometimes difficult for modern observers to sift his legitimate achievements from those he merely took credit for. Because his company built so many guns in so many grades over such a long period, many today think of the firm as primarily a maker of mid-grade boxlocks for colonial markets; what W.W. is less-well remembered for is being the inventor and maker of one of Victorian England's most fascinating "best"-quality guns: the G-Gun.

My first encounter with a G-Gun was nothing short of a revelation—and I don't mean that loosely. It was in 1996 during a visit to the workshop of David J. Dryhurst, then one of Britain's premier independent gunmakers to the trade and, incidentally, one of the last apprentices trained at the original Greener factory. Along with Graham Greener (the great-great-great-great-great grandson of W.W.), Ken Richardson and fellow gunmaker Richard Tandy, Dryhurst was also a director of W.W. Greener, Ltd., and the revitalized firm was beginning to take seriously the task of raising its public profile. There were new best-quality Damascus-barreled guns on the way—built with a stock of unused vintage tubes that Dryhurst had accumulated since the 1960s—and these were destined to become centerpieces in the batteries of wealthy American collectors. Some would be built as sidelocks, but a small number would be made as smallbore and double-rifle G-Guns.

After giving me a tour of the facilities, Dryhurst asked: "Have you ever seen a best-grade vintage G-Gun?"

"No."

Taking a gun from the safe, Dryhurst handed me a gorgeous scalloped-action gun with Damascus barrels. The stock was magnificent French walnut, but what really caught my attention was the gun's sumptuous engraving. What seemed like acres of fine scroll surrounded game-scene vignettes and left scarcely any metal untouched. The fences were the most elaborately sculpted I'd seen on a hammerless gun, each swirling like a nautilus captured in steel.

But engraving alone does not a best gun make. As impressive as the gun's external aesthetics were, it had the balance and handling characteristics to match. This Greener simply possessed the most dynamic "between-the-hands" weight distribution of any hammerless shotgun I'd ever picked up.

"This is one of the presentation-grade G-Guns built for the 1893 Columbian Exposition," Dryhurst explained. "It is a best-quality hammerless ejector with intercepting sears."

"I had no idea Greener built boxlocks of this quality," I said.

There followed a moment of stony silence. "No self-respecting gunwriter should *ever* call a G-Gun a boxlock," Dryhurst finally said. "This is not a boxlock; it is a Greener Self-Acting Ejector. The G-Gun is out there on a design limb of its own, like the Dickson Round Action or a Westley Richards hand-detachable droplock. In their day G-Guns cost just as much to build as a very best London sidelock. There was no difference in quality between them; they were simply of different design."

The most famous G-Gun:
The St. George gun.
(Courtesy of W.W. Greener, Ltd.)

Of course there was one very famous G-Gun I had heard of: the "St. George" gun, whose story has been well chronicled by Geoffrey Boothroyd and others. But I had assumed the St. George was essentially a one-off built only for promotional purposes.

Dryhurst informed me otherwise: "Between 1880 and the First World War there were thousands of G-Guns made. We haven't counted exactly how many yet, but in just one archive book, which spans from 1892 to 1894, the ledger indicates Greener built about 2,700 guns. Of that, 486 were G-Guns, and 88 of them were exhibition-grade models.

"Outside of a small group of connoisseurs, virtually no one realizes these guns exist or the level of craftsmanship they embody. For all intent, they are lost to history."

That was then. In 1998 I returned to visit with Dryhurst and Tandy and spent several days poring through the Greener archives. To comprehend the development of and, ultimately, demise of the G-Gun, one must first consider sporting-gun development in the mid-1870s. Until that time the epitome of a British best gun had been a London-made sidelock with external hammers—first the flintlock, then the percussion muzzleloader and finally the centerfire breechloader. But the 1875 patent by Westley Richards craftsmen William Anson and John Deeley, employing the fall of the barrels to cock internal hammers, rendered the hammergun technologically obsolescent, if not operationally obsolete. And the race for a successor was on.

During the next two decades gunmakers from London, Birmingham and Scotland vied with each other to establish a new best-gun paradigm in the shooting-public's eye, inventing and marketing a staggering variety of hammerless sidelock, boxlock and trigger-plate actions. And W.W. Greener, with his fertile imagination and prolific pen, was always in the thick of the fray.

Greener probably had started the process of creating his new hammerless design as early as 1874, when he purchased the firm of J.V. Needham, a gunmaker who had just patented the world's first self-cocking ejector gun. Of course Greener couldn't ignore the genius of Anson & Deeley, so he licensed their patent from Westley Richards in the late 1870s, all the while working out his own proprietary designs.

In 1880 Greener unveiled the Facile Princeps, a hammerless action whose apparent mechanical similarity to the A&D precipitated a lawsuit by a Westley Richards director. But in an influential legal case, the court struck down the Westley suit. "The reason Westley's lost the case was that a different principle was utilized to cock the Greener gun," explained Graham Greener. "In the Anson & Deeley design the forend acting on the cocking dogs actually cocks the gun as the barrels are opened. In the Facile Princeps it is a cocking lever in the front barrel lump that acts on the tumbler to cock the gun as the barrels are opened."

One year later came the Self-Acting Ejector, essentially an amalgam of the Facile Princeps action with much-modified Needham ejectorwork located in the front barrel lump. Greener called it his G-Gun.

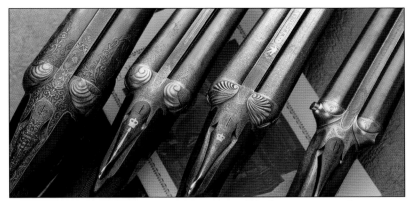

*Best-grade G-Guns showcase a fabulous variety of
sculpted fences. Greener's current directors believe there
were at least 25 variations, likely more.* (David Grant)

Although it was neither the world's first successful ejector gun nor its
first successful hammerless gun, the G-Gun was unquestionably one
of the first commercially successful hammerless ejector guns.

During the course of their production, G-Guns were built on two
different but related designs: Greener's aforementioned patent of 1881
and Harry Greener's "Unique" Ejector of 1889. The two were similar in
that the mainsprings powered both the hammers (tumblers) and ejec-

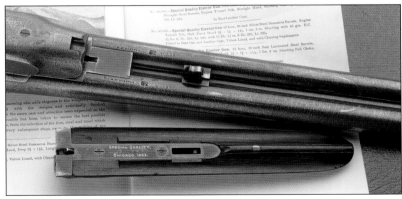

*G-Gun No. 40535 was one of eight exhibition-grade guns
built for America's 1893 Columbian Exposition to showcase
Greener's gunmaking capabilities. Its 30-inch Damascus barrels
are described as "silver steel."* (David Grant)

tors. They differed principally in that with the 1881 patent, the gun ejected the fired cartridge first, just before cocking. With the Unique design, the tumblers were articulated (or jointed), permitting the gun to cock first, and then eject the fired cartridge (see illustration "How a G-Gun Works" on facing page). Guns built on both designs handle superbly, in part thanks to the locks and ejectorwork being contained within the action body, which concentrates the weight there. The highest-grade models also had a concealed crossbolt top fastener.

Interestingly, both G-Gun designs were made concurrently, at least

Mechanism of the Greener "Unique" Ejector as fitted to all G 60 and G 90 Grade Guns.

This cutaway illustration from an early 20th Century Greener catalog shows not only the Unique's ejectorwork but also its articulated tumblers.

until shortly after 1900, when the Unique design seems to have fully superseded the Self-Acting Ejector. A Greener catalog circa 1900 still lists both versions, whereas a 1906 catalog shows only the Unique.

Although Greener would go on to make and sell London-style sidelocks, he clearly believed in the superiority of his own designs. After all, G-Guns possessed the most desirable attributes of best side-locks—intercepting safety sears, sweet trigger pulls, perfected ejectors and a wide gape to facilitate loading. They were also elegant and could be made across a wide range of weights. What they were not, how-ever, was easy to build.

Of their design, Greener noted: "The gun requires most careful ad-justment, and—although the parts are few and most simple—to en-

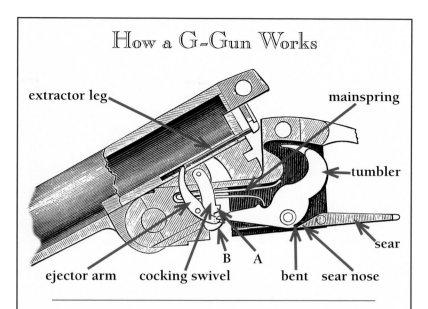

How a G-Gun Works

The illustration shows the major components of the left lock and ejector mechanism of Greener's Self-Acting Ejector patent of 1881. Bear in mind that the forearm of each tumbler curves in near the knuckle of the action and that the cocking swivel and ejector arms flanking each side are built into the front lump of the barrel. The tumbler initially is lifted (as the barrels fall) by the cocking stud (A), protruding from the cocking swivel. As the tumbler rises, its forearm slips off the cocking stud and is propelled downward by the mainspring onto the ejector arm, which in turn pivots and strikes the extractor leg, ejecting the fired cartridge. (The drawing illustrates this action in process.) As the barrels continue to fall, the tumbler's forearm then contacts the second cocking stud (B), at the bottom of the cocking swivel, which lifts the tumbler again, allowing the sear nose to slip into the bent, cocking the gun. The gun's intercepting sears are not shown in this simplified drawing.

sure perfect working the utmost precision is necessary in centering and shaping the various limbs. Consequently, the gun can only be made by experienced workmen, and must be made of best quality throughout."

And in this case his words weren't hyperbole. The archives show that out of a factory that employed hundreds, just more than 20 craftsmen—essentially the same craftsmen—worked on best-grade G-Guns from 1880 to 1916. They were Greener's élite, a workforce hand-picked for its skills and experience. For 45 years the same surnames appear in the archives under each of the 14 major stages in building a G-Gun: Kilby, barrelmaker; Hadley & Barton, jointers; Dalloway, locks; DeBarr, Camm & Dodd, action filers; Evans, bolt fitter; Goldsmith, stocker; Bates & Ilsley, finishers; Smith, shooter; Doughty & Watson, smoothers; Jones, polisher; Stokes, namer; Perry, Tomlinson, Miles & Horrocks, engravers; Fletcher, browner; and Sadler & Taylor, freers.

"Unfortunately we know very little about these men—not even their first names—other than that they were among the best craftsmen of their day and that they spent their entire working lives in the employ of Greener's," Tandy explained. "We do know they were extraordinarily well paid for their era. It was quite normal for them to earn 100 shillings per week in the 1880s, when the average Birmingham trade worker was only taking home about 20."

Dryhurst and Tandy admire all these men and admit a particular affinity for Camm, Greener's finest action filer. When they speak of him, they do not call him Camm but always Mr. Camm. "Whenever Greener was building a very best gun," Dryhurst said, "for about 45 years it was Mr. Camm filing it off to these exquisite shapes. But all of them were superb craftsmen and worked well together, because the fit and finish of every component of these guns is consistently perfect."

Because of attendant labor costs, G-Guns were the best of Greener's proprietary line. Although the Self-Acting Ejector also could be had in less elaborately embellished grades, its base price invariably meant it was expensive relative to the rest of the Greener line. The Unique model always began with the G-60 Royal grade, which had umbrella-arcaded fences. Next up was the G-70 Imperial grade, usually inlaid with a gold crown and scepter on the toplever. The Presentation and Exhibition grades enjoyed engraving patterns and fence designs unique to each order.

"If you ordered a Presentation or Exhibition G-Gun, you were personally dealt with by one of the heads of the Greener family, usually Harry [W.W.'s son]," Dryhurst said. "Harry and his engraving team would meet with you to discuss what types of engraving and fences you'd like. They always tried to make each Presentation-grade slightly different from the others."

Although their operation was simple in principle, G-Guns demanded superlative craftsmen to build them. In their late 19th Century heyday, G-Guns were the flagbearers of the Greener line. Pictured are a single-trigger G-60 Royal with umbrella-arcaded fences and gun No. 50477, a G-70 Imperial with seashell-sculpted fences. At the time they were built, they cost as much as the most-expensive sidelocks made in London. (Top: David Grant; above: Richard Rogers)

The St. George gun is famous for its deep-relief chiseled engraving, but there were many other Presentation and Exhibition G-Guns that approached its ornamental splendor. Dryhurst thinks there are at least 25 variations of sculpted fences, probably more. Many of them play off variations of seashell designs: fluted clams, scallops and nautiluses. Others have Continental-type game scenes and ornamentation.

In short, the G-Gun was an innovative and successful design that handled superbly, had gorgeous decoration, was widely promoted and sold well for decades. Which begs the question: Why aren't they better known today?

There are likely many reasons for this. Graham Greener, who maintains the company archives, has yet to fully analyze the records, but it appears that most best-grade G-Guns were sold internationally rather than on Britain's domestic market. Many went to Paris, Berlin or St. Petersburg; many more came to the US or Canada. According to Dryhurst: "The mechanical ingenuity of a G-gun appealed to Germans and Americans, and their engraving to the Russians and the French."

This global dispersion of G-Guns may partly explain their relative obscurity, at least in the English-speaking world. Many of those sold to the Continent were undoubtedly lost in the two world wars; others remain tucked away in European collections. (There is, for example, incredible interest in Greeners in Italy today—a veritable "cult of Greener," notes Dryhurst.)

G-Guns are also the most aesthetically "Victorian" of any British best. They were products of an age that was historicist to a fault, and Victorian decorative arts were profoundly influenced by stylistic "revivals"— Classical, Gothic, Baroque, Renaissance and more. G-Gun scroll & game-scene engraving was typical enough, but judging from the sculpting on the guns' fences, Greener's probably had a special predilection for the neo-Rococo style, with its marine motifs. Today, with all of their luxuriant engraving and metalwork, the guns have something of a period appearance about them—unlike, say, the timeless aesthetic of a London-type bar-action sidelock adorned with classic rose & scroll.

There is also the issue of their mechanical reliability (see sidebar, "The Unreliable G-Gun?"). Nor was the G-Gun or its maker helped in the long term by a streak of corporate stubbornness. A good example is the Greener side safety, which the firm clung to long after top safeties had become the industry standard.

The Greener action shop in the late 19th Century at the firm's famous factory in Birmingham's gun quarter; master gunmaker—and a current W.W. Greener director—David J. Dryhurst at the bench today.

Perhaps the biggest pitfall, though, was their resemblance to standard Anson & Deeley boxlocks. Although the G-Gun clearly was recognized as a best gun when introduced in the early 1880s, this would change over time simply through guilt by association. "Once the rest of the Birmingham trade started churning out poor- to middling-quality A&Ds, the term 'boxlock' became inexorably associated with a lower grade of gun," Tandy said. "Birmingham sadly sank its own reputation—and that of boxlocks—by making hundreds of thousands of A&Ds of appalling quality." By sometime before the First World

The Unreliable G-Gun?

Because G-Guns were extremely difficult to build, they were never copied by other makers. They hence remain poorly understood by most craftsmen, and many of them have been ruined by those unfamiliar with G-Gun design, saddling the gun with a reputation for unreliability.

Most mechanical problems begin with someone attempting to alter trigger-pull weights, specifically by shortening the noses of the sears. Remember that in both G-Gun designs the ejectorwork is connected directly to the cocking mechanism and triggers & sears.

"Although the Self-Acting Ejector and the Unique are very strong mechanisms that are quite simple in principle, they are extremely sensitive to any form of unskilled regulating," said W.W. Greener director Richard Tandy. "Once the sear nose is shortened by even a minute amount, it throws the ejectorwork regulation out and sets up a chain reaction of disasters."

What happens is this: If the sear nose is shortened, it makes the tumbler forearm slip forward, which often will cause the ejectors to trip upon opening, whether the gun has been fired or not. To prevent unwanted ejection, many repairers then have filed off the nose of the tumbler's forearm. "At that point it becomes a spiral into gunmaking hell," Tandy said. "They've basically ruined everything.

"It is sometimes possible to re-regulate them, but if this has happened, they are rarely perfect again. You really need to make new internal components and refit them, which is incredibly expensive."

G-Guns are also sometimes encountered with cracks or bulges in the water table, leading some to think the gun has a weak action. Not true. The problem results from bodgers who have attempted to "tighten" the action by squeezing the bar. The bridges between the barrel-lump slots are relatively thin and often will crack.

According to the principals at W.W. Greener, there are only a handful of craftsmen alive today capable of properly regulating or repairing G-Guns. If you have a high-grade G-Gun in need of such work, contact the maker.

War, the tastes of the discerning shooting public had changed, and the hammerless sidelock, as made by the top London houses, had carried the day.

The final death knell for the G-Gun would be the demise of Greener's élite craftsmen. After a half-century of service, the top 20 craftsmen were aging out of the workforce. "By the end of 1916," Dryhurst said, "the G-Gun team was finished. Their like would not be replaced."

W.W. Greener himself, already retired a decade, died in 1921, taking with him the fiercely competitive spirit that stoked the fires of the firm's success. After the First World War the firm continued to build a few G-Guns but, according to Dryhurst, most were not to pre-war standards. By 1929 the G-Gun had disappeared from the company's catalog. The firm claimed that "maladjustment" made by repairers in the trade had become so frequent—and created so much customer ill will—that the Unique was abandoned "in favor of one that was more widely understood and easier to service and repair."

Until its revival in the 1990s, Greener would mostly build mid-grade guns for a desiccated empire and shriveled world market. The lights had gone off in Europe with the onset of WWI, and so too at W.W. Greener.

But in the G-Gun, the brilliance that was Greener's shines on.

XVII.
The Return of
Westley Richards' Ovundo

There is innovation in gunmaking that is interesting as a technical achievement—say, a self-cocking hammergun—and then there is a singular sort of innovation that changes the nature of gunmaking itself.

John Robertson's over/under of 1909 was a game-changer as such. By buttressing the barrels with bifurcated, bolted lumps and hinging them into the sides of the action, the owner of London's Boss & Co. transformed the over/under configuration from a gawky Continental curiosity to a sleek thing of beauty and mechanical ingenuity. In an age increasingly sated with perfected side-by-sides, the Boss O/U was indeed an item new and improved—and was bound to find a market.

As such, rival gunmakers in England could hardly ignore it: Over the next five years they patented a welter of competing O/Us—among them from the likes of C. Lancaster, E. Green, W. Baker and F. Beesley. Conventional wisdom has held that only J. Woodward's design from 1913 has proven worthy competition, but this is hindsight built mostly on perspectives of the present, rather than necessarily an accurate reflection of any contender's historical success.

Next to the Woodward, the Ovundo from Westley Richards came closest to besting the Boss—and like the latter the Ovundo was a design unique to its maker. This in itself would have come as no surprise to gun buyers of the day: Since its founding in Birmingham in 1812, Westley's continually had pushed the boundaries of firearms technology, introducing notable innovations in percussion, breechloading and military gunmaking as well as in ammunition.

With their own singular patent of 1875, Westley's William Anson and John Deeley had created the genesis for the modern sporting shotgun—a gun with concealed hammers as well as locks that cocked with the fall of the barrels. The firm's doll's-head top extension and bolting system were enormously influential, its mechanical single trigger and ejector systems proven, and its forend fasteners were (and still are) trade standards. Westley's hand-detachable locks—more commonly known in America today as "droplocks"—were nothing short of a stroke of genius.

By 1910 or so, Leslie B. Taylor, the latest in a long line of enterprising Westley leaders, would have known a response to John Robertson (who once had worked at Westley's) was utterly necessary. Taylor was described in 1912 by *The Field* as "a man of virile and energetic personality . . . [who] has kept the firm to the fore during an epoch when invention was proceeding at a rapid rate."

*A resurgent Westley
Richards has reintroduced
its Ovundo over/under. This
new example is a 20-bore engraved
by Alan Portsmouth with birds of prey and Westley's bold scroll.*
(David Grant)

His response—the Ovundo—would incorporate many of Westley's most famous patents and showcase a few new ones as well. In retrospect Westley's over/under was the final flourish of a golden age of gunmaking at the firm—a precursor, in fact, to the modern Perazzi-type detachable-trigger gun. It became popular in the blowsy decade after the First World War before vanishing as the Second World War approached. And now, after more than a half-century absence, Ovundos are once again being made by a revivified Westley Richards in an expansive new factory in Birmingham.

Westley's initial effort came in 1912 with a gun described in its 211-page Centenary catalog as its "Under & Over" gun. In the fall of 2006 at the firm's old factory in Bournbrook, I sat down with Westley's owner and Managing Director Simon Clode and foreman of gunmaking operations Ken Halbert for an exclusive look at the new Ovundo as well as to document the design's history. (Halbert has since retired but still works part-time.) Neither had seen an example of an Under & Over, but if the sketchy catalog illustration is accurate, then it is possible it was a different design from the Ovundo, which would succeed it two years later. Just how different—if at all—awaits detailed examination of an extant example, should one survive.

The Under & Over first appears in the 1912 Westley record books as gun No. 17431. It was advertised as being available in 12, 16 and 20 gauge and was priced from 30 to 40 guineas for a non-ejector version and 40 to 50 guineas for an ejector version—well below the 70 to 95 guineas charged by Westley's for its "best"-grade hand-detachable side-by-sides.

Under & Over No. 17431 was possibly a prototype model, as the record books indicate it was never sold and its barrels were described as "waste" in 1930. The first gun to specifically bear the "Ovundo" name is listed as No. 17500, made in 1913. This gun was not sold until 1930, and it was perhaps another prototype. It appears that one Norman Goodenham placed the first order for a production Ovundo in July 1914, for gun No. 17530.

While London's makers concentrated on sidelock O/Us, Leslie Taylor and his gunmakers modeled their version on the house designs Westley's had invented and made famous. Today we know little of the Ovundo's actual development process; Henry "Harry" Payne Sr., a craftsmen who later would become Westley's works manager during the First World War, is known to have played a major role in its making along with Taylor, but to what extent is poorly documented. The record books, however, indicate that an individual named "Payne" actioned many of them. This was certainly Henry.

In its most elemental form the Ovundo was a boxlock with either fixed or Taylor-patent hand-detachable locks with superposed barrels that hinged on a conventional hook located beneath the lower tube. What was novel and new was its barrel-bolting system (Taylor's patent No. 4853 of 1914): two hooks, which extended from buttresses

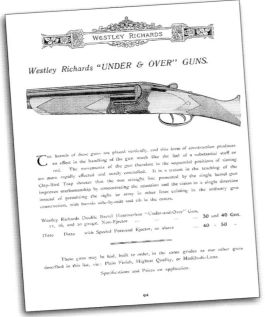

An early advertisement for
Westley's "Under & Over" guns shows
an Ovundo design still evolving.

*Harry Payne Sr. was the
craftsman responsible for much
of the Ovundo's development.*
(Courtesy of John Payne)

on either side of the barrels, fitted into slots in the face of the action. When the gun was closed, bolts actuated by the toplever rested atop the hooks and locked down the barrels. At the same time any forward motion of the barrels upon firing was prevented by the bearing surfaces of the hooks contacting corresponding bearing surfaces in the slots in the action face.

The Ovundo was unique in that it was entirely of Westley Richards' design: In addition to its locks and Taylor's bolting system, its toplever, top safety bolt, ejectors, hinged cover plate and mechanical One-Trigger single trigger were in-house inventions. Moreover, the gun showcased a new patented hinged trapdoor on the sideplates that allowed access for lubricating the selective Westley One-Trigger.

Unfortunately, the Ovundo could not have been introduced at a worse time; the guns of the summer of 1914 did not sound on the grouse moors of Scotland but across bloody fields in France and Belgium. For the next four years sporting-gun production essentially ceased as Westley's concentrated on war work.

Westley's left the war years behind on better legs than many of its notable Birmingham competitors. For one, Leslie Taylor was still at the helm. Under his expert leadership, the company was in a position to tap a burgeoning American market and, most importantly, the patronage of fabulously wealthy Indian princes. Ovundo production restarted in 1919.

According to Ken Halbert there were four major Ovundo variants: a fixed-lock gun with a scalloped (or rebated) action back, a fixed-lock version with sideplates, a detachable-lock version with a scalloped back, and the detachable-lock version with sideplates—the latter being the best-known and most-expensive variant. Another variant of the fixed-lock non-sideplated model was a version with a flat (straight) action back instead of scalloping. These were sold as Special Model Ovundos and marketed as "trap and field" guns. The Ovundo was available with single or double triggers, and Halbert says that single-trigger guns are most common and that sideplated versions might or might not have the hinged trapdoor.

Unlike Boss or Woodward O/Us, which invariably were built as best guns (with best-gun prices), the Ovundo was available from mid-grade to best-grade, a deliberate attempt to bring the British O/U to a broader range of potential consumers. It was advertised in 12, 16 and 20 bore—"or smaller bores," although it appears that only one 28-bore was made. In 1925 the non-sideplated Special Model started at £65, whereas the Highest Quality best sideplated gun with all the bells & whistles commanded £150. (A best Woodward O/U also sold for £150 at the time, and a best Purdey side-by-side was approximately £130.)

Archival research conducted by Westley's Gun Room Manager Anthony Alborough-Tregear indicates that most Ovundos feature the more-expensive droplocks. "Only the first few were fixed locks," Tregear said. "Then over 90 percent were detachable locks. It seems when people ordered our over/under they wanted the detachable lock."

The Ovundo was fully capable of being built in double-rifle configurations, from .22 HP to .425 bore, with the company's .318 Westley being the most popular chambering. It also was made in Westley's proprietary rifled-choke ball & shot configurations, as the 12-bore Explora or the 20-bore Fauneta.

By the mid-'20s Westley's was promoting the Ovundo as its "modern masterpiece" and "the perfect modern gun." Americans (among others) were becoming increasingly fond of the over/under configuration, especially for live-bird competitions and the growing sport of clay shooting. The records show a sizeable number of Ovundos being shipped to one Bob Smith, evidently an importer in Boston. A good number of these were non-ejector guns. Also at that time company literature touted Belgium's Henry Quersin, editor of *Chasse et Peche*, as winning several clay- and pigeon-shooting championships with his Ovundo. The Indian princes were particularly partial to Ovundos in double-rifle configurations as well as in the Explora and Fauneta versions. The Maharaja of Alwar, for example, between June 1922 and December 1925 ordered 10 Ovundos—one in .240, one in .318 WR, six in .350, and a pair of Fauneta 20-bores.

An examination of record books makes it clear that the Ovundo was at its pinnacle of popularity in the Roaring '20s. The '30s, on the other hand, ushered in tougher times. Not only had the Great Depression descended, but also Leslie Taylor died in 1930. As the decade wore on, Ovundo production tapered off; by 1938 the gun essentially had ceased to be made on a regular basis. A few scattered references to Ovundos continue to pop up at later dates in the archives, but most appear to be either rebarreling jobs or guns finished from orders or actions started years earlier. Judging by the main record books, it appears that at least 200 Ovundos of all configurations were produced.

That makes the Ovundo one of the more successful British over/unders of its era—even if its era was short-lived and its long-term influence nowhere as pervasive as those of Boss and Woodward O/Us. Like any vintage British O/U, the Ovundo was a challenging, expensive gun to build, especially in its detachable-lock versions, and it was ill suited to the world's desiccated economies of the Depression.

The demise of the Ovundo also was indicative of the declining health of the company. To make matters worse, in 1940 Henry

Payne was killed in a tram accident, and then the Second World War wrecked a tottering British Empire—and so, too, the firm that depended on it. Capt. E.D. Barclay purchased the bankrupt business from liquidators in 1946, and Westley's muddled through another decade before being sold to Capt. Walter Clode in 1957. Clode kept Westley's gunmaking going through some lean years—largely through repairs and renovations to secondhand guns that he was buying from the armories of Indian princes—but he also concentrated on modernizing the firm's engineering and toolmaking operations. It was a move that would pay great dividends when his son, Simon, joined the firm in 1987.

Simon set about integrating the CNC millers, spark-eroders and wire cutters of Westley's engineering division with the files and chisels of the firm's bench-trained craftsmen. At the time, the gun Westley's was best known for—its great hand-detachable-lock side-by-side—was still being made in 12 gauge, but it was being made sporadically and by hand and virtually on a one-off basis, making it very costly and inefficient to produce.

Simon's goal was to bring the detachable-lock gun back into regular production using the latest manufacturing technology married to traditional gunmaking skills. In the late 1980s he launched this process with the .410 version, only six of which had ever been made. Initially, 10 were produced to great success, and since then Westley's has followed up with 28-, 16-, 20-, 12- and 10-bores as well as rifles in a host of calibers. Even an 8-bore is currently under construction. Significantly, all are built on scaled frames appropriate to each gauge or caliber.

With the hand-detachable back as its core product in shotguns and rifles, Westley's now also makes bolt rifles and sidelock shotguns and rifles as well as its own proprietary rifle ammunition. Under Clode's tutelage, the company also has diversified into making its own best-quality gun cases and leather goods. Virtually everything, save the ammunition, is made in-house. In 1997 the firm opened a US agency to better market its goods and guns to the American market.

As Westley's approaches its second full century of continuous operation, Clode has invested massively in the company's future. In May 2008 the firm moved from its historic Bournbrook factory to a new 4-1/2-acre complex near the heart of Birmingham's old gun quarter.

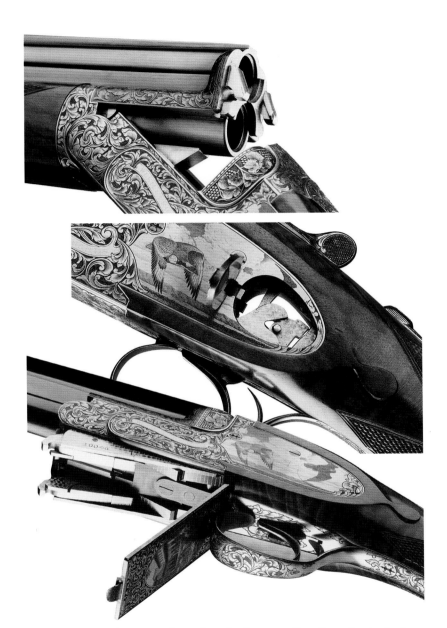

Proprietary features of Westley's highest-quality Ovundos include (from top): a bolting system with hooks fitted on the barrel fitted into slots in the action face; trapdoors on the sideplates that allow access to the One-Trigger; and a hinged cover plate permitting access to the detachable locks. (David Grant)

Located in what was an old enameling factory, the 20,000-square-foot building has been fully refurbished. Westley's engineering division, which designs and manufactures press tools for automotive and general industries, also has moved into a new 20,000-square-foot facility next door.

Clode's vision and Westley's unique guns—and the quality with which they are made—have garnered Clode a loyal and discerning client base as impressive as any since the halcyon days of the Empire. Among them number not only the bulk of the world's most prominent collectors but also kings and princes from across the globe. It was largely his customers' interest in a new Westley O/U, according to Clode, that led to the Ovundo's reintroduction. "The new Ovundo has been a long time in the making," Clode said. "We needed to get our side-by-side shotguns and double rifles going first.

"From the outset, I had no intention of introducing a modern competition-type O/U into the market. The Ovundo was historically our gun, a traditional English gun, and we decided to build it on that basis."

The first to be completed were a matched pair of sideplated 20-bores engraved by Alan Portsmouth with birds of prey and Westley's bold scroll. Built for a customer in the Middle East, they were impeccably made and, at 6 pounds 4 ounces each, as lively and well balanced as any best British side-by-side. Compared to a Boss, the Ovundo has a tall action but is by no means ungraceful—particularly in 20 bore—and in the hand it handles superbly.

New Ovundos currently are available in 20 and 16 bore on scaled frames, and a rifle version in .318 is under consideration. The configuration is Westley's Highest Quality version: hand-detachable locks, sideplates with trapdoors, the 1909-patent selective single trigger, a Deeley forend latch and an ebony forend cap. Double triggers are an option, as are a number of top-rib configurations.

Mechanically, the new Ovundo remains largely faithful to its predecessor. Apart from making a lock-locating stud integral with each lockplate (rather than drilling it in the action), little was done to improve the original design. "The Ovundo hasn't changed, really," Halbert said.

There were no craftsmen left at the factory who had helped build the original Ovundos, so Clode and Halbert appointed actioner Henri

A period illustration showing three "grips"—at A, B & C—
for bolting the rifle version of the Ovundo. Extension C is the
firm's famous doll's-head.

Laurent, a 30-year-old French-born gunmaker, to head up the project. Laurent—a graduate of the Liège School of Gunmaking who's served time at Holland & Holland and E.J. Churchill—had the task of discerning any problems in development, coordinating between the engineering and gunmaking departments, and creating a manufacturing procedure. "To graduate in Liège, you have to be able to build an entire gun," Clode said. "Henri is very good and, with his broad range of skills, he was the right man for the job."

The fact that the Ovundo is back and that there are young men making them speaks volumes about the current state of affairs at a firm that is only a couple of years short of being two centuries old.

Fourteen craftsmen, young and old, work at benches in the manner their predecessors did a century ago. Modern engineering has indeed been integrated into the gunmaking process, but Clode has deliberately restrained it from supplanting traditional craft. "Our machinery could make a new gun to near-finished specs," Clode said, "but then you quickly lose traditional gunmaking skills. Once those skills are gone, they are gone for good.

"Every Ovundo—every gun, for that matter—that you look at here will be filed up slightly different, and if someone makes a tiny surface error filing it, it has to be blended in. That's part of the beauty of a hand-crafted gun." As of early 2010, Westley's had 20 Ovundos on order or under construction.

Founder William Westley Richards had a simple motto: "To make as good a gun as can be made."

The Ovundo is new all over again, but Westley's motto has remained the same.

XVIII.
Watson Bros. Lightweight O/Us

Scarcely as many guns are made nowadays in Britain as a century ago, and they are all eye-wateringly expensive, but the finest makers in and around London, Birmingham and Glasgow are crafting shotguns that are literally masterpieces of the gunmaker's art. The best of these guns possess a distinctiveness that separates them from their peers—either by mechanical design, unique aesthetics or sometimes a bit of both.

It is fair to note, however, that England's makers have looked mostly to the past to revive their glory. The flag-bearer designs at Purdey's, for example, are the Beesley self-

A 20-bore round-body over/under with ornamental engraving by Martin Smith. One of a pair, this gun weighs only 6 pounds 1 ounce. Note the distinctive style of the Watson fences—and the gun's racy lines. (David Grant)

opener (patented 1880) and the Woodward over/under (1913); at Holland & Holland, the Royal side-by-side (1883); and at Boss & Co., its over/under (1909) still fitted with its single trigger (1894).

Though London began introducing new over/under models in the 1990s, the guns have tended to be on modern Anglicized Italian designs, notably H&H's detachable-trigger Sporter (1990) and of late Purdey's similarly configured Sporter (2006).

London gunmaker Michael Louca, who owns Watson Bros., has charted a different course with his over/under. His vision was to create a new O/U—mechanically and aesthetically—but using only English gunmaking influences inside and out.

Louca's over/under today features a pared-down ejector system that in itself not only is simple but also has made the gun's forend and action smaller, thereby intrinsically reducing the gun's overall size and weight. A new Watson O/U is consequently a sidelock of remarkable elegance—and possessed of aesthetics that are simultaneously classic and contemporary—and as thoroughly British as a Supermarine Spitfire.

Louca trained as a barrelmaker at James Purdey & Sons, joining as an apprentice in 1977 and leaving in 1984 to become an outworker to some of the best makers in the British trade. Building his own guns was a consuming dream and, when presented with the opportunity, he purchased the mostly dormant Watson Bros. name in 1989.

Louca liked Watson Bros. because of its historic association with smallbores—which in the late 1980s were becoming increasingly popular in English shooting circles. His initial goal was to make new Watsons as slender round-body sidelocks, particularly in 20 and 28 bore, initially as side-by-sides, and then as O/Us. He also planned to make them in his own gun factory—a workshop proper where as much production as possible could be performed in-house by a dedicated team of employee craftsmen. It was an ambitious dream.

In 1992 Louca rented the upper floor of 39 Redcross Way, an old printer's workshop on the south bank of the Thames, just a few blocks from London Bridge. He assembled a small team of craftsmen trained by the likes of Purdey's, Holland's and Boss's and began building guns. When real estate began to boom in London, Louca scraped up cash and courage and in 1998 purchased Redcross, renting the lower level out while retaining the upper floor for his factory.

When I stopped by Watson's in the spring of 2005, it had been six years since my last visit. Louca had opened up the factory floor and altered it slightly, but its ambience remained much the same: benches scattered with work-darkened hand tools, metal shavings on the floor, racks of oil-finished gunstocks drying and, always, the sound of men

The Watson Bros. team in 2005 (from left): Ryan Glyde, barrelmaker; Michael Louca, director; Alex Torok, actioner; and Thomas McGuire, ejectorman. (David Grant)

rasping files over steel. There was more machinery, most of it traditional: a pair of lathes, a milling machine, a lapping bench, an upright drill, equipment for guilding locks, a fly press, a surface grinder and a forge. A single compact spark eroder was the sole concession to contemporary gunmaking technology.

There were also three new faces at the bench: Ryan Glyde, barrelmaker; Thomas McGuire, ejectorman; and Alex Torok, actioner. Glyde and McGuire had joined Watson's in 2000 as apprentices, replacing older craftsmen who had departed; Torok joined in '04 after leaving Purdey's, where he'd worked since 1975 (having been trained as an actioner by Ben Delay). A familiar face was engraver Martin Smith, another talented Purdey-trained craftsman who had been at Redcross going on a decade and was responsible for developing several of Watson's "house" engraving patterns. Louca, having trained Glyde and McGuire in their respective specialties, was now finisher and foreman.

Over mugs of coffee we caught up on the changes that had occurred at Watson's since my last visit. "Five or six years ago we were still developing our own over/under and at the same time turning out a handful of guns per year," Louca said. "Today we have perfected our over/under and are now concentrating on manufacturing guns—meaning getting our production line efficient and, importantly, tightening delivery times."

Building guns largely in-house was always central to Louca's strategy for distinguishing Watson's from competitors. As he explained it, there are many advantages to building guns this way—not the least of which is greater efficiency. "If I employ a craftsman here in the factory and I think something can be changed or improved on, I can just pop over to his bench and say, 'Let's try this,'" Louca said. "If you've farmed something out to an outworker and the same thing happens, you can find yourself running up many, many hours of bills to change it; it can also take longer, and you still don't know what's going on."

Not only that, Louca added, but concentrating production and craftsmen in the same building fosters creativity, which has helped Watson's achieve its own house style, or "pedigree." Louca also elaborated on an evolving strategy of training his own apprentices rather than relying solely on craftsmen trained by others. "I find craftsmen you train as apprentices want to keep learning," he said, "and they also have a lot of vision, both of which are important qualities here."

As noted, Watson's initial focus was on smallbore round-body side-by-sides. The first new round-body Watson was an elegant 20-bore Louca built for himself, a gun with aesthetics similar to those made famous by Boss & Co. but built on a self-opening Beesley-type action.

Like the Boss, Watson's round-body side-by-side has its beads filed smooth and the bar dressed down, but the height of each lockplate was reduced and the top strap made narrower and shorter. The latter two changes left more wood in "the horns"—that is, where the wood meets the action between the lockplates and the top and bottom straps—so the head of the stock and the locks could be filed rounder. When viewed from below, Watson actions have a discernable coffin-shaped taper—narrow at the knuckle, flaring subtly at the midpoint of the action, and then tapering off gracefully back toward the standing breech. Mechanically, Louca altered the geometry of the ejectors and self-opening system, making the lifters longer and the mainspring slightly weaker so to make the gun easier to close.

Although side-by-sides have staged a mini-revival in the US over the past couple of decades, British buyers of bespoke "best" guns have during the same time flocked to over/unders, particularly 20-bores. Louca, for example, reports that eight out of 10 new orders from British customers are for O/Us.

From the get-go, Louca wanted the new Watson O/U to be distinctive, and if Britain's classic side-by-side designs have left little room for substantive mechanical improvement, the same cannot necessarily be said for its over/unders. "Ejector systems, especially, on most British over/unders are far too complicated and are prone to breaking down too often," Louca said.

The inspiration for the Watson over/

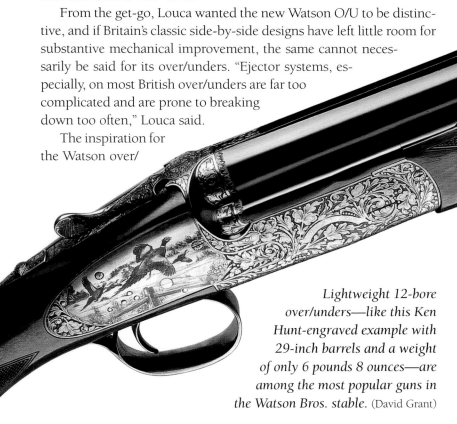

Lightweight 12-bore over/unders—like this Ken Hunt-engraved example with 29-inch barrels and a weight of only 6 pounds 8 ounces—are among the most popular guns in the Watson Bros. stable. (David Grant)

under was originally the Woodward design, although Louca noted, "With our many changes, the Watson gun no longer bears a great deal of resemblance to that."

Louca retained the Woodward's classic features—side-mounted hinge pins and bifurcated lumps—but he realized that substantial changes were otherwise necessary. "If there are already London over/unders that are absolutely beautiful and built to traditional designs," he said, "what is the point of us bringing out copies of the same thing?" Moreover, existing O/U sidelock designs could not be built as sleek and round—or as light in weight—as Louca wanted.

"Initially, most of our over/under orders were for 20-bores," Louca said. "When you'd ask a customer 'why,' he'd say he wanted an O/U with the weight and handling of a traditional English 12-bore side-by-side, which is typically 6¹/4 to 6³/4 pounds. New English sidelock over/unders are mostly quoted at 7 to 7¹/4 pounds, but many actually come out at 7¹/2 pounds.

"Consequently, we worked very hard at getting the Watson 12-bore O/U to come in at only 6¹/2 pounds. Since we've accomplished this, there's been a big change in what guns are ordered. Today 70 percent of our over/under orders are for lightweight 12s. Shooters like getting the ballistic benefits of the 12 without having to resort to using a 20 with a heavy load." Watson customers who do want a 20-bore over/under can have one that weighs only 6 pounds—one-half to three-quarters of a pound less than many other London-built 20-bore sidelock over/unders.

Achieving these weight reductions in the Watson O/U was a long, often-difficult process marked by much experimentation. Louca's first change was to reduce the distance between the vertical walls of the action by about ¹/8". This was accomplished by bringing down barrel-wall thickness at the breech to safe minimum thicknesses and also pro-portionally reducing wall thicknesses at select points along the tubes. "These reductions were actually similar to what has been around on side-by-side barrels for years," Louca said, "so it is not like we changed anything that compromises the safety or strength of the gun."

Louca also reduced the length of the top strap as well as its width, similar to what he'd already done on his side-by-sides, to allow more wood in the horns. He then reduced the vertical height of the walls of the action by about ¹/8", eliminating the step-down on the top of the sidewalls (as seen on traditional Woodward/Purdey-type actions). "The straighter line makes for a much sleeker-looking gun."

Paring down the height of the sidewalls necessitated fitting the barrels (and locking bolt) lower in the action, which in turn reduced the action height by .100" (a Watson 12-bore is merely 2.270" tall; a 20 stands 2.100"). The height of the lockplates was reduced by .075" to accommodate the lowered top strap, and this change necessitated some lock redesign.

It is easy enough to install smaller locks in a 12-bore gun to achieve lockplate-height reduction, but a potential problem is an increase in misfires as the size and power of the mainspring decreases. To overcome this, Watson's experimented in the late '90s using rebounding locks with swivels—a swivel being the connecting link between the mainspring arm and the tumbler designed to reduce the friction that can deaden the blow to the striker. Since 2002, however, Watson's has returned to traditional roller locks. "The advantage of swivel locks is that they tend to be more efficient on paper," Louca said, "but in reality swivels are so small that you can start to lose the inertia of the hammer blow. With a roller lock, you lose inertia the more the spring opens, but if you set your locks up right, you can compensate with a beefier mainspring. It is also more robust and easier to regulate, and with rollers we don't get any misfire problems." Watson's also offers pinless locks for those who prefer an uninterrupted surface on the lockplates for engraving.

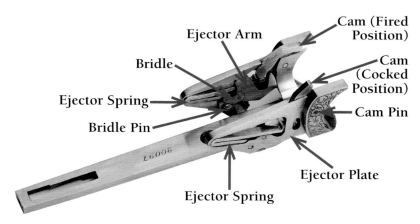

Ejectorwork for a new Watson Bros. over/under. Designed by Louca to be compact and light, it has helped reduce the size and weight of the Watson O/U. (David Grant)

Critical in the evolution of the Watson O/U was Louca's development of the ejector system—one designed from the ground up to be smaller than those found on traditional Woodward-type over/unders, which in turn would allow substantial reductions to size of the Watson forend and action. Louca labored countless hours over three years through numerous prototypes and two major design variants before declaring it perfected in August 2001.

The Watson O/U ejector operates on the over-center principle—the same simple and efficient principle employed by the famed Southgate-type system commonly found on side-by-sides. Watson's first ejector variation had five moving parts per side (or barrel) and employed a small piece screwed into each extractor, which re-cocked the ejector locks as the gun was closed. Watson guns with this first ejector variant can be identified by a stop pin, visible in the bar on either side of the lower barrel.

The second variant, patented by Louca and still used today, has only three moving parts per side—the cam, the spring and a special ejector arm. This arm—Louca dubs it the "magic arm"—is actuated by an ejector cocking rod running through the knuckle of the action. The arm not only trips the ejectors but also compresses the spring, re-cocks the mechanism and prevents it from ejecting shells live.

Because the mechanism was purpose-designed to be compact, this allowed Louca's gunmaking team to make the action even narrower. Today's Watson O/Us also have a true U-shaped interior action bar rather than the traditional squared-off interior, and this shaves off about two ounces and allows the radius of the lower barrel to fit the action "like a glove." A narrower action also has decreased the overall width of the forend by .100", creating a straighter—and racier—transition from wood to metal. All told, the changes resulting from the new ejector design have pared about six ounces from the weight of the gun.

In the hand, a new Watson over/under handles very much like a classic English side-by-side game gun—lithe, fast-swinging and feeling very much *alive*. These qualities have made the guns popular with shooters who prefer the dynamics of the side-by-side coupled with the superior pointing qualities and reduction in recoil torque of the O/U. Most current Watson clients are British or Irish shooters who use them for driven shooting, where the benefits of the over/under configuration are increasingly appreciated. "The vast majority of the guns we make are shot regularly and shot a lot," Louca said. "So our guns have got to work."

In October 2006 Louca moved Watson Bros. to a new factory at 54 Redchurch Street, closer to the heart of central London. Despite a challenging global economy, Louca reports his business is better than

Watson Bros. side-by-sides are typically made in the round-body style, with their actions sculpted with a coffin-shaped taper.
(Courtesy of Michael Louca)

Watson Bros. History

The late Don Masters has an excellent chapter on Watson Bros. up to the firm's 1935 merger in his book *Atkin Grant & Lang* (Safari Press, 2005). An abbreviated list of company milestones is presented below:

- **1875**—Founded by Thomas William Watson at 4 Pall Mall in London.
- **1884-'85**—Firm becomes Watson Bros., named after Thomas William and brother Arthur Henry. Develops a reputation as London's specialist for smallbore guns.
- **1894**—Firm relocates to 29 Old Bond Street.
- **1929**—Firm moves to 13a Pall Mall.
- **1933**—T.W. Watson dies.
- **1935**—A.H. Watson retires; Watson Bros. assets purchased by W. Robson of Stephen Grant & Joseph Lang, Ltd.
- **1984**—Owners of Churchill, Atkin, Grant & Lang names sell Hellis, Beesley & Watson names to Frederick Buller, of Amersham.
- **1989**—Michael Louca purchases Watson Bros. name and records from Buller.
- **1991**—First new round-body side-by-side completed; new Watson serial numbers beginning at No. 20,000.
- **1995**—First new round-body over/under completed.
- **1998**—Louca purchases 39 Redcross Way and starts apprenticeship program.
- **2001**—Watson Bros. perfects proprietary over/under ejector system.
- **2006**—Factory relocated to 54 Redchurch Street.

ever. He is confident that Watson Bros. is now making its finest guns ever. Consumers have noticed. "Ten years ago I was spending vast amounts of time developing the Watson over/under and its ejectors *and* finishing off guns," Louca said. "Today I'm free to concentrate only on finishing off guns—and these are guns I'm happy with."

Gun Proof & Proof Masters

IXX.
Memories of a Proof Master: Roger Lees

I am late to this interview. "You are 15 years too late," said Roger Lees. "Too many people I knew are now dead. And my memory isn't what it was."

Roger Preston Lees was 89 when I interviewed him in November 2008. He was bald and wore glasses with lenses as thick as headlamps. Hearing aids sprouted from each ear. Decades of shooting, war years served in an anti-aircraft battery, and a half-century working at the Birmingham Gun Barrel Proof House had nearly deafened him.

Roger Lees in 2006. (Courtesy of Roger Lees)

For all his years, there was no indication that Lees' mind or memory were any worse for wear. The day before I had shared a field with him in the Shropshire Hills shooting driven pheasants with the syndicate he headed up with British gun photographer David Grant. Lees didn't shoot—time's toll on his legs had nixed that—but he keenly watched those who did. He recalled—in excruciating detail—birds I missed.

Lees was ribbing me—with a wink and a smile—but in the decade I have known him I have learned that he possesses a peregrine's eye for detail. He is a man who likes things done well and done right—the shooting of pheasants included.

One might expect a certain fastidiousness from a man who became Birmingham's youngest-ever proof master and, eventually, its longest serving. As Lees' friend, the late great gunwriter Gough Thomas, put it: "All guns . . . have a powerful and innate tendency to burst." For 35 years it was Lees' task to ensure that if a gun indeed did burst, it was safely in the confines of a proof-house firing chamber and not in a shooter's hands.

We were at the home that Lees and his wife, Audrey, share near Lichfield, about 15 miles north of Birmingham. Displayed on the table between us were the photographs, journals and mementos of a life and career that span most of the 20th Century. Thumbing through them, it was evident that Lees was entirely correct in one critical point: Most of those pictured or mentioned have long since shuffled off this mortal coil. Lees is one of the last living links to an era of British gun-making the likes of which will never be witnessed again.

I was late to my interview, even very late, but not too late.

Britain has two proof houses, in London and Birmingham, and a proof master for each. Proof houses conduct the tests—centered on subjecting firearms to excessive pressures—that all guns must pass before they can be legally sold. It is the proof master's job to administer his respective house and its staff. Proof masters are appointed—by a board of Guardians in Birmingham and in London by a committee for the Worshipful Company of Gunmakers. Each answers to his own board—a balancing act that makes proof masters both regulated by the gun trade and also regulators of it.

Britain's proof laws date to 1637, when the London Company obtained a royal charter of incorporation. Birmingham built its proof house in 1813. Lees was only the seventh official proof master of the latter, and there have been but two since he retired.

During his half-century at the Birmingham Proof House, Lees

*In his youth, Lees was a keen hockey player
and secretary of the Walsall Hockey Club.*

witnessed—and grappled with—developments such as metallurgical changes in guns and gun barrels; the advent of progressive powders and other new propellants; cartridge improvements, such as star-crimping, plastic hulls & wads; and the sleeving of barrels. Lees was there to help get a new Proof Act through Parliament in 1950 and again in 1978. He assisted with the adoption of 1954's Rules of Proof, the longest running of any of Britain's proof rules. He helped Britain join the international proof commission—*Commission International Permanente pour l'Epreuve des Armes a Feu Portatives* (or CIP)—in 1980, and from 1982 to '84 he served as its president.

But when pressed to name his greatest personal accomplishment during a career so long and consequential, Lees momentarily went quiet. "I made a fair number of mistakes during my tenure," he finally replied.

"But . . . I kept my staff safe. No one was ever seriously injured under my watch."

Lees was born in May 1919 in the town of Bournville, near Birmingham, the second son of an enlisted soldier returning badly wounded from the First World War. Lees sprung from neither a gunmaking nor a shooting family, but he spent his childhood as many boys would have done in semi-rural Britain: playing with toy guns.

His neighbor was one Lt. Col. Charles Playfair, then proof master of the Birmingham Proof House, a post he had held since 1914. "Col. Playfair lived in a big house up at the top of the lane, and we lived in an old farmhouse lower down," Lees said. "I suppose you could say he watched me grow up."

Playfair is regarded by many as the father of the modern proof system in Britain, in large part because he expanded the proof house's ballistic laboratory, which was started by his predecessor, Samuel B. Allport. Although London's proof house predates Birmingham's by more than 150 years, the lab and testing facilities modernized by Playfair made Birmingham the undisputed leader in ballistic research and proof matters.

"Col. Playfair had two daughters but no sons," Lees said. "When I was 17, he asked my father if he thought I might like to work at the proof house." Lees would not go so far as to say he was Playfair's surrogate son, but the colonel was clearly more than just a mentor.

Lees jumped at the chance for employment, in his words "perhaps too hastily" leaving school, where he was studying for admittance to university. He joined the proof house in February 1937, his starting salary being 50 pence a week. "It paid the bus fares into Birmingham and maybe a little more," Lees recalled. His title was "learner."

I asked Lees what a "learner" was. "You learned everything," he explained. "They started me on the dirty jobs—cleaning barrels after blackpowder provisional proof. I also prepared barrels for proof in the 'Big Hole' [the provisional proofing room famously illustrated by W.W. Greener in the 19th Century]." Lees assisted with office work as well and also worked in the ballistic laboratory. "In short I learned a little bit about everything in how the proof house works."

Young Lees reported directly to Playfair. He had landed a job in a dire economy and without the benefit of gun-trade experience—something that rankled a few of his proof-house coworkers. "I must admit there were a number of chaps who did not want me there," he said. "One of them encouraged me to disassemble a lot of new revolvers without proper turnscrews and tools. I should have been under supervision, probably wasn't, and I damaged the screw heads. They were brand-new weapons, and obviously there were going to be complaints.

"Col. Playfair backed me up. He didn't even reprimand me—though he could have." When I asked Lees what qualities led Playfair to believe in him, his response was a furrowed brow. "This is a very hard thing to answer, because you are talking about yourself, and for me that is very difficult." Like many Englishmen of his generation,

Lt.-Col. Charles Playfair —the father of modern proof in Britain and mentor to Roger Lees.

LT.-COL. CHARLES PLAYFAIR
1914—1941

Lees exhibited a congenital aversion to public confession of personality and character traits.

I later asked Peter Powell, director of gunmaker William Powell & Sons and former Chairman of the Proof House Guardians, to assess Lees' qualities. Powell's family has been deeply involved in Birmingham proof-house matters since its founding, and Powell has known Lees since the early '60s. "His strength was always an incredible ability to believe in himself," Powell said. "Shy he was not."

Lees soon would be tested by events more serious than ruining the pins of a few revolvers. War was brewing in the late 1930s, and in September '39 it boiled over. At the recommendation of Playfair—himself a decorated veteran of the First World War—Lees had joined Britain's Territorial Army in '37. When Hitler pushed into Poland, Lees was activated in a heavy anti-aircraft unit as a gunner—as the "lowest of the low," he said. But by 1941, at the age of 22, he made officer and served in "ack-ack" units most of the war in the Mediterranean Theater, campaigning in North Africa, Sicily and up the Italian Peninsula.

"Service as a Junior Officer was very helpful in later life," Lees said. "Getting on with other ranks, knowledge of explosives, organizational skills—such experience made running the proof house a lot easier than it might have otherwise been.

"If you have faced shell fire, other problems seem slight."

Before his discharge from the Army in the spring of '46, Lees wrote to the proof-house Guardians asking if there were any jobs available. "They replied, 'Yes,' but did not say what job it was going to be or how much I would be paid," Lees said. Upon his return, he began working in the proof-house administrative office.

Like the British nation—and its gun trade—the Birmingham proof house was in shambles in the immediate post-war period. It had been without an official proof master since Playfair died in '41. (The acting proof master, A.A. Edwards, had been killed in '44 in a vehicular accident, and Clive Harris, his successor, had died soon after the war due to intestinal illness.) According to Lees, the war had taken many of the best proof-house employees, and most would never return. Sporting-arms production had virtually ceased in Birmingham from 1939 to 1945, and military arms had been proofed at service facilities, not the proof house, leaving the latter short of work.

Lees—now working as an accountant and clerk—impressed the Guardians, then chaired by Eric Bewley, Secretary of Webley & Scott. In September '49, encouraged by Bewley, the Guardians appointed Lees acting proof master—a "two-year trial run" for the official position. As an article in a 1950 edition of the *Birmingham Post* makes clear, appointing a proof master was a task that proof authorities did not take lightly: "Because the terms of the [Proof] Act under which they operate authorizes them to make the appointment, but gives them no power, except under exceptional circumstances to discharge . . . the Guardians of the Birmingham Gun Barrel Proof House proceed with caution in appointing a proof master—they must be 'abundantly satisfied' they elect the right man.'"

After one year the Guardians were "abundantly satisfied," and in August 1950, at age 30, Lees was officially confirmed as proof master, making him, in the words of Birmingham's *Express & Star*, "the youngest man to ever hold the responsible post of the ancient Birmingham Proof House." Not only that, but Lees also was the first in Birmingham to have come from outside the gun trade—all proof masters to that time had been gunmakers or members of gunmaking families.

Lees' first major task was to rebuild the capabilities of the proof house—it had, in his words, "gone to bits during the war." Because

Lees (center, front row) with the proof house staff in 1965.
(Courtesy of Roger Lees)

he was not a gunmaker, Lees was dependent on a professional staff of technical experts, particularly the inspectors charged with evaluating the guns before and after proof tests. "I was lucky enough to be put in touch with Sam Scott, chief inspector before the war," Lees said. "He was a very capable chap, and I got him back."

Lees also relied heavily on gunmakers he could trust when dealing with issues of the day, notably Graham Holloway, of G&S Holloway; Bernard Powell, of William Powell & Sons (and Peter Powell's father); Charles and Leighton Greener, of W.W. Greener; and Albert Brown, of A.A. Brown & Sons. He credits Eric Bewley for much of his success. "Bewley was without question the best Chairman I knew in my 35 years as proof master," Lees said. "I leant on him for advice of all sorts in the early years. He was responsible for a lot of the modernization of the proof house during his tenure."

Reviving the proof house was critical, because as the war years receded there came a pent-up worldwide demand for sporting arms. In Birmingham companies like BSA and Parker-Hale did a huge business in converting surplus military weapons into "sporters." By the mid-'50s, more than 300,000 guns were going through the Birmingham Proof House. At the peak Lees had more than 30 inspectors and technicians working under him. Retaining staff during this era was always a challenge, Lees recalled, as the Birmingham gun trade was competing for skilled employees lured by better-paying jobs in the auto and manufacturing industries.

Roger Lees in 1978.
(Courtesy of Roger Lees)

So acute was this shortage of craftsmen that in the '50s the Guardians charged Lees with recruiting an engraver from Brescia—one Italo Zoli—to work for the Birmingham trade at large, which was suffering from a shortage of engravers. As Lees then noted in a local paper, "For the time he is working for the City's gun trade as a whole and not for any firm in particular."

"In the end," Lee told me, "he eventually ended up taking a job with Webley & Scott."

Although it is natural to associate Lees' position mostly with proofing guns, Britain's Proof Acts gave him the larger mandate of protecting the public on many firearms-related issues. One of his respon-

Retirement from the Proof House, 1984. (Courtesy of Roger Lees)

sibilities was providing expert witness at trials where firearms were involved. Occasionally these were murder trials. More often, however, Lees was assisting prosecutors in cases involving violations of British proof laws—notably the sale of out-of-proof guns.

As proof master, Lees was involved with more than 90 prosecutions of this sort, and he issued many more warnings.

If the safety of the shooting public was his overarching duty, protecting the staff of a facility where hundreds of guns were being overloaded and overstressed on a daily basis was never far from his mind. "First and foremost the thing you do when testing guns is to ensure the safety of your workers," Lees said. "I had only one chap who dropped a loaded gun, it went off, and a pellet ricocheted off an electric switch and nicked his head. It could have been much worse."

Lees retired in September 1984 at age 65, and Alfred Scott, ex-managing director of BSA and a former Chief Guardian, succeeded him at the post. (Scott, in turn, was succeeded by current proof master Roger Hancox.)

Proof master or not, Lees has never strayed from the *leitmotif* that has dominated his life. "Roger is still deeply passionate about all things connected with guns and shooting," said his stepson, Adrian Chadwick. Until recently Lees was an avid rifle and game shooter and, according to David Grant, he remains an excellent clay shot. ("When Roger's eyes were better," Grant said, "he was formidable with a gun.") The annual proof-house shoot bears his name, as does its award: the Roger Lees Cup.

In recent years Lees has had a hip replaced, but neither titanium joints nor treacherous ground prevent him from accompanying his syndicate shoot afield. "Several of us have been known to manhandle him over walls and fences," Chadwick said. "But he *has* to be out there beetling around the hills with us. Roger is tough as old boots."

Nine decades are plenty proof of that.

XX.
The Rules of Proof

Old doubles rarely come with operator's manuals. How often we wish they did. Who hasn't had questions about their condition and safety, especially about what shells can be safely fired through a gun that could be a century old, maybe older?

If the gun originated in England or Europe, however, it *will* have operating instructions of sorts—its proof marks. These impressions, usually located on the action- and barrel-flats, certify that at some time in its life the gun was tested at a proof house to reveal any structural weaknesses. The markings are "proof" that it passed those tests. The

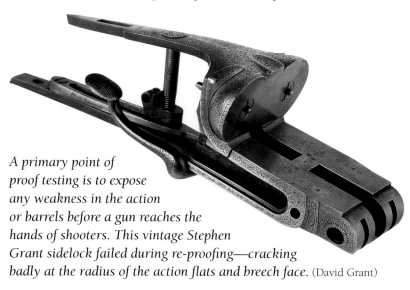

A primary point of proof testing is to expose any weakness in the action or barrels before a gun reaches the hands of shooters. This vintage Stephen Grant sidelock failed during re-proofing—cracking badly at the radius of the action flats and breech face. (David Grant)

proof process consists of firing heavier-than-normal loads through a gun, then carefully examining it to ensure the elastic limits of the metal in the barrel and action have not been exceeded. The specific proof marks on an individual gun also will reveal important clues about the gun's original specifications and the uses its maker intended it for. These two factors—and its current condition—will in large part determine the sorts of shells you should use in it.

To the uninitiated, decoding the world's proof marks is unfortunately a cryptic task at best—and even those with working knowledge will admit the subject's complexities. Americans, with no government-sanctioned proof houses to turn to for advice or guidance, are at a particular disadvantage.

No chapter of this length can do justice to a subject so vast, but the novitiate can gain a better understanding of what shells to use in an older double by better understanding the issue of pressure, in this case using England's Rules of Proof as a guide, specifically key tenets of the Rules of Proof of 1925 and '54. Though these Rules have since been superseded, their principles regarding safe pressures for fine doubles retain relevance undiminished by time.

Rules of Proof are the working instructions for Britain's two proof houses. Authorized by the Gun Barrel Proof Acts—which are acts of Parliament—the Rules specify in detail how guns are to be proofed and marked. In addition to certifying that a gun has at some time passed proof in either London or Birmingham, the marks—depending on the Rules in effect when impressed—will specify matters such as the gun's nominal gauge, nominal bore diameter, chamber lengths, what sorts of propellants it was proofed for, and either its intended service loads (or service pressures) or the pressures the gun was proofed at.

The Rules have never been cast in stone, and they have been revised as circumstances demanded by proof authorities. Through most of the 20th Century these revisions were driven chiefly by technology—the interplay between advances in propellants & cartridges and improvements to the materials used in gunmaking.

The end of the 19th Century, for example, saw the appearance of various smokeless powders as well as the gradual supplanting of Damascus tubes with those of fluid steel. The First World War (and Second) drove great improvements in metallurgy, with subsequent alloying of nickel, chrome, vanadium and molybdenum increasing the tensile strengths of steels. Concordant with better steels have come vastly improved powders—specifically progressive (slow-burning) powders that allow heavier shot loads to be propelled without increases in peak pressures.

The Rules of 1954 replaced those of 1925, which had replaced those of 1916, which had replaced those of 1904. And back it went. Those of 1925 provide important perspectives necessary to understand those that were to follow. For the first time the actual length of the chambers was marked, and for the last time the weight of the shot load of the normal service cartridge was impressed (the latter having been a practice since the Rules of 1896). To use the case of the 12-gauge, a British game gun with then-standard 2½" chambers was proofed and marked for a service load of 1⅛ oz; a 2¾" gun for 1¼ oz; a 3" gun for 1½ oz.

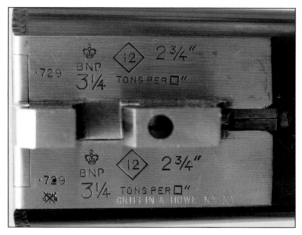

Birmingham proof marks from the 1954 Rules on a circa-1960s Churchill boxlock. Proof marks provide a clear indication of a gun's original purpose and the ammunition suitable for it—in this case the gun was proofed for 2¾" cartridges. They also provide a guide for comparing a gun's original specifications to its current condition. (The Griffin & Howe markings are recent importer stamps, not original proof marks.) (Richard Rogers)

It's important to understand that in Britain there had been an immutable relationship between cartridge length, chamber length and shot load—for example, through the '25 Rules no 12-gauge 2½" gun would have been proofed for a greater payload than 1⅛ oz, with either blackpowder or smokeless "Nitro" shells. (During the First World War, payloads in 2½" shells actually dropped to 1 oz or 1¹/₁₆ oz to conserve lead, but regardless none would have exceeded 1⅛ oz.)

The weight of the shot load played a vital role in capping pressures during an era when blackpowder and many early smokeless powders were volumetrically similar. "The markings on the 12-bore game gun implied that the shot load should not exceed $1\frac{1}{8}$-oz," wrote then-Birmingham Proof Master Roger Lees in a January 1955 article in *The Field* explaining the new Rules of '54. "Its real meaning was this was the maximum shot load to be used so long as the standard load of black powder or its equivalent in smokeless powder was employed."

But Britain's proof authorities had not anticipated cartridges like the Maximum, introduced in the mid-1930s by Eley/Imperial Chemical Industries (ICI). Popular with rough shooters, the Maximum packed $1\frac{3}{16}$ oz of shot into a $2\frac{1}{2}$" 12-gauge cartridge.

An extra $\frac{1}{16}$ oz may not sound like much, but it upended proof's proverbial applecart. Now a $2\frac{1}{2}$" cartridge was available with a shot load that exceeded the $1\frac{1}{8}$-oz limit to which $2\frac{1}{2}$" guns were proofed and marked for. The proof houses viewed the Maximum as setting a potentially dangerous precedent that the ammunition industry at large would follow.

Eley, in fact, used newly introduced progressive powders in the Maximum so that the load actually developed no greater peak pressures than the standard $1\frac{1}{8}$-oz load—making it safe for an in-proof $2\frac{1}{2}$" game gun. To the proof authorities, however, that was not the point. Charles Greener (of W.W. Greener), then chairman of Birmingham's Proof House Guardians, called the Maximum "illegal;" ICI threatened a lawsuit in response. After consulting lawyers, proof authorities backed down, but the stage had been set for drafting new Rules of Proof.

New Rules, however, would have to wait. The Depression, the Second World War and Britain's subsequent economic dislocation—indeed, the funk into which England's post-war gun trade sank—all conspired to delay their drafting for nearly 20 years.

The Rules of 1954 were enacted in October that year and became effective February 1, 1955. They remained in effect until the Rules of 1984, making them the longest running of any of the 20th Century's. They remain recognizably "modern" in the sense that they codified proof principles still in use today, and for the layman their clarity makes them the easiest of any to understand. As Roger Lees noted at the time: "In the English-speaking world they will be far better under-

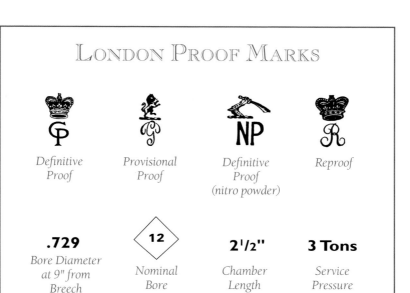

LONDON PROOF MARKS

Definitive Proof

Provisional Proof

Definitive Proof (nitro powder)

Reproof

.729 — Bore Diameter at 9" from Breech

12 — Nominal Bore

2¹/₂" — Chamber Length

3 Tons — Service Pressure

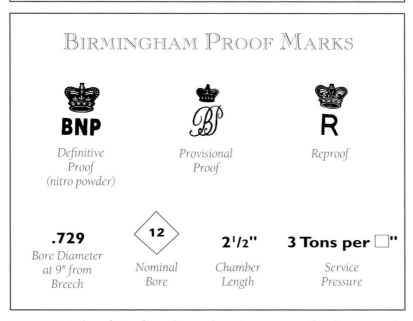

BIRMINGHAM PROOF MARKS

BNP — Definitive Proof (nitro powder)

BP — Provisional Proof

R — Reproof

.729 — Bore Diameter at 9" from Breech

12 — Nominal Bore

2¹/₂" — Chamber Length

3 Tons per ☐" — Service Pressure

Britain's Rules of Proof are the working instructions for the country's two proof houses. They also specify the proof marks impressed on the guns—in the case of side-by-sides on the flats of the barrels and actions. Illustrated are examples from the 1954 Rules.

stood and appreciated, for they are comprehensive, unambiguous and written in a language intelligible to all."

The number of markings was reduced and simplified, and for the first time the nominal bore size was marked as a decimal part of an inch—12-bore was now shown as .729" (as measured at 9" from the breech), which replaced the more coded system of marking bore diameters with gauge sizes or fractions thereof (see chart on facing page). Excessive bore enlargement (to remove pitting, rust and so on) is one of the most common ways in which a gun is taken out of proof. The decimal system allows anyone with a bore gauge to easily

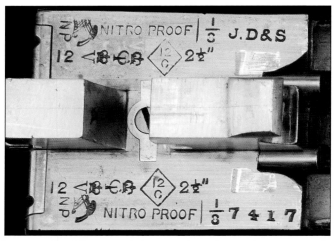

Made in Scotland but proofed in London, these John Dickson barrels show proof marks that state they were chambered for 2¹/₂" cartridges.
(Courtesy of James D. Julia Auctioneers)

check this. Under the '54 Rules (and those preceding it) a bore could be enlarged by .010" before going out of proof—for example, a gun proofed at .729" would not be out of proof until its bore reached .740". It then would have to be re-proofed if it were to be legally sold in Britain. A gun remains in proof, incidentally, so long as the parameters set down by the original Rules under which it was proofed have not been exceeded or the gun has been subsequently weakened in specified ways (such as cracks in the action, gas welds to the action or barrels, failure of the brazing of the barrel lumps, among others). But

NOMINAL BORE SIZES

Bore	Rules of 1925 Old Marking Nominal Size	Rules of 1954 Nominal Diameter	Rules of 1986-1989 Metric Marking
12	$\frac{12}{1}$	.740"	18.9mm
	12	.729"	down to
	$\frac{13}{1}$	.719"	
	13	.710"	18.2mm
16	$\frac{16}{1}$	.669"	17.3mm
	16	.662"	
	$\frac{17}{1}$	.655"	down to
	17	.649"	
	18	.637"	16.8mm
20	19	.626"	16.2mm
	20	.615"	down to
	21	.605"	
	22	.596"	15.6mm

The nominal bore sizes under the 1989 and 1954 Rules of Proof and the corresponding nominal figures under the Rules of 1925.

if a gun is re-proofed under new Rules, the parameters established by the latter take precedence. Remember: To be legally sold in Britain a gun must be in proof at the time of sale. If a gun has been re-proofed, it will have a special marking that denotes this. It also will have added impressions from the Rules it was re-proofed under as well as those of its original proofing.

The most important result of '54, though, was the explicit marking of the mean service pressure of cartridges intended for the gun rather than marking their maximum shot load. Progressive powders—and cartridges like the Maximum—had rendered the latter practice obsolete.

"Since the powders and loads now available giving safe pressures are many and varied, no proof marking of load alone can cover the possible range of loads," explained Roger Lees in *The Field*. "It is considered that the proof marking of highest mean service pressure is measurable and can be expressed in terms that are universally understood."

"Mean service pressure" is the average pressure of the normal service load intended for a particular gun. This was expressed in English long tons and so marked on the barrel flats (see markings chart on p. 203). Under the Rules, ammunition also was marked for pressures so that shooters were assured they were buying cartridges that developed pressures appropriate per the chamber lengths of their guns (see pressure translation chart, opposite).

Though the '54 Rules spelled out for the first time that definitive proof was to be 60- to 80-percent greater than normal service pressures, authorities emphasized that these pressures would not set up stresses greater than those of proof loads from earlier in the century. "The proof loads now set down in writing [in the '54 Rules] are almost in every instance the proof loading in use under the 1925 Rules," wrote Lees. "In general it may be said that under the new Rules of Proof no arm will receive a more severe proof than hitherto. Some, such as the 12-bore 2-inch and 4- and 8-bore guns, will now receive a less severe proof than they received heretofore." Lesser proof pressures were possible in some instances, Lees went on to explain, because of greater understanding of the ballistics of these loads.

The world of proof, gunmaking and ammunition has changed dramatically since 1954. Britain joined the *Commission Internationale Permanente pour l'Epreuve des Armes à Feu Portatives* (CIP) in the 1980s, and new Rules were adopted in 1984, '86, '89 and 2006. Proof marks are now expressed in metric rather than Imperial measurements, and the pressure markings on guns are now proof pressures, not service-load pressures. The methods of measuring those pressures also have changed, from using crusher-gauges to more-accurate transducers. Nontoxic shot and a global proliferation of new loads, many of them of high pressure, have muddied what was once an easily understandable relationship between cartridge size, chamber length and pressure.

Yet the Rules of '54 and its Imperial predecessors remain as instructive as ever in certain regards. For one, the proof marks of this era will provide a clear indication of a gun's original purpose. English makers traditionally built their guns around a specific maximum load: a 12-bore game gun almost always will have 2¹/₂" chambers and bear proof marks for 1¹/₈-oz loads (1925 Rules and earlier) or for 3 tons

BRITISH 12-GAUGE SERVICE-PRESSURE CHART

Chamber Length	1925 Rules	1954 Rules	Approximate conversion to CIP radial-transducer service pressures
2½"	1⅛-oz	3 tons	8,943 psi
2¾"	1¼-oz	3¼ tons	9,686 psi
3"	1½-oz	3½ tons	10,427 psi
3" Magnum	N/A	4 tons	11,913 psi

Chart info supplied by C.W. Harding BSc, Birmingham Proof House Historian. Note: The CIP transducer pressures are approximate only and are not marked on the gun, but are shown for comparison only to 1925 and '54 markings.

of pressure (1954 Rules); a heavier pigeon gun will have 2¾" chambers and marks for 1¼-oz or 3¼ tons; a stout wildfowler will have 3" chambers and marks for 1½-oz or 3½ tons. (Yes, there are no doubt odd exceptions to the guidelines listed above.) Remember that these early shot-load markings should be thought of as an alternative expression of suitable service pressure (as the '54 Rules later would codify).

With this is mind, the shooter can pick appropriate loads for the gun in question. The most conservative approach for Americans is to shoot CIP-approved loads from the same country of origin as the gun, choosing a shell based on appropriate chamber size and on the markings on the ammunition box that indicate shell specifications. Take care not to juxtapose the service-load markings of guns proofed by 1925 Rules and earlier with modern shells carrying the same shot load. For example, one of today's 70mm (2¾") 1¼-oz shells loaded to American magnum pressures will not be appropriate for a vintage gun proofed for 1¼-oz shells from the era of the 1925 Rules or earlier.

Another alternative for Americans is to shoot appropriately sized low-pressure shells as made by specialty US-based producers such as RST/Classic Shotshell Company or Polywad. Both companies specialize in producing a wide range of shells for the vintage-gun market.

Neither publishes pressure figures on its boxes but often will supply them at request. Another option is to reload low-pressure loads. I am admittedly giving short shrift to a complex subject, but bear in mind that because of differences between the ways pressure is measured by CIP and by America's Sporting Arms and Ammunition Manufacturers Institute (SAAMI), there are no direct mathematical conversions from one pressure measurement to the other. It is therefore incumbent on the reloader to very much err on the side of caution when it comes to pressure in working up suitable loads.

Perhaps most enduringly, proof marks are your guide when comparing a gun's specs as it left the factory to the condition it is in today—particularly in regard to its bore diameter and chamber length. It is a caveat worth repeating to have any old gun vetted by a competent gunsmith before firing, regardless of the pressures of the shells you use.

The Rules were written to be followed.

Old Guns & Restoring Them

XXI.
Restoration the
Atkin Grant & Lang Way

Ken Duglan hung up the phone in his basement office at Broomhills Shooting Grounds. "That was a gentleman who wants a matched pair of secondhand 12-bores for driven game," Atkin Grant & Lang's owner said. "Thirty-inch barrels, 2³/4" chambers, 16-inch stocks and Prince of Wales grips."

Duglan leaned back in his chair and shook his head. "He'd have to look long and hard to find a pair like that. But . . ."

This pair of Joseph Langs, restored by the maker, would cost less than half the price of a new pair. (David Grant)

he said, pausing as the hint of a smile creased his face, "I think I can help him."

From the gun rack lining his office wall, Duglan pulled a pair of sidelocks and placed them on his desk. "Joseph Langs—plainly engraved but made on perfectly good actions. They should work nicely."

I looked them over—12-bore bar-action game guns of conventional design with 28-inch barrels, well-used but not abused, with simple border engraving over actions gone silver from most of a century's shooting.

"I'll propose to fit in new barrels to his required length and chokes, then restock them with wood he's picked to his fitted dimensions," Duglan said. "We'll put in new springs and lock components, make new pins, re-engrave both to a pattern of his choosing, case-color them, then add a case and accessories.

"In 18 months or so he'll have two like-new bespoke London guns—for less than half the price of a new pair."

At noon a sleek green Jaguar XK convertible arrived at Broomhills, and from it Duglan's caller appeared. An hour or so later both emerged from Duglan's office beaming and then shook hands. As the Jag sped off, Duglan pushed his head into the Broomhills workshop where three men stood at benches with files in hand. "Carl, let's get those Langs from my office up here . . . ."

Since purchasing London gunmaker Atkin Grant & Lang in 1995, Duglan and his associated craftsmen have made something of a specialty of rebuilding fine British guns to as-new condition—particularly those by makers Henry Atkin, Stephen Grant and Joseph Lang. The firm, today based at Broomhills, in Hertfordshire, north of London, still builds a handful of new guns annually under each of those respective names, but the bulk of its customers are interested in vintage English guns that have been, depending on the gun in question, partially restored to completely rebuilt by AG&L's craftsmen.

For the consumer, one advantage is price: A vintage sidelock as sold by AG&L—fully rebuilt lock, stock and barrel—will average £15,000 to £20,000; new British "bests" built to similar designs begin at £35,000 and run to well over £50,000. Buyers get an utterly bespoke gun that promises to work like new but is imbued with the nostalgia and romance only vintage pieces offer.

Finisher Alan Bower at work in AG&L's workshop.

Sums of this sort, of course, still represent a heavy investment, so the integrity of craftsmanship involved in restoration is paramount. One needn't visit too many gun shows in the US to encounter a flood of poorly restored guns. Nothing screams "tarted up" quite so loudly as an old gun wearing fresh case colors over worn engraving and buggered pins; examples of such are legion and seem increasingly common. Disassemble and examine such, and problems often only multiply—the gun's intrinsic collectible value likely will have been obliterated, mechanically it will offer all the reliability of a Yugo and, in worse cases, it may even prove perilous to hand or eye or to other physical attributes commonly associated with good health and sound mind.

Proper restoration, on the other hand, involves skilled craftsmen working sympathetically to the original maker's intent—as well as standards of quality. Best British guns are so desirable—and expensive—because they combine incomparable handcrafted aesthetics with high levels of performance and reliability afield. Restoring these qualities to an older English gun by traditional means is never cheap.

The heart of the matter is, quite literally, first finding a suitable action. Generically speaking, to justify the costs of full restoration, Duglan prefers bar-action sidelocks of "modern" design—typically made on the ubiquitous Holland/Rogers-type action with Southgate-type ejectors.

In AG&L's case, specifically, Duglan also can offer a bit more flexibility to its customers, thanks to the varied designs historically offered by the firm's three incorporated makers. "There are certain actions customers are always interested in," Duglan said. "Atkin was famous for its Beesley-type self-openers. Grants are desirable for their side-lever actions with fluted fences as well as the company's 'Lightweights' [sleek, assisted-opening sidelocks made most famous by Charles Lancaster as the 'Twelve-Twenty' but built on William Baker's patent of 1906]." For those who want a single trigger, Langs offer a good choice, as their design was relatively simple and reliable. Duglan also will pursue best hammergun ejectors and almost any 20- or 28-bore sidelock by any British maker—"because there were so few made and they are in high demand today."

To get these actions, Duglan seeks out what he calls "wrecked guns"—those with out-of-proof, badly sleeved, pitted or thin barrels and stocks that are cracked, broken or otherwise marred by hard use, alterations to LOP or excessive refinishing. "So long as the action remains structurally sound," Duglan said, "they are far too good to waste.

"When we find a gun like this, we put it on the shelf and wait for the right customer. Our objective will be to make a good useable gun from it."

AG&L's restoration is performed by a team of crack Holland & Holland-trained outworkers and in-house craftsmen. The former include barrelmaker Bill Blacker, actioner Gary Hibbert, stockmaker Stephane Dupille and finisher Alan Wey. All work for the trade at large and are assisted by AG&L's in-house finishers Alan Bower and Carl Russell, both of whom originally trained at Ladbrook & Langton, a gunsmithing shop based in Hertfordshire. Under their tutelage, Ian Sweetman recently was taken on as an apprentice.

Once a client is interested in a particular gun, restoration begins in earnest. "First Alan and Carl go through the action to make sure it is as sound as it looks," Duglan said. "They'll strip and clean it to examine if it's ever had cracks welded up or to make sure it hasn't taken a 'set.'" (A "set" indicates the action has actually bent at its root—the juncture between the standing breech and the action flats—catastrophic dam-

AG&L apprentice Ian Sweetman.

age usually resulting from the use of high-pressure loads that have exceeded the elastic limits of the action's metallurgy). If either of the two flaws is encountered, the gun is rejected; if not, it's on to barrels.

Duglan occasionally will retain original barrels if he considers them sound, but if existing wall thickness is much below .024" at the thinnest spot—.020" being absolute minimum—Duglan will opt to have Bill Blacker build a new set. "In good conscience you really can't be selling guns thinner than that," Duglan said. "However, we are in a fairly unique position where we can rebarrel the guns of three high-quality London makers and legally put those names on the new tubes." (If original barrels are deemed good enough to keep, they are normally in a condition where re-proofing is not required.)

Rebarreling is the single most expensive element of full restoration—AG&L charges £6,500, which is considerably less than most other London houses, even though Blacker also builds new barrels to the same quality for those makers.

If the standing breech has pitting around the striker holes—a not uncommon cosmetic flaw with guns dating from the corrosive-powder era—it will be stoned down to present a smooth face for Blacker's new barrels. Once chopper-lump tubes are joined, rough-struck and chambered, they are sent to Gary Hibbert to be machined and jointed in to the action. At this stage the new barrels and action are sent for proof.

"Proof must occur as early as possible in the restoration process," Duglan said. "It doesn't happen often, but we've had guns fail before, so we try to spend the minimum amount of money on the gun until it passes." Under current CIP/proof rules, standard proof pressures for $2^1/_2$" and $2^3/_4$" chambers are identical for 12-bore guns—850 Bars—so the latter, longer chamber length is used.

The new-barrel option allows the customer to pick his length and chokes, and it also offers the readily apparent advantages of modern metallurgy and perfect wall thicknesses. Moreover, Hibbert makes new extractors as well as a new underbolt and hinge pin for each rebarreled action.

Normally when an old gun wears loose and the barrels come off the face of the action, the answer is to replace the existing hinge pin with that of a larger radius, to compensate for wear that usually occurs on the barrel lump. With a rebarreled action, however, Hibbert can start afresh by fitting in a hinge with a small radius, thereby assuring the ability in the future for re-jointing with successively larger-radius pins should wear occur.

On guns originally built with third bites (or top extensions), AG&L offers the option of filling in the recess on the action face and fitting in new barrels *sans* extension. More than a few London guns of the late 19th Century were built with top extensions. In ensuing decades top extensions came to be regarded as mechanically superfluous to bolting the barrels on bar-action sidelocks.

Part of the bias against third bites on London sidelocks is also stylistic convention—the idea that they render, in the words of Sir Ralph Payne-Gallwey, "a clumsy appearance"—and that the extension sometimes inhibits cartridge extraction. "When you don't have a third bite, you can have nice large extractors," Duglan said. "One of the irritating things you can have happen on guns with top extensions is for the cartridge rim to slip over their smaller extractors and then jam in the chamber. Not terribly convenient in the midst of a driven shoot." If a customer chooses to remove the top extension, the recess will be filled and tig-welded and the new barrels made with a straight breech.

After proof, barrels go back to Blacker to have the ribs installed and tubes polished, then Dupille begins stocking using walnut the customer has selected. In the meantime work begins to replace any damaged components as well as those most subject to repetitive stress. Finishers Russell and Bower invariably will fit in new mainsprings and sear springs in the locks and a toplever spring as well.

For replacement springs, AG&L uses those wired out of a block of spring steel by electro-discharge machines (EDMs). Duglan has had these tested for compression strength and durability. "We attached one to a revolving wheel with a cam on it and checked it after 800,000

On guns with barrels originally fitted with a top extension (left), AG&L offers the option of filling in the recess on the action face and fitting in new barrels sans extension (right).
(David Grant)

compressions," Duglan said. "It hadn't weakened in the slightest. In this sense I am a modernist. Today's components made with today's steels are far better than those of the past."

Strikers are also replaced and, if necessary, new disks fitted should the gun have them. Often new tumblers are required, as the originals may have cracked or broken at the highly stressed hinges where they engage the swivels attached to the mainsprings. Swivels are also routinely replaced and a full set of new pins made. "If a pin is buggered or doesn't line up right, it just jumps out at you no matter how good the rest of the restoration is," Duglan said.

Perfectly functioning ejectors are critical, and new springs are always fitted for them. "Normally we prefer to restore guns with Southgate-type ejectors," Duglan said. "The Southgate's advantages are simplicity, strength and reliability."

Duglan does make exceptions for certain sought-after house actions: Many best-grade Grants, for example, date from the era when the maker employed his own proprietary ejector design. "Grant ejectors work perfectly well if they are still mechanically correct," Duglan said, "but over the course of 100 years many have springs that have never been replaced and are not performing as they should. So we've had components machined for them and make a practice of restoring them to full order."

Though some prefer to leave the action as is, many choose to have it re-case colored. With the latter option, the action first will be annealed to relieve the stresses in the metal. Re-hardening without annealing runs the risk of distortion emerging in the re-hardening process. "It doesn't take much distortion to produce an unseemly gap in metal-to-metal fit," Duglan said. Moreover, annealing must take place if the gun is to be re-engraved.

If the engraving on the trigger guard and other "soft" furniture is worn, it is customary to have it touched up. In general, however, Duglan said he prefers to not re-engrave actions—and in the case of a gun bearing full scroll there is rarely a need to. "If the action was properly worked in the first place," he said, "it will be very hard and the engraving won't have worn with normal use."

However, upgraded guns (such as the pair of Langs mentioned earlier) allow the customer to choose engraving to his own tastes. Because an action is annealed in either case, Duglan's engravers usually "pick out" the maker's name with discreet gold lettering—quite handsome against the vibrant colors of a re-cased action. Triggers and pins are also case colored. After hardening, a few customers prefer to have the exterior colors removed for a silver or gray finish but, per tradition, the colors are retained on the action flats and face. For the time-honored pack-hardening process used, Birmingham's Richard St. Ledger is the obvious choice.

Dupille's new stock—which is completely inlet by hand and shaped by traditional stocking tools—is then sent to outworker Alan Wey, who checkers it. Wey sometimes applies the oil finish, although during my visit I watched Alan Bower rubbing in a finish to a pair of stocks in the workshop. "One of the hardest things to get is a really good oil finish," Bower said. "A good finish has about three months work into it."

The barrels, which have come back from Blacker's final polishing gleaming like chrome, are sent to John Gibbs, in Bath, for traditional rust-blacking. Bower and Russell will then finish the gun, freeing up any sticky parts and regulating ejectors and locks.

After final assembly, Duglan wraps the stock of the gun in a protective covering and steps out back at Broomhills to fire it for functioning. "When I test a gun," Duglan said, "I shoot it horizontally, vertically, upside down and on each side—at least 10 times in each position. We don't just take it out and go 'bang-bang'—that proves nothing."

The gun is then sent to casemaker Ian Tomlin, in Kent, for a full set of accessories and a custom-made case. Upon its return, Duglan shoots the gun one last time and makes a final inspection. "I need to know everything is right before we release it," Duglan said. A fully restored gun will carry a five-year warranty.

Duglan describes vintage English guns as "practical art." The gun craft of restoring them is no less artful.

XXII.
J.P. Morgan's Atkin

It likely will remain a mystery why in 1899 one of the world's richest and most powerful men picked Henry Atkin to build his guns, but Atkin's records leave no doubt that the London firm was *the* gunmaker for John Pierpont Morgan Jr.

From August '99, when Morgan placed his first order, until the early 1930s, the American tycoon ordered a dozen or so Atkins for himself, his family and his friends. One of those was gun No. 804, a 20-bore sidelock that recently has been fully restored to original glory by its maker in the UK—but only after an odyssey involving cocaine addicts, a stolen gun safe and an improbable recovery in an Alabama pawnshop.

J.P. "Jack" Morgan Jr. was the son of J.P. "Pierpont" Morgan, and at the turn of the 19th Century he was the heir apparent to the transatlantic banking empire known as the House of Morgan. These days it is difficult to conceive of the sheer economic clout the Morgan family wielded at the time. "The old pre-1935 House of Morgan was probably the most formidable financial combine in history," writes Ron Chernow, author of *The House of Morgan*. "The House of Morgan was something of a cross between a central bank and a private bank. It stopped [international economic] panics, saved the gold standard, rescued New York City three times, and arbitrated financial disputes . . . .

Though this was the Gilded Age of robber barons—men like Andrew Carnegie and Jay Gould—the Morgans were by contrast patrician, the family having crossed the Atlantic only 16 years after the arrival of the *Mayflower*. Jack Morgan was of the fourth generation to be involved in building his family's financial empire. Born in 1867, Jack grew to physically resemble his legendary father—with a balding pate, large nose and expansive frame—but he proved more genteel than the mercurial Pierpont. Differentiating him from many robber-baron peers, *Time* Magazine noted in its 1943 obituary that Jack was "A tycoon by inheritance, he was not a buccaneer by nature."

Educated in England and Europe and in 1899 in charge of Morgan's powerful London branch, Jack was also an unabashed Anglophile. He and his wife were granted audiences with Queen Victoria, and he hobnobbed in the highest echelons of British society.

Given shooting's popularity during the era amongst Britain's (and America's) upper classes, it is no surprise that Jack was an avid sportsman. In the US he belonged to an exclusive duck club in Georgia and had a magnificent quail lease in North Carolina; in Great Britain he enjoyed an estate full of pheasants and made frequent visits to the grouse moors of Scotland.

It's little surprise he shot English—rather than American—shotguns. What is somewhat surprising is not that he didn't pick Parker Bros. as his gunmaker but why he didn't pick James Purdey & Sons—then as now arguably the world's most prestigious

Henry Atkin No. 804:
a 20-gauge sidelock ordered
by banking magnate J.P. Morgan Jr.
more than a century ago and now
restored by its maker. (David Grant)

marque—over Henry Atkin. It was no lack of money or taste that influenced his choice.

It's worth noting that members of the Rothschild and Coutts families were at the same time loyal customers of Atkin's. Baron de Rothschild, for example, was a member of the Continental banking dynasty, and H.B. Money-Coutts belonged to the banking family that served England's royal family. Could it be that Atkin became the de facto gunmaker to the Gilded Age's greatest bankers? The answer is likely lost to time.

What we do know is that by the 1890s Henry Atkin had in short order earned himself a superb reputation as craftsman and gunmaker. Atkin had learned his trade at James Purdey & Sons, having been apprenticed there to his father, Charles. In the mid-1870s he had become confident enough to open his own shop in Oxenden Street; in 1890 he was successful enough to move to a more prestigious address at 2 Jermyn Street. It bears emphasizing that for a craftsman like Atkin to climb from the bench in class-conscious Victorian Britain to owning a shop patronized by aristocracy and the social elite was no mean feat.

G.T. Teasdale-Buckell, at the time the influential editor of *Land and Water*, noted: "When a man has got a pair [of Atkins] he may be sure he has got excellent work with balance, style or proportion, and neatness of workmanship." Teasdale-Buckell went on to praise not only Atkin's ability to work to the highest standards but also to perceive those standards in the work of others—an invaluable talent when overseeing a team of craftsmen responsible for building "best" guns.

Jack Morgan's first order with Atkin was for a cased pair of best-quality single-trigger 12-bores priced at £129 and change. When a gentleman of the era placed an order with a bespoke London maker—for shoes, shirts, shotguns, whatever—it was to enter into a relationship that could last decades, even from generation to generation, between the client's family and the maker. There was no shopping around for a better price or cheaper product. Morgan's patronage survived Henry Atkin's death, in 1907, and lasted with the company until Morgan's final decade. According to Ken Duglan, current owner of Atkin Grant & Lang: "It appears to have always been a good day at Atkin's when Mr. Morgan walked through the doors."

In later years Morgan grew especially fond of Atkin's best-quality spring-openers built on modified Beesley/Purdey-type actions, which Atkin's introduced to its line in 1907. But I'm getting ahead of myself. Morgan followed his first order at Atkin's by placing three commissions in 1903: one for a 12-bore for himself to match his first pair, another for a pair of best 12-bores for business partner W.P. Hamilton, and the third a 20-bore—No. 804—as a gift for his eldest son, Junius Spencer Morgan Jr., then age 11.

True to form, smallbores in Britain at the time mostly were regarded as "boys" or "ladies" guns and often were built as modestly priced boxlocks or otherwise finished quite plainly. No. 804, however, was a fully engraved toplever bar-action hammerless sidelock ejector with 29-inch barrels. Cased "as compactly as possible" and accompanied by a set of best-quality cleaning tools, it cost £50—about £10 to £15 less than a typical best-quality London sidelock of its day. Said Duglan, "It still would have been quite an extravagance to buy a gun of this quality for a boy." "J.S.M." was engraved on the stock oval, "J.S. Morgan" was stamped on the case, and the gun was sent to Morgan on December 10, 1903.

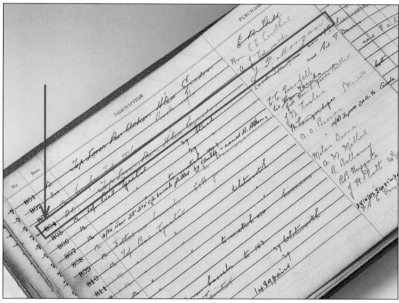

Atkin's record books reveal that Morgan was a faithful customer of the London firm. (David Grant)

No. 804 evidently was well liked—and used hard—by the young Morgan scion, and as with the majority of Atkins that Jack commissioned, it remained within the family until recently. In time Junius passed No. 804 to his son, John P. Morgan III, who in turn passed it to his sons, Junius Morgan II and Frederick Converse Morgan.

No. 804 was gifted to Junius II around age 10 or 12—just as it had been to his father and grandfather. Junius II was left-handed and had the stock altered. He remembers using the gun mostly to shoot "squirrels and crows." Subsequently, the little Atkin passed into the hands of his younger brother, Frederick, who recalled shooting it at clay targets as a young man.

Frederick, however, did not inherit his grandfather's love of shooting and hunting, and in recent years the gun remained mostly in storage. After the chronometer from J.P. Morgan's legendary steam yacht—the *Corsair*—was stolen from Frederick in a burglary, he thought it best to place the gun in safe keeping and loaned it to Fitz Hudson, an old friend from boarding-school days.

Hudson secured No. 804 in a gun safe in his father's home in Alabama that contained about 20 other firearms. It was therefore a shock to Frederick and Fitz when the entire safe and its contents disappeared in a well-planned burglary in March 2004. After four generations in Morgan hands, No. 804 appeared gone for good.

Which is where gunmaker Atkin Grant & Lang enters the picture. Within the space of a couple of months, Ken Duglan was contacted by both Fitz Hudson and Nick Tooth, the latter then in charge of Bass Pro Shops' expanding fine-gun program. Hudson was asking about the cost of a new 20-gauge Atkin to replace a stolen gun; Tooth was trying to find out the market value of a rather tired Atkin 20-gauge he'd been offered by a pawnshop dealer in southern Alabama.

It didn't take Duglan long to put one and one together and, by matching information to serial number, it became clear that No. 804 had been found. Now it needed rescuing. Duglan put Hudson in contact with Tooth, the latter having been unaware the gun was stolen, and Hudson then contacted a private investigator who had worked at the FBI and had contacts in law enforcement. A raid by authorities on the pawnshop produced Atkin No. 804 along with a bevy of stolen merchandise. (Sadly, Hudson would recover only one other of his father's missing guns.) Subsequent investigation revealed that the safe had been stolen by three "crackheads" (as Hudson described them), and No. 804 eventually had been bought by the pawnshop.

Frederick Morgan was overjoyed to regain No. 804, but he then was confronted with what to do with it. He didn't shoot, and his children weren't interested. After consideration, he decided to offer the gun for sale to Duglan. Given the scarcity of British 20-bore sidelocks and the strong demand for them, the offer was one Duglan would not turn down.

"When I received the barrels and stock, they were in very poor condition," Duglan said. "The barrels were worn out—bores pitted and the walls were thin. The stock had been shortened and then lengthened again. The checkering was mostly gone. During its life, it had obviously seen a terrific amount of use.

"However, the action's engraving was still very crisp, and mechanically the gun remained sound. It hadn't been messed about with inside." In other words, for Duglan it would be a prime candidate for rebuilding and restoration (see "Restoration the Atkin Grant & Lang Way," p. 211).

"I called an American client—Dr. John S. Thalgott—who was looking for a smallbore, and described it to him," Duglan said. "Before I could even finish, he said, 'It's mine!'"

Because of the gun's provenance, Duglan decided to restore it to original specs—though to Thalgott's personal stock measurements. In addition to re-stocking, Duglan had a new set of 29-inch barrels made, and new pins, mainsprings and ejector springs were fitted. The action's fine scroll did not require re-engraving, but the Atkin name and serial number were picked out in gold and the gun was re-color hardened. It was fitted into a new case—"as compactly as possible"— with tools that matched the originals. (The original case had not been recovered.)

Before the gun was delivered to its fortunate new owner, I had a chance to examine and handle it during my visit to AG&L headquarters in November 2007. At 5 pounds 15 ounces, it was beautifully balanced and appeared virtually indistinguishable from new. Closer examination showed that the gun exhibited many of the hallmarks of a top-quality London sidelock of its era—bar-action locks with three-pin bridles, the action fully stocked to the fences, and barrel lumps fully contained (in other words, not protruding through the bottom of the action). However, the gun did have a top-extension more typical of Birmingham provenance and an unconventional cocking and ejector system.

Unlike a standard sidelock, there were no Rogers-type cocking levers (lock lifters) protruding through the knuckle, rather recesses for rods, one per lock. On the action flat to either side of the bridge between the slots were two pins and also two separate patent-number inscriptions: Pat. 10679-86, No. 930, and Pat. 14526-84, No. 343.

On the action face was W&C Scott's well-known patent gas-check rings (Pat. No. 617). The ejectors in the forend appeared to be a derivation of the "Westley box" mechanism.

It was an action I was utterly unfamiliar with. Duglan, likewise, could not recall seeing a design like it, and even AG&L finisher Alan Bower, who spearheaded restoration of No. 804, had encountered only one previously. Moreover, the Atkin ledger book in Duglan's possession is remarkably scanty in its details of early guns. No. 804 is listed simply as "20 bore top lever, bar, hammerless ejector J. P. Morgan," with no details of the craftsmen involved.

This presented a puzzle and a call for more research. A check through British sporting-gun patents revealed that Pat. 10679-86 was T. Perkes' ejector patent of 1886; Pat. 14526-84 was John Deeley's (of Westley Richards) ejector patent of 1884. The numbers following the patent numbers (930 and 343) were "use numbers," which recorded the number of times the patents had been licensed for use by their inventors.

In the meantime I contacted Valerie Masters, widow of Don Masters, the latter having authored the definitive tome *House of Churchill* and also *Atkin Grant & Lang*. It was clear from details about Atkin guns in the *AG&L* book that Masters had had access to more-extensive production records. During his long tenure at Churchill Atkin Grant & Lang, Masters had rescued many of those companies' archives and related correspondence from the trash heap—invaluable primary source material that distinguishes his books from many others. (Always a gentleman and freely offering assistance to writers, Masters unfortunately passed away in 2004, and his untimely death was a loss to the British gun trade and historians of it.)

Valerie Masters soon replied after checking some of the records in her possession. She confirmed that the gun was built for Morgan. "The action was purchased 'in the soft' or 'in the white' from [W&C] Scott & Sons, before they joined forces with [P.] Webley," she wrote. That would explain the Scott-patent gas checks on the action face. This information in hand, I consulted *The History of W.&C. Scott Gunmakers*, by J.A. Crawford and P.G. Whatley. According to the authors: "Scott manufactured several types of sidelock ejector guns [in the 1880s] . . . the largest number were based on a design by Thomas Perkes in 1886 . . . . Deeley ejectors, patented in 1884, occasionally were used on guns built on the Perkes action . . . . Guns made on the Perkes action can be distinguished . . . by the presence of two screws on the water-table." (These very distinctive screws [pins] retain the Perkes cocking rods and ejector trips.)

W&C Scott's was, of course, a great supplier of guns to the trade, and Atkin and his craftsmen would have finished out the Perkes action to their high standards. As the records indicate, No. 804 was purchased as an action in the white from Scott's in 1894, and it is likely to have sat in the storeroom for years awaiting an order—in this case that placed by Morgan in 1903. Orders for 20-bore sidelocks of this quality and high price were not particularly common, as most were destined for boys.

Although the Atkin superficially appears to be a London bar-action sidelock of conventional design, some of its mechanical features reveal origins in Birmingham, such as a top extension (more typical of guns from the Midlands) and Scott-patent gas-check rings around striker holes in the action face. The gun also bore two patent inscriptions, revealing that it was built on a Perkes-patent action and fitted with Deeley-patent ejectors. (David Grant)

Although Atkin's is today associated with best London sidelocks—guns that would have been made in-house or with the assistance of London outworkers—the company also sold boxlocks, rifles and, as evidenced by No. 804, at least some sidelocks that had origins in Birmingham. Admitted or not, it was a ubiquitous practice in London.

According to Crawford and Whatley, Scott's stopped production of Perkes bar-action guns in 1897, superseding them with Rogers-action guns fitted with Southgate-type ejectors. The latter designs were simpler, ultra-reliable and no doubt easier and less expensive to make. Toby Barclay, of England's Heritage Guns, specializes in researching and selling British sporting guns of this era and offered this take on Scott's Perkes bar-action sidelocks: "The Perkes/Deeley action and ejectorwork, especially the latter, is complicated, with at least two small springs per barrel, with swivels, sears et al. Southgates, on the other hand, can be as few as two parts per barrel. Also, the Perkes cocking rods do require some very neat and accurate boring of the rods' tunnels through the action, which required jigs the rest of the trade did not have, hence the Scott monopoly of this action."

Perkes bar-actions were built for a decade in evidently considerable numbers, and if more complicated than what has become the standard "modern" sidelock, it has proved a sound design. No. 804 was shot extensively for the better part of a century without any evidence of internal repairs. "Everything about it appeared original and was working," Alan Bower said. "The mechanism had never really been messed about with, so although there was a lot of time involved in refurbishing everything, it all came together really well. It will happily be around shooting for at least another 100 years."

Its new owner—a founding member of the Anglo-American Shooting Society—already has put the gun to good use in England on driven game. "I took a nice left and right on ducks," Thalgott said. "I'm proud to be a keeper of a truly historic work of art."

XXIII.
The Frederick C. Scales Gun

In retrospect it seems inauspicious—foolish even—for an English-man to have commissioned an exhibition-grade gun in the summer of '39. Franco had triumphed in Spain, fascist Italy had just occupied Albania, and Hitler was preparing to march in Central Europe. A war like no other was looming, and everyone in England knew it. For Brit-ons, what lay ahead was not only uncertain but also frightening.

But none of this halted work on a most unusual side-by-side for a most unusual client. Begun on the eve of the Second World War and finished sometime the next year, it was a 12-gauge sidelock with 30-inch chopper-lump barrels, a matte rib, a fluted action, an articu-lated front trigger, Southgate-style ejectors, Chilton locks, a Silvers re-coil pad, Holland-type locks with a hand-detachable pin, and a stock of well-figured French walnut. All were fairly standard features for an English sidelock of its era, but the stock was distinguished by a capped full pistol grip as well as a cheekpiece on its left side more ap-propriate to a Continental double rifle than a British game gun.

The gun's engraving, too, was anything but standard: The barrel breeches were carved with superbly executed bold acanthus scroll, with portions of the top rib, action, lockplates and furniture featuring the same against a matte background. Inlaid in gold on the lockplates were mythological winged animals reminiscent of a gryphon and phoenix. The toplever had a gold-inlaid pheasant; the trigger guard had a partridge. On the underside of the action was the glowering face of "The Green Man" in gold. On the forend in a diamond was another smaller Green Man, his features also in gold. The Green Man motif appeared a third time in miniature atop the safety.

There was no maker's name anywhere on the exterior, but depress-ing the Anson pushrod and removing the forend revealed the top of the scroll-engraved forend iron, which was inscribed: "Made by Fred-erick C. Scales, 38 years with J. Purdey & Sons, London 1940."

Fine as the intrinsic workmanship and ornate engraving were, these attributes were not what fully stood the gun apart; rather it was the man who built it. Frederick C. Scales was employed at the time at London's James Purdey & Sons, and although he was reputed to be the firm's best stocker, it was virtually unheard of for a man on the bench to build a gun of such quality and lavish ornamentation for himself. Though the world was changing fast, this was still the era of "masters & men," when Britain's social and class distinctions were far more rigid than those of today. In this sense the Scales gun is almost as anomalous as a scepter built by a crown jeweler for himself rather than a regent.

As is the case with many craftsmen of the day, confirmed details about Fred Scales' life are scanty. Presently, we know nothing of when and where he was born or his eventual fate and only fragments from his time at Purdey's. After he spent the war years at the firm's Great West Road factory, company wage books indicate that Scales retired from Purdey's on January 4, 1946, vanishing thereafter for all intents and purposes.

Had his gun not caught the eye of British gunwriter Geoffrey Boothroyd in the late 1980s, almost all historical details of Scales' life—and his unique creation—would have faded into the gauzy mists of time.

That we know more about this gun today than at any time since it left the bench in 1940 is largely thanks to Boothroyd as well as to the dogged detective work of David Trevallion, a craftsman trained as a stocker at Purdey's in the same factory, on the same floor, at the same bench and by the same men who worked hand in hand with Scales.

Boothroyd brought the gun to the British public's attention in an article titled "Guns at the Game Fair," in the August 24, 1989, edition of *The Shooting Times & Country Magazine*. He initially had examined the gun when its then owner brought it to the Game Fair for him to photograph. Describing it as "one of the most interesting guns to come in front of my camera lens during the Game Fair," Boothroyd briefly noted its unusual engraving and the inscription on the top of the forend iron and recounted what he'd learned of its history: "Mr. Scales, then employed by James Purdey, was given permission to build a double gun, in the factory, but during his own time. The gun is based on a Holland & Holland action and was engraved by Mr. Harry Kell, who did most of the Purdey engraving at the time the gun was made." Where Scales' gun had been in the intervening years, from 1940 until the '89 Game Fair, was not revealed.

The Frederick C. Scales Gun is distinguished by its stock configuration and engraving—and the fact that the maker is identified only in an inscription inside the forend iron. (Courtesy of Richard Raymond)

Shortly thereafter Boothroyd contacted Trevallion, one of the world's finest independent stockmakers and co-author (along with Michael McIntosh) of the book *Shotgun Technicana*. Although working walnut is his profession, those who know Trevallion know his true passion is helping preserve the history of the British gun trade—and especially that of the craftsmen upon which the glories of that trade were founded.

Because of James Purdey & Sons' long and storied history, its celebrated centuries-old standards of craftsmanship, and the peculiarities of its formal apprenticeship program, Purdey craftsmen inevitably have a certain weight of history present in their handwork—even, sometimes, a palpable sense of long-gone predecessors peering over their shoulders as they work. There is a company tradition of sons and their sons succeeding fathers on Purdey workbenches, and it is to this sense of a lineage of ancient skills passed from one generation to the next that Trevallion is acutely attuned.

Trevallion told Boothroyd that, yes, he'd heard of Scales and the gun—Scales had been known as a "real character" by workmates, and his gun had become part of the "folklore" of the factory floor—but he remembered little beyond the barest details. "Boothroyd called it the 'beast gun' and seemed fascinated by it," Trevallion said.

Trevallion had joined Purdey's in 1953. His gaffer, or teacher, had been William ("Bill") O'Brien, who had started work at the firm's "No. 2" factory at Irongate Wharf in 1936 as a trainee stocker under Sid Block, who'd worked next to Scales. On a bench lit with gas lamps, Scales and O'Brien had worked side by side. "Bill often talked about Fred," Trevallion said. "Lots of stories, most of which I've unfortunately forgotten."

"Fred's bench and vise were the ones I went on to use, so I always felt there was a connection between Scales and myself." At some point in his research Boothroyd contacted Purdey's and evidently gained access to company wage books and also interviewed employees—notably Chris Gadsby, then factory manager and a craftsman at Purdey's since 1926, as well as Gene Warner, at the time Purdey's longest-serving employee, having worked at Audley House since 1918.

In a follow-up article titled "Made to Impress" (*The Shooting Times*, March 15, 1990), Boothroyd updated the Scales-gun saga, admitting that he'd been unhappy with some of the information he'd published in his initial article.

One apparent anomaly Boothroyd mentioned was a mismatch between the forend iron inscription "38 years with J. Purdey & Sons London 1940" and the length of time that Boothroyd said the Purdey wage books indicated Scales had served: according to Boothroyd, Scales is first mentioned in the books on April 17, 1907. Were that his actual starting date, his service in 1940 would have been 33 years, not 38.

From his sources at Purdey's, Boothroyd also learned that Scales "was a big bluff man of six feet, considered by many to be the best gun stocker in the country. The story—from yet another source—goes on to say that Scales married a German girl and that when he was asked to go shooting with his German in-laws, he decided to build a fine gun for himself to uphold the dignity of the British gun trade.

"Unable to obtain an action from Purdey, he bought a second-hand Holland & Holland and this became the gun which was in effect rebuilt by Fred and his friends in the gun trade and is known as the 'Fred C. Scales Gun.'"

It is largely thanks to British gun historian Geoffrey Boothroyd and his articles that the history of the Scales gun was not lost to time.

Boothroyd wrote that, according to Gadsby, the Holland's action, barrels and ejectors were reworked by Alf Winter, then foreman of Cogswell & Harrison's factory (Alf's brother, Frank, was at the time an actioner at Purdey's). Scales then stocked the gun and sent it on to Harry Kell to be polished and re-engraved. The gun was finished by Mick Miles, one of Scales' friends at Purdey's.

"The gun has survived and it is undoubtedly a Holland & Holland and the engraving is certainly from the hand of Harry Kell," Boothroyd said. "The German heraldic birds which are inlaid with gold were no doubt added to impress Fred's German in-laws. Since the gun was finished in 1940 one cannot help wonder if they ever saw the gun. If not it was a great shame after all the work Fred and his friends had carried out."

Harry Kell was regarded as perhaps the finest—and most versa-

Taken in 1936, this photograph of gunmakers with more than 25 years' service to Purdey's is the only known picture of Frederick Scales (third from left in back row, beside window). (Courtesy of David Trevallion)

tile—British engraver of his day, and he and the craftsmen he employed contracted to almost all of the best gunmakers. Kell had started his engraving career around the turn of the century, working with his father, Henry, until the late '20s, and then setting up on his own upon his father's death. Purdey's was, of course, an important customer, especially for guns requiring exhibition-grade engraving. Kell was noted particularly for naturalistic game scenes as well as carving, chiseling and elaborate foliate work—all exemplified in the Scales gun. Kell's most famous apprentice, Ken Hunt, joined Purdey's in the late '50s and subsequently helped revolutionize British gun engraving.

Boothroyd briefly described the Scales gun for an American audience in an article titled "Gun Engraving," in the Winter 1992 issue of *The Double Gun Journal*. In this piece he again remarked on the gun's "German heraldic beasts."

A decade later the gun came up for sale at Holt's June 2003 auction. With a full-page color photo montage illustrating the gun's action from the left, right and underneath, Holt's described it thus: "The Frederick C. Scales Gun, a fine Kell-engraved Holland & Holland 12-bore sidelock." After a description of the gun's specifications and

Harry Kell's most famous apprentice, Ken Hunt (left), identified his teacher's engraving on the Scales gun and repaired a gold inlay on it.
(Courtesy of David Trevallion)

It is believed that Harry Kell (right), one of the most talented British engravers of his day, embellished the Scales gun.
(Courtesy of David Trevallion)

Bill O'Brien (left), in 1953, working at Scales' former vise and bench.
(Courtesy of David Trevallion)

The Frederick C. Scales Gun   235

engraving, the catalog noted, "The makers have kindly confirmed that the gun was made by them in 1899. The Holland & Holland name does not appear on the gun."

Lot No. 594 caught the eye of Richard Raymond, a collector and owner of the Gun Vault on Fox Hill, a shop in Fort Kent, Maine, specializing in fine guns with historical provenance. Raymond, who employs Trevallion to vet all of his guns for condition, noticed the Purdey connection and asked Trevallion if he knew anything about the Scales gun. "I didn't need to ask Richard 'what gun?'" Trevallion said. "I told him, 'You need to *own* that gun.'"

After a rather circuitous purchasing process, Raymond became the owner. Trevallion could hardly contain himself; after all, the gun had been stocked at the very bench and with the very vise he'd used as a young apprentice. It had been engraved by one of the greats of British engraving and the teacher of his close friend, Ken Hunt. The Scales gun was not just another Purdey; to Trevallion it represented something more: a personal totem of the craftsmanship and craftsmen so central to his life's work and passion. "Bill O'Brien was still alive at the time," Trevallion said, "so I called him about it, and his reply was, 'Bleedin' 'ell; wonder where that's been all these years?'"

With the gun still in England, Raymond and Trevallion sent it to Cogswell & Harrison's Alan Crewe to determine if any repairs were needed before importation to the US. Originally trained as an actioner at Purdey's, Crewe is not only a first-rate craftsman in his own right (he was apprenticed to Peter V. Nelson at Purdey's), but his association with Cogswell & Harrison also provided a historical link to the work that Coggie's was said to have done when the gun originally was being reworked from the Holland action.

Crewe thought the gun "a top-quality sidelock" and gave it a thorough strip & clean, discovering that it was in excellent condition aside from a frozen triggerplate pin, which was drilled out and another made. At the time, engraver Marcus Hunt—Ken's son—was renting bench space at Coggie's. Trevallion asked him to engrave the head of the new triggerplate pin to match the original and also to take the gun's lockplates to his father to confirm that they were, indeed, Kell-engraved, as they were not signed.

Kell lived in an era when craftsmen worked in utter anonymity, and he virtually never signed his work. As Kell's protégé, however,

Engraver Marcus Hunt (top) embellished the head of the Scales gun's new trigger-plate pin, made by Cogswell & Harrison's Alan Crewe (right). (David Trevallion)

Ken Hunt can recognize genuine Kell engraving by a number of stylistic signatures. In the case of the Scales gun, specifically, he noted that the writing on the inscription was identical to Kell's. (According to Hunt, Kell was the only craftsman in his workshop who lettered the guns.) Moreover, the gold-inlaid beasts were a Kell specialty, so in Hunt's estimation the gun clearly had been engraved by him. Finally, Hunt noted a missing leg on one of the golden beasts and inlaid a repair to bring it back to its original appearance.

After Crewe's new pin and Hunt's & Hunt's gentle engraving restoration, the gun was shipped to John Foster Gunmakers, in northern England, for export. In addition to his import/export services, Foster operates a well-known barrel-sleeving and gun-restoration business, and he and his associate, Graham Bull, examine and repair many British guns annually. As Foster and Bull examined the gun, some telling inconsistencies began to surface regarding the action's provenance.

The gun clearly had a number of features consistent with H&H guns: Holland-style locks, the 10-to-5-o'clock position of the tumbler cocking indicators (when cocked), and the diamond on the underside of the forend. "However, the overall shape of the action was intrinsically wrong for that of a Holland gun," Bull explained. "The top strap was of a typical Birmingham pattern, not that of a London gun, as was the ejector cam. At this point instinct and 35 years of working on double guns told me this was not a reworked Holland action but rather a Birmingham-built gun."

A check with Holland & Holland revealed that its records indicated the Serial Number—H 22269—corresponded to a Holland Royal built in 1899, but *sans* the H prefix. Curiously, the gun featured what appeared to be a Holland hand-detachable lock lever on its left lock. This device, however, was not patented by Holland's until 1908. (Actually, the Scales gun does not have true hand-detachable locks, because another lockplate retaining nail is located at 4 o'clock behind the fences.) Though the lever could have been retrofitted in 1939-'40, its presence seemed incongruous on a gun reportedly built in 1899.

More important, the gun's proof marks clearly belonged to Britain's 1925 Rules of Proof, meaning the gun was built post-1925 but before the new rules of 1954. This in itself did not rule out a Holland & Holland provenance but, assuming original barrels, it certainly precluded a build date of 1899.

Foster and Bull also noted the letters "JA" stamped on the underside of the left barrel just in front of the flats and above the keel rib. Initially, Trevallion had thought the initials might be those of Jack Aldous, a barrelmaker at Purdey's in the '30s; however, Bull reported that "JA" was also the trademark of Joseph Asbury, a highly regarded actionmaker and machinist to the trade in Birmingham from the late 19th Century until the firm's purchase by gunmaker A.A. Brown & Sons after the Second World War.

Moreover, Bull informed Trevallion that H-prefix serial numbers are typically found on guns made by Birmingham's G&S Holloway, a well-regarded gunmaker to the trade in the Scales era. Holloway guns are often found engraved with many "makers'" names, but guns they built for the trade often have an H-prefix serial number on the keel rib—precisely where it was located on the Scales gun. "I began to suspect the gun had been built by Holloway's by the position and style of the number on the tailpiece [keel rib] behind the forend loop," Bull said. "On comparison with another Holloway gun, I found that the style and face of the number and stamps were identical. I pointed out these findings to John [Foster]; he agreed wholeheartedly and immediately said, 'Holloway's!' on seeing the barrel number." Bull told Trevallion that in his opinion the Scales gun originally had been a Holloway gun, itself possibly built on a J. Asbury-machined action.

Until now Trevallion had been compiling as much information as he could on Scales and other Purdey craftsmen who may have had a hand in making the gun. Given Foster and Bull's dramatic findings, however, he shifted efforts to learning more about G&S Holloway. An original '30s-era Holloway catalog was procured, though its pages did not illustrate an exact match for a Scales-type gun.

Trevallion's conversations with Douglas Tate, author of the book *Birmingham Gunmakers*, prompted Tate to send Trevallion a copy of a Scales-era Midland Gun Co. advertisement illustrating the firm's Supreme Ejector Gun, described as a "London Pattern Side Lock." The Supreme's bold scroll and beast motifs were, if not an exact match to the Scales gun, very close, indeed. Kell is known to have done work for the Birmingham trade, and it's plausible that he had a hand in creating the Midland's engraving pattern.

In 2005 British gun-trade historian Nigel Brown published his magisterial tome *British Gunmakers: Birmingham, Scotland & the Regions*, in which he detailed the history of G&S Holloway as well as the company's serial numbers and records to the extent that they survive in the hands of Christopher Holloway, son of the last family proprietor of G&S Holloway, Graham Holloway. Tellingly, the published records confirmed not only the common use of H-prefix serial numbers on Holloway guns built for the trade but also that guns with serial numbers falling between 22185 to 22289 were built between 1939 and '40—a perfect match for the Scales gun.

A letter was sent to Christopher Holloway asking for any details he might have regarding gun H-22269. Months passed without a reply.

(Trevallion was later to learn that Holloway had changed addresses before the book's publication.)

In the meantime we also contacted Robin Brown, director of Birmingham's A.A. Brown & Sons, which, as mentioned, purchased J. Asbury in the early '50s. Brown replied that he was "99.9 percent certain" that the gun's "JA" stamp belonged to Asbury.

We also contacted Daryl Greatrex, Holland & Holland's managing director, for any additional information he might shed on gun No. 22269. "Regarding number 22269, originally the gun was made in 1899 and rebarreled with 27-inch barrels in 1931," Greatrex said. "It is currently owned by a customer we know, as one of a pair, matching gun 22268." The information about Holland Royal No. 22269's current ownership would in itself preclude the Scales gun having the Holland provenance reported. Moreover, had the gun been a real Holland, any H-prefix number would be merely a parts number. "It would not be the serial number that the gun ultimately featured," Greatrex elaborated. "The serial number should be featured elsewhere on the barrels, action and trigger guard."

A note to Nigel Brown soon produced Chris Holloway's updated address, and another letter to Holloway in short order produced this welcome response:

"Sir:

"The records are taken from hand-written ledgers with varying degrees of clarity. The following are the written facts for the Holloway gun you quoted (22269):

"Order No. 571-62
"Barrels: Steel 12.30.2.5
"Chopper Lump: LO.5 RI
"RI Asbury 8759
"Scott Lever Dble Bolt
"Fluted bars
"Betts 8790
"Connect Southgate
"Fence Purdey
"Locks Sidelock
"Snap Marlow
"Sold: 16/09/1939
"To: E. Gale, 20 Joy St., Barnstaple, Devon, England

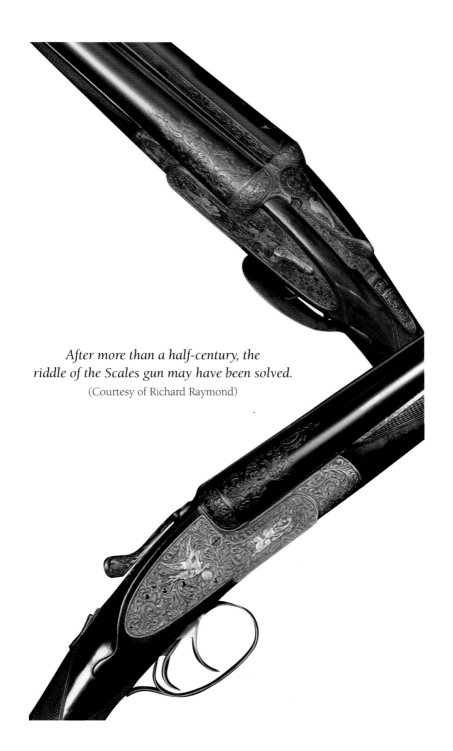

*After more than a half-century, the
riddle of the Scales gun may have been solved.*
(Courtesy of Richard Raymond)

"I regret that I did not receive [your] post from the earlier address
. . . . I also regret that I am unable to explain some of the 'vernacular'
used by my relatives' annotation[s] in the records.

"Best Wishes, Chris Holloway."

Holloway's letter makes it appear virtually certain that the Scales
sidelock was built by G&S Holloway, probably on a barreled action
machined by Joseph Asbury. Although the meaning of some of the
"vernacular" remains a mystery, other specifics clearly match the
Scales gun. For example, the gun's barrels are 30" chopper-lump steel
12-gauge tubes with $2^{1}/_{2}$" chambers—precisely as described in the records. The "RI" in the "RI Asbury" notation is probably a transcription
error from illegible handwriting and should be a "J."

Our understanding of the Scales/Gale connection is more tenuous—
and from this point our conclusions admittedly more speculative. At
the time, Edward Gale & Son was an established shop in Devon that
sold guns under its own name, though the guns would have been made
in the trade. According to British barrel-blacker Paul Stevens, whose
grandfather worked for Gale, the latter (or another Gale family member) was Purdey trained—and if this is the case, it is possible Gale knew
Scales and was picked for this reason. Indeed, in a log from a Purdey's
June 7, 1930, Workmen's Dinner there is a "Gale" listed in attendance
(along with Scales); unfortunately, his first name is not shown.

As Chris Holloway's letter makes no mention of stocking, engraving or finishing, the Holloway likely would have been in an unfinished state. "Almost certainly it was purchased as a barreled action in
the white," Graham Bull said. Boothroyd's account of the craftsmen,
including Scales, who finished the gun seems entirely plausible—the
specificity of names and details lends the account an aura of legiti-
macy. Ken Hunt has authenticated Kell's engraving, and it would have
made sense for Scales, a master stocker, to stock it to his own tastes
and requirements, cheekpiece and all.

What about the engraving's reported *raison d'etre* to impress Scales'
German in-laws? It would take much more research into Scales' life
and family history to know for certain but, to me at least, certain aspects of the account have something of an apocryphal ring about them.
Remember that Germany had invaded Poland on September 1, 1939,
and when Holloway sold the gun to Gale on September 16, Britain already had been at war with Germany for nearly two weeks. Scales likely

had not sent the gun to Kell's workshop for engraving yet, so with the two nations locked in mortal combat, it is arguable that any "shooting" invitations issued from Germany would by this time have involved stakes more serious than the "dignity of the British gun trade."

Moreover, the carved engraving and beast motifs—although atypical for a British "best"—are not necessarily Germanic, as the Midland Supreme of the same era reveals. The mythological beasts are as much generically Medieval in inspiration as they are "German." The Green Man grotesques, appearing thrice, are particularly interesting. An ancient allegorical symbol of death and rebirth, depictions of the

Former Purdey craftsmen David Trevallion (left) and Bill O'Brien at the grave of Joseph Manton. Trevallion is responsible for picking up the trail of the Scales gun where Geoffrey Boothroyd left off.
(Courtesy of David Trevallion)

Green Man are found across Europe—and were especially common in Britain from the Middle Ages on. Kell utilized a number of grotesque types in his engraving, so there is little evidence to suggest its inspiration was perforce Teutonic. That said, the genesis for the gun and its engraving could have taken place long before the outbreak of hostilities—so a German connection cannot be ruled out.

There is no doubt that the gun is unusual. Graham Bull offered his own insights into the gun's decorative and technical features. "Scales probably spent most of his working life with Purdey, who at the time made one style of gun with very little variation," Bull said. "It's my personal opinion that when it came to his own gun, he let his imagination run wild as to what he thought a gun should look like, or what looked good to him."

Aesthetically, the Scales gun is miles apart from the chastely engraved Beesley-type self-openers he would have worked on for nearly 40 years. Why, indeed, would he have wanted to duplicate the same in a gun that was very much an emblem of self-expression and personal pride in his career as a craftsman?

Like any good story, the saga of the Frederick C. Scales Gun resonates on several levels. In one sense it should be read as a cautionary tale—that readers (and writers) should not necessarily take as gospel everything seen in print, past or present, regardless of source. Despite diligence and best intentions, research dependent on personal recollections combined with subjective interpretations, informed speculation and missing primary sources inevitably invites errors. As this chapter, too, incorporates to some extent aspects of all of the above, it is not only possible but also almost certain that it will stand factual corrections in time.

It's well worth remembering that Boothroyd was a true pioneer in writing British sporting-gun history and worked without the benefit of some of the more detailed and extensively researched histories published subsequent to his writings. The Scales gun was, indeed, built on a Holland-type action, and the names "Holloway" and "Holland" are only a few letters apart and certainly sound similar. Given this, it's not surprising that aged craftsmen—interviewed by Boothroyd a half-century after the gun was built—might confuse the two, especially given Holland's fame and Holloway's relative obscurity. And as we know, once errors find their way into print they can assume lives all their own.

The veracity of the printed word aside, on a more elemental level this is really a story as much about people as it is one of an object made of wood and steel. Incomplete though it may be, it is the tale of a craftsman, his life and aspirations, and how he and his magnificent gun have intrigued and fascinated generations to the present day.

The great gun writer Gough Thomas once distinguished between guns made by craftsmen whose traditions were "traceably descended from that of a medieval armorer" and those designed for mass production. Today, with modern engineering increasingly able to duplicate not only the function of handmade guns but also the handwork of traditional craftsmen, it is well worth noting that no machine-made gun—however beautiful—will ever tell a story so rich and dramatic as that of Frederick C. Scales and his gun of golden beasts.

Appendices

A Glossary of Terms

Traditional gunmaking has a language all its own, varying from country to country and even from gunmaker to gunmaker within a respective country. Because of the emphasis in *Gun Craft* on English gunmaking—or at least English-influenced gunmaking—I have chosen to retain British terms of definition as used by UK craftsmen, though the reader will note that there is still room for considerable variation. Though not a complete list, the terms included span the topics discussed herein.

— Guns —

Assisted-opener: a design in which a spring (or springs) eases the opening of a gun. Sometimes called an "easy-opener."

Boxlock: in a traditional gun, an action with its locks mounted in slots in the base of the action, per the Anson & Deeley patent of 1875. Often boxy in appearance, hence the name. Today the term is increasingly used to describe a wide range of non-sidelock guns, including many modern over/unders that are more accurately described as "triggerplate" guns.

Hammerless: a traditional term to describe guns with their lockwork mounted internally and out of view—hence "hammerless."

Self-cocking: in this context, a gun cocked by the fall of the barrels rather than manually.

Self-opener: in the classic Beesley/Purdey design, the gun is sprung open by its mainspring as the gun is opened, whether it has been fired or not. Sometimes called a "spring-opener."

Sidelock: a gun with its lockwork mounted on lockplates, either internally or with the hammers exposed. "Sidelock" is the preferred definition for guns with internally mounted tumblers, whereas "hammergun" describes guns with externally mounted hammers.

Triggerplate: an action design with the lock mechanism mounted on the triggerplate. The German Blitz and Scottish round action are notable traditional designs. Many modern over/unders are triggerplate designs, with Italian-inspired detachable-trigger units an increasingly popular variant.

— Action —

Action: the body or frame of the gun.

Action face: the vertical face of the action that mates with the breech face of the barrels. Sometimes called the "standing breech" or "breech face."

Action flats: the slotted flats of the action bar through which the barrel lumps pass. Sometimes called the "table" or "water table."

Action slots: the slots in the action flats into which the barrel lumps fit.

Back action: a sidelock with its mainsprings mounted to the rear of the lockwork (behind the tumbler) and inlet into the stock. Often used in double rifles because the back-action's bar remains stronger. Sometimes called a "back lock."

Bar: the action body from the breeches forward; also a term for the decorative filing on the bar itself.

Bar action: sidelock with mainsprings mounted in front of the lockwork, which fits into recesses machined in the bar of the action. The classic shotgun sidelock.

Beaded fence: a fence with decorative raised or carved fillets at its back. The latter is sometimes called the "bead."

Bolt: in the classic Purdey design of 1863, a flat sliding bolt that engages bites in the barrel assembly to lock the gun closed. Sometimes called an "underbolt" or "double underbolt." Also, a similar component in an Anson-type forend that locks the forend assembly to the barrels at the forend loop.

Bottom plate: a plate in the base of a boxlock that covers the locks and associated components. In some designs (Westley Richards) it is hand-detachable to allow access or removal of locks.

Breech pin: in a traditional gun, the large screw that passes vertically through the top strap just behind the breech to secure the action to the stock. Typically, it screws into a box on the triggerplate.

Bridge: the bridge on conventional guns that separates the front action slot from the rear slot.

Cam: a projection fitted into the knuckle—or a device fitted into the forend iron—that pushes the extractors/ejector legs out as the gun is opened. Sometimes called the "extractor toe."

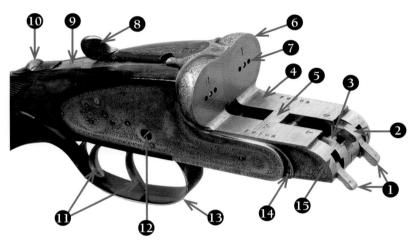

A bar-action sidelock with main components labeled: 1) cocking dogs, 2) ejector cam, 3) hinge pin, 4) action flats, 5) bridge, 6) action face, 7) striker disks, 8) toplever, 9) top strap, 10) safety, 11) double triggers, 12) cocking indicator, 13) trigger guard, 14) bar, 15) knuckle.
(Richard Rogers)

Cocking dogs: levers protruding through the knuckle that pivot as the gun opens to cock the locks as the barrels drop.

Cocking indicators: on a modern sidelock, typically the visibly marked (often in gold) tumbler axle (or pivot) that protrudes through the lockplates, denoting if a lock is cocked or in the fired position. Vintage designs included faux hammers, small glass windows (W.M. Scott's Patent Crystal Indicators) to allow observation of the lockwork, and pins that protruded through the action.

Ejector: generically, the mechanical system employed to eject empty cartridges. Describing a specific component, the split rod bedded in the barrel-breech assembly with semi-circular rim designed to push out cartridges.

Extractor: one-piece rod with semi-circular rim that lifts cartridge clear of the chamber so it can be removed by hand.

Fence: the ball-like projections behind each barrel from the action face back; at Purdey's this is called the "detonating."

Furniture: a term describing any number of external components, including the triggerplate, trigger guard, triggers, toplever (or other opening levers), safety and base plate.

Hinge pin: the cylindrical component running across the action at its knuckle, upon which the barrels hinge. Can be of removable or integral design. Sometimes called the "cross pin."

Kicker: the spring-driven, hammer-like component in an ejector mechanism that strikes (or "kicks") the tip of an ejector rod to clear an empty cartridge from the chamber.

Knuckle: the front of the action bar radiused to mate with the back of the forend iron.

Leverwork: a term used to describe the bolting system and its associated components.

Pin: gunmaking term for any number of screws used in the assembly of the gun and its components.

Radius: the radiused junction at the action flats and breech face shaped to alleviate stresses from bending forces generated when a gun is fired. Sometimes called the "root."

Safety: a mechanism to prevent a gun from firing unless disengaged. Usually mounted on the top strap on traditional guns, with some exceptions mounted on the side (Greener's designs).

Scalloped action: typically a boxlock with the rear of its action rebated (or "scalloped") to break the straight line at the junction of the stock. Sometime called "fancy back" or, in the Birmingham trade, the "Westley back."

Sidelever: lever mounted under the action to retract the bolt and shaped to curve up one side of the action so that a user could push it down. Once an elegant alternative to the toplever with English makers such as Stephen Grant and Boss & Co., it has been revived in modern times by Italian makers and is again being incorporated on new guns in the UK.

Striker: the small cylindrical rod impacted by the falling tumbler or hammer to fire a cartridge. In some designs—many boxlocks, for example—the striker is integral with the tumbler. Also called "firing pin."

Striker disks: threaded metal disks machined into the action face to allow access to the strikers. Sometimes called "bushings" or "bushed pins."

Toplever: the lever on top of the action connected to a spindle and used to retract the bolt so the gun will open. The most common was invented by W.M. Scott in 1865 and married to the Purdey underbolt.

Top strap: the projection extending from the top of the rear of the action. In traditional "best" guns it is made integral with the action. Sometimes called the "tang."

Triggerplate: in traditional guns, the component accommodating the trigger blades; a plate or strap on the bottom of the action inletted into the stock. Sometimes called the "bottom strap."

— Locks —

Bent: the notch in the tumbler that is engaged by the nose of sear.

Bridle: a flat component that sandwiches lock components between it and the lockplate, providing support for the tumbler.

Hammer: normally refers to an externally mounted limb used to deliver a blow to detonate a cartridge.

Mainspring: the spring that powers the tumbler and the largest spring in the gun. In a traditional design, the mainspring is a leaf spring formed in an elongated V shape.

Roller: typically a back-action-lock design that uses a cylindrical roller in one end of its mainspring to bear on the tumbler and reduce friction in the transfer of energy from the mainspring to the tumbler. Sometimes called a "roller lock."

Safety sear: a limb in the lock designed to catch or otherwise impede the fall of the tumbler unless the trigger has been deliberately pulled. Many sidelocks have this safety feature, as do some high-grade boxlocks. Sometimes called the "intercepting sear" or "interceptor."

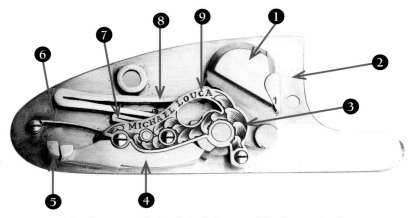

A back-action (roller) lock for a sidelock over/under:
1) tumbler, 2) tumbler block, 3) bridle, 4) interceptor, 5) sear,
6) interceptor spring, 7) sear spring, 8) mainspring,
9) mainspring roller (under bridle). (David Grant)

Sear: the limb that holds the tumbler in a cocked position until the trigger is pulled.

Sear springs: both the sear and safety sear have springs. The primary sear spring positions the sear so that its nose engages the bent when the lock is cocked. A safety sear spring keeps the interceptor in position until the trigger is pulled.

Swivel: a link to connect the mainspring to the tumbler and fitted to reduce friction in the transfer of energy.

Tumbler: the hammer of a gun with internally mounted locks. Also can refer to the hammer component of some ejector designs, such as the Deeley.

— Barrels —

Barrel face: the flat area at the back of the breech that mates with the breech face. Sometimes called the "breech end."

Barrel flats: the flat area under the breech portion of the barrels of a side-by-side gun onto which proof marks are applied.

Bite: in a side-by-side with Purdey bolts, the notch (or notches)—usually rectangular—machined in the back of the lump where the bolt engages to lock the barrels to the action.

Breech: the rear of the barrels into which cartridges are inserted.

Chamber: the portion of the barrels at the breeches that is machined out larger than the bore to accept the cartridge.

Choke: the constriction at the muzzle used to increase or decrease the density of a shot pattern.

Choke cone: a transitional tapered cone leading from the bore to the parallel at the muzzles that establishes the amount of constriction.

Chopper-lumps: Lumps machined integral with the tubes upon which the barrels hinge. In Britain, a feature of a best gun; in Spain, they are ubiquitous regardless of grade.

Circle: on a side-by-side with Purdey bolts, the concave face of the rear barrel lump that mates with the draw at the front of the rear slot in the action flats. Also describes the mating surfaces of certain top extensions, such as the Westley Richards doll's-head.

Crossbolt: a lateral bolt behind the action face that engages a recess in the top extension to bolt the gun. Like the doll's-head, it is extremely strong when properly fitted and shaped.

Doll's-head: a top extension with a larger head behind a neck that fits into a recess in the top and face of the action. It may or may not be locked down with a top bolt. When properly fitted "on the circle," it is an extremely strong and effective bolt.

Dovetail lumps: lump assembly made separate from the tubes and dovetailed in.

Draw: the convex face of the front of the rear slot (or at the rear of the bridge). In a side-by-side the draw, in conjunction with the circle on the rear barrel lump, helps cam the barrels into the action as the gun is closed. It also helps distribute stresses generated by firing over a wider area of the action, preventing the hinge pin and hook from bearing all of the stress. In a Boss-type over/under the draw is on the bifurcated lumps in the action walls. In a modern gun, the draw may have a replaceable hardened insert dovetailed in to aid rejointing.

Forcing cone: a transitional tapered cone between the end of the chamber and the barrel bore. Sometimes called "lead in."

Forend iron: the metal component of the forend assembly that houses the ejectors and fastening system. It forms a frame for the wooden forend and can act as a cam to cock the gun when the barrels drop.

Forend loop: a lug brazed into the barrel assembly onto which the forend attaches. Sometimes called the "bolt loop."

Hook: the concave face on the front lump that allows the barrels to rotate on the hinge pin.

Keel rib: the strip of steel—or short rib—between the flats and forend loop on the bottom of a barrel assembly.

Lumps: in a side-by-side, the lugs (or lug, depending on design) protruding from the bottom of the barrel assembly. The front lug is fitted with the hook that allows the gun to pivot around its hinge pin. In a Purdey-bolted gun, the lumps also contain the bites. Sometimes called the "steels," although many craftsmen use the latter term to describe the sides of the lumps.

Parallel: the straight portion of some choke designs at the muzzle.

Profile: the exterior shape of the barrels, which helps determine not only their appearance but also how metal (weight) is distributed along them.

Proof marks: marks impressed by proof authorities onto a gun to denote pressures that the gun was officially tested at or intended for, as well as supplementary information such as nominal gauge, nominal bore diameter, chamber length, propellant types and age.

Rib: the strips of steel between the barrels used to help join barrels together to provide strength to the assembly, and to provide a sighting plane.

Ride: on a side-by-side, the rear surface of the front barrel lump that prevents the bolt from engaging the bites until the gun is closed. Sometimes called the "run up" because the front of the bolt "runs up," or "rides," the surface until going home into the bite.

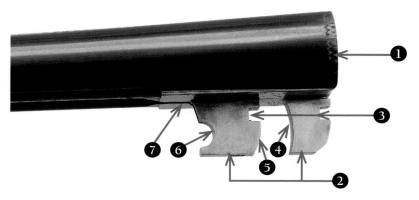

The breech area of side-by-side barrels fitted to a gun with Purdey underbolts: 1) barrel face, 2) lumps, 3) bites, 4) circle, 5) ride, 6) hook, 7) barrel flats. (Richard Rogers)

Striking: the longitudinal filing and burnishing used by barrelmakers to obtain the final concentricity, wall thickness and exterior profile of the barrels.

Top extension: generic term for any number of bolting systems that use an extension off of the barrel breeches to fit into a recess in the action to bolt the gun. Two of the most important are the doll's-head and crossbolt.

Select Bibliography

After nearly a half-century drought on the subject, the past two decades have witnessed a flowering of books on fine guns and gunmakers from both sides of the Atlantic, including many superb histories of individual firms. The following list is in no way a complete catalog for the specialist, but it includes my choices for the core of any library on the craft of artisanal gunmaking or making double shotguns.

— A Core Reading List —

Adams, Cyril S., and Braden, Robert S.; *Lock, Stock & Barrel* (Safari Press, 1996).

Akehurst, Richard; *Game Guns & Rifles* (The Sportsman's Press, 1992).

Austyn, Christopher; *Modern Sporting Guns* (The Sportsman's Press, 1994).

Burrard, Maj. Sir Gerald; *The Modern Shotgun*, Vols. 1, 2 & 3 (reprint, Ashford Press Publishing, 1985).

Garwood, G.T. (Gough Thomas); *Shotguns & Cartridges* (A&C Black, Ltd., 1963).

Garwood, G.T. (Gough Thomas); *The Gun Book* (A&C Black, Ltd., 1969; reprint, The Gunnerman Press, 1994).

Garwood, G.T. (Gough Thomas); *Gough Thomas's Second Gun Book* (Winchester Press, 1972).

Garwood, G.T. (Gough Thomas); *Shooting Facts & Fancies* (A&C Black, Ltd., 1978).

Greener, W.W.; *The Gun and Its Development* (ninth edition, 1910; reprint, various publishers).

Grozik, Richard; *Game Gun* (Countrysport Press, 1986, 1997).

Hughes, S.D.; *Fine Gunmaking: Double Shotguns* (Krause Publications, 1998).

Hughes, S.D.; *Double Guns & Custom Gunsmithing* (Shooting Sportsman Books, 2007).

Potter, Lewis; *The Art of Gunsmithing* (The Crowood Press, 2006).

McIntosh, Michael; *Best Guns* (first revised edition; Countrysport Press, 1998).

McIntosh, Michael, and Trevallion, David; *Shotgun Technicana* (Countrysport Press, 2002).

Mills, Desmond, and Barnes, Mike; *Amateur Gunsmithing* (Boydell Press, 1986).

Nobili, Marco; *Fucili D'Autore: The Best Guns* (second edition; Il Volo srl, 1991).
Tate, Douglas; *Birmingham Gunmakers* (Safari Press, 1997).
Zutz, Don; *The Double Shotgun* (revised expanded edition; Winchester Press, 1985, 1991).

— Further Reading by Chapter —

Where possible—and in the vast majority of cases—*Gun Craft* chapters are based on personal visits to gunmakers and craftsmen as well as follow-up interviews and, where appropriate, research in primary sources—gunmaker records, archives, period catalogs and so on. Following are published secondary sources arranged by date for those who wish to explore topics in greater detail.

Chapter I. The Unknown Gunmaker: Bob Turner

Adapted from Guncraft column "The Unknown Gunmaker," *Shooting Sportsman*, May/June 2010.

Unless they were owners of companies, individual craftsmen—especially those working anonymously for the trade—have historically been poorly documented. This is partly because of the traditional secrecy of craftsmen themselves, a secrecy fueled by the perception of needing to protect hard-earned knowledge from competitors, real or imagined. In an age when craft gunmaking was a normal mode of production, workers and their skills were mostly taken for granted and consequently deemed barely worth recording. In Britain, particularly, this was magnified by an acutely class-conscious society that marginalized those who made a living with their hands. Only lately—too late in many cases—are the gaps in the history of craft gunmaking being recognized. The following provide some idea of the richness of Britain's craft tradition.

Boothroyd, Geoffrey; "The Birmingham Gun Trade," *Boothroyd on British Shotguns* (Amity, Oregon, 1993). An interesting look at the Birmingham gun trade and some of its craftsmen in the 1960s. Boothroyd was unquestionably a pioneer in the renaissance of double-gun literature.
Tate, Douglas; *Birmingham Gunmakers* (Long Beach, California, 1997). Tate picks up where Boothroyd left off and offers original insights into Britain's gunmaking tradiitons.
Masters, Don; *The House of Churchill* (Long Beach, California, 2002). One of the finest—and most comprehensive—of the single-maker histories, this book included much on craftsmen in the British trade, particularly in the troubled 1960s and '70s.

Brown, Nigel; *British Gunmakers, Vols. One, Two and Three* (Shrewsbury, England, 2004, 2005 and 2009). Indispensible for the British gun buff.

Williams, David; *The Birmingham Gun Trade* (Gloucestershire, England, 2004). The book's emphasis is on industrial history, but it includes a good explanation of the eventual division of British gunmaking into mechanized and "craft" production methods.

Hadoke, Diggory; *Vintage Guns* (New York, New York, 2008). Hadoke's focus is on buying and collecting vintage British guns, but good chapters on craftsmen past and present.

Muderlak, Ed; *Parker Guns: Shooting Flying and the American Experience* (Paducah, Kentucky, 2008). Muderlak has mined period primary sources for his interpretations on American guns and gunmaking in the golden age of doubles.

Chapter II. Jointing & The Circle

Adapted from Guncraft column "Jointing and the Circle," *Shooting Sportsman*, July/August 2010.

Walsh, J.W.; *The Modern Sportsman's Gun & Rifle* (Horace Cox, 1882; reprint Wolfe Publishing Co., 1986).

Greener, W.W.; *The Gun and its Development*.

Mills, Desmond, and Barnes, Mike; *Amateur Gunsmithing*. Includes good chapter on jointing.

Potter, Lewis; *The Art of Gunsmithing*. Good chapter on rejointing.

Chapter III. Jointing & The Doll's-Head

Adapted from Guncraft column "A Well-Jointed Westley," *Shooting Sportsman*, September/October 2010.

Crudgington, I.M., and Baker, D.J.; *The British Shotgun, Volume One 1850-1870* (Shedfield, Hants, 1990).

Boothroyd, Geoffrey; "The Top Extension," *Boothroyd on British Shotguns* (Amity, Oregon, 1993).

Chapter IV. The Hunter One-Trigger

Adapted from Guncraft column "The Hunter One Trigger," *Shooting Sportsman*, March/April 2010.

Sharp, Henry; *Modern Sporting Gunnery* (London, England, 1904). A detailed (though biased) look at guns & gunmaking—and the Lard trigger—at Westley Richards in the firm's historical heyday.

Brophy, William S.; *L.C. Smith Shotguns* (Highland Park, New Jersey, 1977).

Houchins, John; *L.C. Smith: The Legend Lives* (Winston-Salem, North Carolina, 2006).

Schuknecht, Larry B.; "Biography of Allan Lard," *L.C. Smith Speaks for Itself*, Volume 5, Issue 1, 2007. A well-researched article in the L.C. Smith Collectors Association newsletter on the inventor and his life.

Chapter V. The Case for Concentricity

Adapted from Guncraft column "The Case for Concentricity," *Shooting Sportsman*, September/October 2009.

"Shotgun Barrel Making," *The Holland & Holland Collection 1976*. Informative article in a Holland & Holland publication on tube- and barrelmaking at the firm in the 1970s.

Chapter VI. 'Best' Barrelmaking

Adapted from Guncraft column "Best British Barrel Making at Holland & Holland," *Shooting Sportsman*, November/December 2009.

Boothroyd, Geoffrey; "The Barrel Builder's Art," *Boothroyd on British Shotguns* (Amity, Oregon, 1993).

Boothroyd, Geoffrey; "Shotgun Barrels—Their History and Development," *Boothroyd on British Shotguns* (Amity, Oregon, 1993).

Rowe, Jack; "Barrels: Buying an English or European Gun," *The Double Gun Journal*, Summer 1990.

Wilkin, Russell; "Factory Tour: Barrels," *The Shooting Field*, Volume 10. Short but good article by H&H's director of technical gunmaking in the firm's house publication.

Chapter VII. Hand-Regulating Chokes

Adapted from Guncraft column "Hand Regulating Chokes at H&H," *Shooting Sportsman*, January/February 2010.

The art and craft of hand-regulating chokes traditionally has been one of the gun trade's more arcane secrets, with almost as many theories on choke and choke-cone formation existing as there are guns. The 2007 DVD "A Look Inside Holland & Holland: The Royal Gunmaker" provides excellent insights into full-time regulator Steven Cranston's views on the subject.

Allsop, Derek; "Choke Profiles: The Different Ways of Shaping Up For A Shot Pattern," British Association of Shooting & Conservation.

Brindle, John; "Shooting: Chokes and Their Classifications," *Shooting Sportsman*, January/February 1992.

Boothroyd, Geoffrey; "G.T.'s Gun," *Game & Gun*, July/August 1992.

Chapter VIII. Toys No More: The New Purdey .410s

Adapted from the feature "A Toy No More," *Shooting Sportsman*, January/
February 2008.
Beaumont, Richard; *Purdey's: The Guns and the Family* (London, England,
1984).
Dallas, Donald; *Purdey: The Definitive History* (London, England, 2000).
Gabriel, Ronald S.; *American & British .410 Shotguns* (Iola, Wisconsin,
2003). An excellent book on the development of the .410.

Chapter IX. The Art of Finishing: David Sinnerton

Adapted from the feature "The Best Finish Last," *Shooting Sportsman*, Sep-
tember/October 2005.
McIntosh, Michael, and Trevallion, David; "Protocol at Purdey's," *Shotgun
Technicana* (Camden, Maine, 2002). Excellent chapter on gunmaking at
Purdey's in the 1950s, including a discussion on finishing.
Yardley, Mike; "David Sinnerton Gun Review," *The Field*, November 2006.

Chapter X. British Color Case Hardening

Adapted from Guncraft column "The Black Art of British Color Case Hard-
ening, Parts 1 & 2," *Shooting Sportsman*, May/June and July/August 2009.
Boothroyd, Geoffrey; "Let's Build A Best Gun," *Sidelocks & Boxlocks: The
Classic British Shotguns* (Amity, Oregon, 1991). An excellent discussion of
A.A. Brown's ultra-traditional gunmaking methods and in-house workforce
in the 1970s and '80s.
Boothroyd, Geoffrey; "A.A. Brown & Sons, Birmingham," *The Double Gun
Journal*, Spring 1993.
Gaddy, Oscar L.; "The Color Case Hardening of Firearms, Parts I & II," *The
Double Gun Journal*, Winter 1996 and Spring 1997.

Chapter XI. Gianfranco Pedersoli: Italian Super-Engraver

Adapted from Guncraft column "Gianfranco Superstar," *Shooting Sportsman*,
November/December 2008.
Abbiatico, Mario; *Modern Firearms Engraving* (Gardone, Val Trompia, Italy,
1980). The book that arguably launched the Italian revolution in modern
sporting-arms engraving.
Nobili, Marco E.; *Il Grande Libro Delle Incisioni* (fifth edition, Milan, Italy, 2001).
Great photos and text but marred by poor Italian-to-English translation.
Hands, Barry Lee; "An American Engraver in Italy," *Shooting Sportsman*, No-
vember/December 2006. A noted American engraver's perspectives on some
of Italy's best engravers, Pedersoli included.

Sundseth, Dag (edited by S.P. Fjestad & Elena Micheli-Lamboy); *Gianfranco Pedersoli: Master Engraver* (Minneapolis, Minnesota, 2007). The *definitive* book on Pedersoli and one of the most beautifully designed gun books ever published. The Pedersoli book is the first in a series on Italy's master engravers, and following volumes on Firmo & Francesca Fracassi and Giancarlo & Stefano Pedretti, written by Stephen Lamboy and Elena Micheli-Lamboy, are equally impressive. Must-haves for engraving buffs.

Chapter XII. Last Gasp in Liège

Adapted from the feature "In the Country of Vulcan's Furnaces," *Shooting Sportsman*, May/June 1998.

The history of Auguste Francotte—and the artisanal Liège trade at large—remains poorly documented, certainly in the English language. The best source on the Liège trade is Claude Gaier, curator of Liège's famous arms museum.

Park, Will K.; "Guns and Gunning: Some Views Upon the Gun Question," *Sporting Life*, November 14, 1896.
Gaier, Claude; *Four Centuries of Liège Gunmaking* (Liège, Belgium, 1985).
Hammond, W.R.; "Three Fine Francottes," *The Double Gun Journal*, Spring 2000.

As inheritor of the records of longtime Francotte importers Von Lengerke & Detmold and Abercrombie & Fitch, Griffin & Howe can provide information on many of the Francotte guns sold in the US. Contact:

Robert C. Beach, Records Research
Griffin & Howe, Inc.
33 Claremont Road
Bernardsville, NJ 07924
tel.: 908-766-2287
e-mail: research@griffinhowe.com
www.griffinhowe.com

Chapter XIII. The SuperBritte

Adapted from the feature "The SuperBritte," *Shooting Sportsman*, March/April 2000.
Tate, Douglas; "The Jules Bury Collection," *Shooting Sportsman*, November/December 2009.

Chapter XIV. The Spanish Way

Adapted from Guncraft column "The Spanish Way," *Shooting Sportsman*, March/April 2009.

Kurlansky, Mark; *The Basque History of the World* (New York, New York, 1999). Non-gun-related but entertaining social history of Basque region and its culture, providing insights into the gun trade's adherence to tradition.
McIntosh, Michael; *Best Guns* (Selma, Alabama, 1999). Good chapters on Spanish guns.
Wieland, Terry; *Spanish Best* (Camden, Maine, 2001). The revised edition is a well-researched, well-written, entertaining history of modern artisanal Basque gunmaking. A must-have for Spanish-gun aficionados.
Wieland, Terry; "Crafting in Basque," *Shooting Sportsman*, May/June 2005.

Chapter XV. Manufacturas Arrieta

Adapted from the feature "Arrieta: A Gunmaker's Gunmaker," *Shooting Sportsman*, September/October 2010.
McIntosh, Michael; "Gun Review: Another Look at Arrieta," *Shooting Sportsman*, March/April 1993.
McIntosh, Michael; "In the Shop at Arrieta," *The Double Gun Journal*, Spring 1995.
Venters, Vic; "Gun Review: Arrieta's 2" Light Game Gun," *Shooting Sportsman*, November/December 1997.
Wieland, Terry; "A Family Concern," *Shooting Sportsman*, July/August 1999.
Fergus, Charles; "The Two-Inch 12 Revisited," *Shooting Sportsman*, March/April 2007.
Rawlingson, Richard; "Family Tradition," *Fieldsports*, Winter 2009/'10.

Chapter XVI. Greener's Greatest Boxlock: The G-Gun

Adapted from the feature "The G-Gun," *Shooting Sportsman*, May/June 1999.
Boothroyd, Geoffrey; "The Greener St. George's Gun" and "More on the St. George's Double," *Boothroyd on British Shotguns* (Amity, Oregon, 1993).
Greener, Graham; *The Greener Story* (London, England/Long Beach, California, 2000). Greener's illustrious history written by W.W.'s great-great-great-great-great grandson. Includes a good explanation of Greener's complicated grading system and range of models, including the G-Guns.
Venters, Vic; "G is for Glorious," *Shooting Sportsman*, July/August 2004. An update on the return of Greener's G-Gun to modern production.

Chapter XVII. The Return of Westley Richards' Ovundo

Adapted from the feature "Ovundo Again," *Shooting Sportsman*, January/February 2009.
Boothroyd, Geoffrey & Susan; *The British Over-and-Under Shotgun* (London, England, 1996). A short chapter on the Ovundo is included.

Tate, Douglas; *Birmingham Gunmakers* (Long Beach, California, 1997). Includes a chapter with information on the development of the Ovundo.
Brown, Nigel; *British Gunmakers, Vol. Two* (Shrewsbury, England, 2002). Excellent chapter included on Westley Richards.

Chapter XVIII. Watson Bros. Lightweight O/Us

Adapted from the feature "A Little London Big-Bore," *Shooting Sportsman*, November/December 2005.
Lowther, Tom; "Lock, Stock and Barrel," *Sunday Express Magazine*, March 12, 1995.
Venters, Vic; "Then and Now," *The Double Gun Journal*, Spring 1997.
Tate, Douglas; "Innovation from In-House," *Shooting Sportsman*, March/April 1999.
Venters, Vic; "Gun Review: Watson Bros. Smallbore Round-Body," *Shooting Sportsman*, January/February 2000.

Chapter XVIX. Memories of a Proof Master: Roger Lees

Adapted from the feature "Memories of a Proof Master," *Fieldsports*, Winter/Spring 2009/2010.
Harris, Clive; *The History of the Birmingham Gun-barrel Proof House* (Birmingham, England, 1947).
Boothroyd, Geoffrey; "The Birmingham Proof House," *Boothroyd on British Shotguns* (Amity, Oregon, 1993).

Chapter XX. The Rules of Proof

Adapted from Guncraft column "The Rules of Proof," *Shooting Sportsman*, January/February 2009.
The Gunmaker's Company and the Guardians of the Birmingham Proof House; *Rules of Proof 1925* and *Rules of Proof 1954* (Birmingham, England, 1925 and 1954).
Lees, Roger; "The New Rules of Proof," *The Field*, January 1955.
Willett, Roderick; "Proof Marks, Their Purpose and their Meaning," *The Field*, 6 July 1967.
Harding, Bill; "Proof Positive," *The Shooting Times & Country Magazine*, 4 December 1997.
The Gunmakers Company and the Guardians of the Birmingham Proof House; *Notes on the Proof of Shotguns & Other Small Arms* (various dates). Published by Britain's proof authorities, the "little red book" is a concise guide to modern proof marks and regulations.
The Birmingham Gun Barrel Proof House maintains an informative Website: http://www.gunproof.com.

Chapter XXI. Restoration the Atkin Grant & Lang Way

Adapted from Guncraft column "The Art of Restoration at Atkin Grant & Lang," *Shooting Sportsman*, September/October 2008.

Yardley, Mike; "Re-manufactured Joseph Langs," *The Field*, June 2007.

Calabi, Silvio; "Extreme Gun Makeover," *Garden & Gun*, December 2009.

Chapter XXII. J.P. Morgan's Atkin

Adapted from the feature "An Atkin for Morgan," *Shooting Sportsman*, September/October 2008.

Teasdale-Buckell, G.T.; *Experts on Guns & Shooting* (Sampson, Low, Marston & Co., Ltd., 1900).

Crawford, J.A., and Whatley, P.G.; "The History of W.&C. Scott Gunmakers" (Rowland Ward, 1991). A small volume but packed with good information on one of Britain's most important gunmakers.

Venters, Vic; "Golden Days in the Gilded Age," *The Double Gun Journal*, Winter 1992. An article based on interviews with the son of J.P. Morgan's gamekeeper at his North Carolina quail-hunting lodge, with his comments on Morgan's preferences for Henry Atkin guns.

Tate, Douglas, and Venters, Vic; "The Guns of Henry Atkin," *Shooting Sportsman*, March/April 2001.

Masters, Don; *Atkin, Grant & Lang* (Long Beach, California, 2006). Good discussion of Morgan as a longtime Atkin customer.

Yardley, Mike; "Rebuilding a Piece of History," *The Shooting Gazette*, April 2008.

Chapter XXIII. The Frederick C. Scales Gun

Adapted from the features "The Frederick C. Scales Gun, Parts I and II," *Shooting Sportsman*, May/June and July/August 2007.

Boothroyd, Geoffrey; "Guns at the Gamefair," *The Shooting Times & Country Magazine*, August 24, 1989.

Boothroyd, Geoffrey; "Made to Impress," *The Shooting Times & Country Magazine*, March 15, 1990.

Boothroyd, Geoffrey; "Gun Engraving, Part IV," *The Double Gun Journal*, Winter 1992.

Brown, Nigel; *British Gunmakers, Vol. Two* (Shrewsbury, England, 2002). G&S Holloway chapter.

Tate, Douglas; *British Gun Engraving* (Long Beach, California, 2000). Excellent chapter on Kell.

— Online Resources —

Order of Edwardian Gunners: www.vintagers.org.
The Internet Gun Club: www.internetgunclub.com. Good source for information on British gunmakers.
Doublegunshop: www.doublegunshop.com.
Shooting Sportsman Magazine: www.shootingsportsman.com.
Parker Gun Collectors Association: www.parkerguns.org.
L.C. Smith Collectors Association: www.lcsmith.org.
A.H. Fox Shotgun Collectors Association: www.foxcollectors.com.
Lefever Arms Collectors Association: www.lefevercollectors.com.
German Gun Collectors Association: www.germanguns.com.
Damascusknowledge.com: http://sites.google.com/a/damascusknowledge.com/www/home.

Addresses:
Featured Gunmakers & Craftsmen

Atkin Grant & Lang
Broomhill Leys, Windmill Road,
Markyate, St, Albans, Hertfordshire AL3 8LP
England
tel.: (+44) 1582 849382; fax (+44) 1582 842318
e-mail: info@atkingrantandlang.co.uk
www.atkingrantandlang.co.uk

Arrieta Y CIA
Morkaiko 5, Apartado 93
20870 Elgoibar (Gipuzkoa)
Spain
e-mail: info@arrietashotguns.com
www.arrietashotguns.com

Pedro Arrizabalaga
Errekatxu, 5
20600 Eibar (Gipuzkoa)
Spain
e-mail: pedroarrizabalaga@pedroarrizabalaga.net
www.pedroarrizabalaga.net

The Birmingham Gun Barrel Proof House
Banbury Street, Birmingham B5 5RH
England
tel.: (+44) 121-643-3860; fax (+44) 121-643-7872
www.gunproof.com

A.A. Brown & Sons
One Snake Lane
Alvechurch, Birmingham B48 7NT
England
tel.: (+44) 121-445-5395; fax (+44) 121-445-2113
e-mail: robin@aabrownandsons.com
www.doubleguns.co.uk

Abe Chaber (Gunsmith)
40 Fairmount Road
Danbury, CT 06811

Armas Garbi
Urki 12, Apartado 221
20600 Eibar (Gipuzkoa)
Spain
e-mail: info@armasgarbi.com
www.armasgarbi.com

Gavin Gardiner, Ltd.
Hardham Mill Business Park
Mill Lane, Pulborough
West Sussex RH20 1LA
England
tel./fax: (+44) 1798-875300
e-mail: info@gavingardiner.com
www.gavingardiner.com

W.W. Greener (Sporting Guns), Ltd.
The Mews, Hagley Hall
Hagley, Stourbridge DY9 9LG
England
e-mail: sales@wwgreener.com
www.wwgreener.com

Griffin & Howe
33 Claremont Road
Bernardsville, NJ 07924
tel.: 908-766-2287, fax 908-766-1068
email: info@griffinhowe.com
www.griffinhowe.com

Holland & Holland
33 Bruton Street
London, W1J 6HH
England
tel. (+44) 20-7499-4411; fax (44) 20-7408-7962
e-mail: gunroomuk@hollandandholland.com
www.hollandandholland.com

Holland & Holland
10 East 40th Street, Suite 1910
New York, NY 10016
tel.: 212-752-7755; fax: 212-752-6975
e-mail: gunroomny@hollandandholland.com

James Purdey & Sons, Ltd.
Audley House
57 - 58 South Audley Street
London W1K 2ED
England
tel.: (+44) 20-7499-1801; fax: (+44) 20-7355-3297
e-mail: enquiries@purdey.com
www.purdey.com

Westley Richards & Co., Ltd.
130 Pritchett Street
Birmingham, B6 4EH
England
tel.: (+44) 121-333-1900; fax (+44) 121-333-1901
e-mail: sales@westleyrichards.co.uk
www.westleyrichards.com

David Sinnerton
e-mail: Davidsinnerton@aol.com

David Trevallion
Trevallion Gunstocks
9 Old Mountain Road
Cape Neddick, ME 03902
tel.: 207-361-1130

Dewey Vicknair
Vicknair Restorations
565 Oak Lane
Lititz, PA 17543
tel.: 717-626-4226
e-mail: Dewey@VicknairRestorations.com
www.vicknairrestorations.com

Watson Bros. Gunmakers
54 Redchurch Street
City of London
England
tel.: (+44) 20-7033-0003
e-mail: Michael.Louca@WatsonBrosGunmakers.com
www.watsonbrosgunmakers.com